the **empty boat**

OSHO

This book is a transcript of a series of original talks by Osho given to a live audience.
The talks in this edition were previously published as *The Empty Boat*.
All of Osho's talks have been published in full as books, and are also available as original audio and/or video recordings.
Audio recordings and the complete text archive can be found via the online OSHO Library at www.osho.com
OSHO is a registered trademark of Osho International Foundation, www.osho.com/trademarks

Osho comments on selected excerpts from:
Thomas Merton, from *The Way of Chuang Tzu*, copyright © 1965 by The Abbey of Gethsemani.
Reprinted by permission of New Directions Publishing Corp.

OSHO MEDIA INTERNATIONAL

New York • London • Mumbai
an imprint of
OSHO INTERNATIONAL
www.osho.com/oshointernational

Distributed by Publishers Group Worldwide
www.pgw.com

Library of Congress Cataloging-in-Publication data is available

ISBN 13   978-0-9818341-9-1
ISBN 10   0-9818341-9-1
Also available as an eBook: ISBN 13   978-0-88050-212-2

Printed in China

10   9   8   7   6   5   4   3   2   1

Design by Bookcraft Ltd
Cover design by Terry Jeavons
Jacket image © Dorling Kindersley/Getty Images

the **empty boat**

reflections on the stories of chuang tzu

Contents

Preface

Osho, can you summarize your teaching in short because I am here only for a day or two.

It is impossible. In the first place I have no teaching to summarize. I am not a teacher, I am a presence. I have no catechism. I cannot give you ten commandments – do this, don't do that.

And whatsoever I say today I may contradict tomorrow – because my commitment is to the moment. Whatsoever I said yesterday, I am no longer committed to it. The moment I said it I became free of it. Now I won't bother about it, I won't look at it again. Whatsoever I am saying to you right now is true this very moment; tomorrow I will not be committed to it. Whatsoever tomorrow brings, I will say it. Whatsoever today has brought I am telling you now. And if they are contradictory who am I to make them consistent? I don't make any effort on my own.

My commitment is to the moment. I am never committed to the past. I am like a river: where I will be tomorrow nobody knows, not even I myself. You will be surprised, I will also be surprised.

The question must be from someone who comes from the continent I call "Acirema" – it is "America" read in the reverse order. America is topsy-turvy. Everything has become chaotic. People are in such a hurry that they have forgotten that there are a few things which you cannot get in a hurry, for which patience is a must.

You cannot get truth in such a hurry. Patience is a basic condition for it. It is not like instant coffee and it does not come packed in tins. It does not come ready-made. Truth is not a commodity that somebody can give to you. It grows in you.

That's what I mean when I say I am a presence, I am not a teacher. If you are here, something may grow in you. I say, "may" because it depends on you. I am here. If you are ready to receive me, something will start growing within you. It is like a child becoming a young man. Yes, truth is like that. The false personality drops and the true being arrives. It is like a child becoming a young man, a young man becoming an old one. There is no way to hurry the process. You cannot make a child grow up fast in one night, in a day or two. It will take time. And it is good that it takes time because only through time do things become seasoned.

No, I cannot do that, I cannot summarize. I have no teaching. And even if I had a teaching I would not summarize it, because the more you summarize something, the more it becomes less alive. Love is vast, life is vast; law is limited. Law can be summarized; love cannot be summarized. Law is defined but life is excessive. You cannot summarize life, there cannot be a synopsis of life; you can summarize law. I am life. There is no way to summarize me.

And I am still alive so whatsoever you summarize I will destroy tomorrow.

When you summarize, by and by things become absurd.

Never summarize anything that is alive. I am still alive. When I am dead and gone then people will summarize. And I am going to give them a hell of a lot of trouble. It will not be an easy thing. They will go nuts. It will be impossible to put me into a synopsis.

It has been always so. You cannot summarize Buddha. Because of summarizations many schools were born. Buddha died, then there was a question. People wanted to summarize. For forty years the man had been teaching – morning, afternoon, evening – for forty years. He had talked a lot, he had said many things, and now he had gone and it had to be summarized.

Truth is not like a commodity. When you come to me, if you really want to know what my truth is, you will have to be here. My truth can be expressed to you only when I have come to know your truth too. When I have come to know you and you have come to know me, in that meeting will be the glimpse. It cannot be given to you. You will have to receive it and you will have to prepare for it. You will have to become a very relaxed being. You will have to be able to soak me up and allow me to sink deep into your heart.

It happened …

In the Amsterdam National Museum an elderly couple came to see Rembrandt's masterpiece "The Nightwatch." When, after a long walk through the many corridors, they finally reached the famous painting, the usher overheard the man say to his wife, "Look, what a beautiful frame!"

The frame may have been beautiful, but can't you see that something is missing in the admiration? Something essential is lost. I am not saying that the frame was not beautiful, the frame may have been the most beautiful frame in the world, but to go to see Rembrandt's masterpiece "The Nightwatch" and then to talk about the frame is absurd. Even to see the frame is foolish, stupid. The painting is not the frame. The frame has nothing to do with the painting.

What I am saying is just a frame, what I am is the painting. Look at the masterpiece and don't be bothered with the frame.

Chapter 1

The Toast Is Burned

He who rules men lives in confusion;
He who is ruled by men lives in sorrow.
Yao therefore desired
Neither to influence others
Nor to be influenced by them.
The way to get clear of confusion
And free of sorrow
Is to live with Tao
In the land of the great Void.
If a man is crossing a river
And an empty boat collides with his own skiff,
Even though he be a bad-tempered man
He will not become very angry.
But if he sees a man in the boat,
He will shout at him to steer clear.
If the shout is not heard, he will shout again,
And yet again, and begin cursing.
And all because there is somebody in the boat.
Yet if the boat were empty,
He would not be shouting, and not angry.

If you can empty your own boat
Crossing the river of the world,
No one will oppose you,
No one will seek to harm you.

The straight tree is the first to be cut down,
The spring of clear water is the first to be drained dry.
If you wish to improve your wisdom
And shame the ignorant,
To cultivate your character
And outshine others;
A light will shine around you
As if you had swallowed the sun and the moon:
You will not avoid calamity.

A wise man has said:
"He who is content with himself
Has done a worthless work.
Achievement is the beginning of failure,
Fame is the beginning of disgrace."

Who can free himself from achievement
And from fame, descend and be lost
Amid the masses of men?
He will flow like Tao, unseen,
He will go about like Life itself
With no name and no home.
Simple is he, without distinction.
To all appearances he is a fool.
His steps leave no trace. He has no power.
He achieves nothing, he has no reputation.
Since he judges no one,
No one judges him.
Such is the perfect man:
His boat is empty.

You have come to me. You have taken a dangerous step. It is a risk because near me you can be lost forever. To come closer will mean death and cannot mean anything else. I am just like an abyss. Come closer to me and you will fall into me. And for this, the invitation has been given to you. You have heard it and you have come.

Be aware that through me you are not going to gain anything. Through me you can only lose all — because unless you are lost, the divine cannot happen; unless you disappear totally, the real cannot arise. You are the barrier.

And you are so much, so stubbornly much, you are so filled with yourself that nothing can penetrate you. Your doors are closed. When you disappear, when you are not, the doors open. Then you become just like the vast, infinite sky.

That is your nature. That is Tao.

Before I enter into Chuang Tzu's beautiful parable of The Empty Boat, I would like to tell you one other story, because that will set the trend for this meditation camp which you are entering.

I have heard ...

It happened once, in some ancient time, in some unknown country, that a prince suddenly went mad. The king was desperate — the prince was the only son, the only heir to the kingdom. All the magicians were called, miracle makers, medical men were summoned, every effort was made, but in vain. Nobody could help the young prince, he remained mad.

The day he went crazy he threw off his clothes, became naked, and started to live under a big table. He thought that he had become a rooster. Ultimately the king had to accept the fact that the prince could not be reclaimed. He had gone insane permanently; all the experts had failed.

But one day, again hope dawned. One sage, a Sufi, a mystic, knocked on the palace door and said, "Give me an opportunity to cure the prince."

But the king felt suspicious, because this man looked crazy himself, more crazy than the prince. But the mystic said, "Only I can cure him. To cure a madman, a greater madman is needed. And your miracle makers, your medical experts, all have failed because they don't know the ABC of madness. They have never traveled that path."

It looked logical, and then the king thought, "There is no harm in it, why not try?" So the opportunity was given to him.

The moment the king said, "Okay, you try," this mystic threw off his clothes, jumped under the table and crowed like a rooster.

The prince became suspicious, and he said, "Who are you? And what do you think you are doing?"

The old man said, "I am a rooster, more experienced than you. You are nothing, you are just a newcomer, at the most an apprentice."

The prince said, "Then it is okay if you are also a rooster, but you look like a human being."

The old man said, "Don't go by appearances, look at my spirit, at my soul. I am a rooster like you."

They became friends. They promised each other that they would always live together – and the whole world was against them.

A few days passed. One day the old man suddenly started dressing. He put on his shirt. The prince said, "What are you doing, have you gone crazy, a rooster trying to put on human dress?"

The old man said, "I am just trying to deceive these fools, these human beings. And remember, even if I am dressed, nothing is changed. My roosterness remains, nobody can change it. Just by dressing like a human being do you think I am changed?" The prince had to concede.

A few days afterwards the old man persuaded the prince to dress because winter was coming, and it was becoming so cold.

Then one day suddenly, he ordered food from the palace. The prince became very alert and said, "Wretch, what do you mean? Are you going to eat like those human beings, like them? We are roosters and we have to eat like roosters."

The old man said, "Nothing makes any difference as far as this rooster is concerned. You can eat anything and you can enjoy everything. You can live like a human being and remain true to your roosterness."

By and by the old man persuaded the prince to come back to the world of humanity. He became absolutely normal.

The same is the case with you and me. And remember, you are just initiates, beginners. You may think that you are a rooster but you are just learning the alphabet. I am an old hand, and only I can help you – all the experts have failed, that's why you are here. You have knocked on many doors, for many lives you have been in search – nothing has been of help to you.

But I say I can help you because I am not an expert, I am not an outsider. I have traveled the same path, the same insanity, the same madness. I have passed through the same – the same misery, the anguish, the same nightmares. And whatsoever I am doing is nothing but persuading you to come out of your madness.

To think oneself a rooster is crazy; to think oneself a body is also crazy, even crazier. To think oneself a rooster is madness; to think oneself a human being is a greater madness – because you don't belong to any form. Whether the form is that of a rooster or of a human being is irrelevant – you belong to the formless, you belong to the total, the whole. So whatsoever form you think you are, you are mad. You are formless. You don't belong to any form, and you don't belong to any body, you don't belong to any caste, religion, creed; you don't belong to any name. And unless you become formless, nameless, you will never be sane.

Sanity means coming to that which is natural, coming to that which is ultimate in you, coming to that which is hidden behind you. Much effort is needed because to cut form, to drop and eliminate form, is very difficult. You have become so attached and identified with it.

This *Samadhi Sadhana Shibir*, this meditation camp, is nothing but to persuade you toward the formless – how not to be in the form. Every form means the ego; even a rooster has its ego, and man has his own. Every form is centered in the ego. The formless means egolessness; then you are not centered in the ego, then your center is everywhere or nowhere. This is possible, this which looks almost impossible, is possible, because this has happened to me. And when I speak, I speak through experience.

Wherever you are, I was, and wherever I am, you can be. Look at me as deeply as possible and feel me as deeply as possible, because I am your future, I am your possibility.

Whenever I say surrender to me, I mean surrender to this possibility. You can be cured, because your illness is just a thought. The prince went mad because he became identified with the thought that he was a rooster. Everybody is mad unless he comes to understand that he is not identified with any form – only then, sanity.

So a sane person will not be anybody in particular, cannot be. Only an insane person can be somebody in particular – whether a rooster or a man, or a prime minister or a president, or anybody, whatsoever. A sane person comes to feel the nobodiness.

This is the danger ...

You have come to me as somebody, and if you allow me, if you give me an opportunity, this somebodiness can disappear and you can become a nobody. This is the whole effort – to make you a nobody. But why? Why this effort to become a nobody? Because unless you become nobody you cannot be blissful; unless you become nobody you cannot be ecstatic; unless you become nobody the benediction is not for you – you go on missing life.

Really you are not alive, you simply drag, you simply carry yourself like a burden. Much anguish happens, much despair, much sorrow, but not a single ray of bliss – it cannot. If you are somebody, you are like a solid block of stone, nothing can penetrate you. When you are nobody you start becoming porous. When you are nobody, you are really an emptiness, transparent, everything can pass through you. There is no hindrance, there is no barrier, no resistance. You become a passivity, a door.

Right now you are like a wall; a wall means somebody. When you become a door you become nobody. A door is just an emptiness, anybody can pass, there is no resistance, no barrier. Somebody, you are mad; nobody, you will become sane for the first time.

But the whole society, education, civilization, culture, they all cultivate you and help you to become somebody. That's why I say religion is against civilization, religion is against education, religion is against culture – because religion is for nature, for Tao.

All civilizations are against nature, because they want to make you somebody in particular. And the more you are crystallized as somebody, the less and less the divine can penetrate into you.

You go to the temples, to the churches, to the priests, but there too you are searching – how to become somebody in the other world, how to attain something, how to succeed? The achieving mind follows you like a shadow. Wherever you go, you go with the idea of profit, achievement, success, attainment. If somebody has come here with this idea he should leave as soon as possible, and he should run as fast as possible from me, because I cannot help you to become somebody.

I am not your enemy. I can only help you to be nobody. I can only push you into the bottomless abyss. You will never reach anywhere, you will simply dissolve. You will fall and fall and fall and dissolve, and the moment you dissolve the whole existence feels ecstatic. The whole existence celebrates this happening.

Buddha attained this. Because of language I say *attained* — otherwise the word is ugly, there is no attainment — but you will understand. Buddha attained this emptiness, this nothingness. For two weeks, for fourteen days continuously, he sat in silence, not moving, not saying, not doing anything.

It is said that the deities in heaven became disturbed — rarely it happens that somebody becomes such total emptiness. The whole existence felt a celebration, so the deities came. They bowed down before Buddha and they said, "You must say something, you must say what you have attained." Buddha is said to have laughed and said, "I have not attained anything; rather, because of this mind, which always wants to attain something, I was missing every-thing. I have not achieved anything, this is not an achievement; rather, on the contrary, the achiever has disappeared. I am no more, see the beauty of it," said Buddha. "When I was, I was miserable, and when I am no more, everything is blissful, the bliss is showering and showering continuously on me, everywhere. Now there is no misery."

Buddha had said before: "Life is misery, birth is misery, death is misery — everything is miserable." It was miserable because the ego was there. The boat was not empty. Now the boat was empty; now there was no misery, no sorrow, no sadness. Existence had become a celebration and it would remain a celebration for eternity, forever and forever.

That's why I say, it is dangerous that you have come to me. You have taken a risky step. And if you are courageous, then be ready for the jump.

The whole effort is how to kill you; the whole effort is how to destroy you. Once you are destroyed, the indestructible will come up — it is there, hidden. Once all that which is nonessential is eliminated, the essential will be like a flame — alive in its total glory.

This parable of Chuang Tzu is beautiful. He says that a wise man is like an empty boat.

Such is the perfect man —
his boat is empty.

There is nobody inside.

If you meet a Chuang Tzu, or a Lao Tzu, or me, the boat is there, but it is empty – nobody in it. If you simply look at the surface, then somebody is there, because the boat is there. But if you penetrate deeper, if you really become intimate with me, if you forget the body, the boat, then you come to encounter a nothingness.

Chuang Tzu is a rare flowering, because to become nobody is the most difficult, almost impossible, the most extraordinary thing in the world.

The ordinary mind hankers to be extraordinary, that is part of ordinariness; the ordinary mind desires to be somebody in particular, that is part of ordinariness. You may become an Alexander, but you remain ordinary – then who is the extra-ordinary one? The extraordinariness starts only when you don't hanker after extraordinariness. Then the journey has started, then a new seed has sprouted.

This is what Chuang Tzu means when he says: "A perfect man is like an empty boat." Many things are implied in it. First, an empty boat is not going anywhere because there is nobody to direct it, nobody to manipulate it, nobody to drive it somewhere. An empty boat is just there, it is not going anywhere. Even if it is moving it is not going anywhere.

When the mind is not there life will remain a movement, but it will not be directed. You will move, you will change, you will be a riverlike flow, but not going anywhere, with no goal in view. A perfect man lives without any purpose; a perfect man moves but without any motive. If you ask a perfect man, "What are you doing?" he will say, "I don't know, this is what is happening." If you ask me why I am talking to you, I will say, "Ask the flower why the flower is flowering." This is happening, this is not manipulated. There is no one to manipulate it, the boat is empty. When there is purpose you will always be in misery. Why?

Once a man asked a miser, a great miser, "How could you succeed in accumu-lating so much wealth?"

The miser said, "This has been my motto: whatsoever is to be done tomorrow has to be done today, and whatsoever is to be enjoyed today has to be enjoyed tomorrow. This has been my motto." He succeeded in accumulating wealth – this is also how people succeed in accumulating nonsense.

That miser was also miserable. On the one hand he had succeeded in accumulating wealth, on the other hand he had succeeded in accumulating misery. The motto is the same for accumulating misery also: whatsoever is to be done tomorrow, do it today, right now, don't postpone it. And whatsoever can be enjoyed right now, never enjoy it right now, postpone it for tomorrow.

This is the way to enter hell. It always succeeds, it has never been a failure. Try it and you will succeed – or, you may have already succeeded. You may have been trying it without knowing. Postpone all that which can be enjoyed, just think of the tomorrow.

Jesus was crucified by the Jews for this reason, not for any other. Not that they were against Jesus – he was a perfect man, a beautiful man, why were the Jews against him? Rather, on the contrary, they had been waiting for this man. For centuries they had been hoping and waiting: "When will the messiah come?"

And then suddenly this Jesus declared, "I am the messiah for whom you have been waiting, and I have come now. Now look at me."

They were disturbed – because the mind can wait, it always enjoys waiting – but the mind cannot face the fact, the mind cannot encounter this moment. It can always postpone.

It was easy to postpone: "The messiah is to come, soon he will be coming ... " For centuries the Jews had been thinking and postponing and then suddenly this man destroyed all hope, because he said, "I am here." The mind was disturbed. They had to kill this man, otherwise they would not have been able to live with the hope for the tomorrow.

And not only Jesus, many others have declared since then, "I am here, I am the messiah!" And Jews always deny, because if they don't deny, then how will they be able to hope and how will they be able to postpone? They have lived with this hope with such fervor, with such deep intensity, you cannot believe it. There have been Jews who would go to their beds at night hoping that this would be the last night, that in the morning the messiah would be there.

I have heard about one rabbi who used to say to his wife, "If he comes in the night, don't waste a single minute, wake me up immediately." The messiah is coming and coming, he may come at any moment.

I have heard of another rabbi – his son was going to be married, so he sent invitations to the marriage to friends and he wrote on the invitation, "My son is going to be married in Jerusalem on such-and-such a date, but if the messiah hasn't come by then, my son will be married in this village of Korz. Who knows, by the time the day of the marriage comes, the messiah may have come. Then I will not be here, I will be in Jerusalem, celebrating. So if he has not come by the date of the marriage, only then will the marriage be here in this village; otherwise in Jerusalem."

They have been waiting and waiting, dreaming. The whole Jewish mind has been obsessed with the coming messiah. But whenever the messiah comes, they immediately deny him. This has to be understood. This is how the mind functions: you wait for the bliss, for the ecstasy, and whenever it comes you deny it, you just turn your back towards it.

Mind can live in the future, but cannot live in the present. In the present you can simply hope and desire. And that's how you create misery. If you start living this very moment, here and now, misery disappears.

But how is it related to the ego? Ego is the accumulated past. Whatsoever you have known, experienced, read, whatsoever has happened to you in the past, the whole is accumulated there. That whole past is the ego, it is you.

The past can project into the future – because future is nothing but extended past. The past cannot face the present – the present is totally different, it has a quality of being here and now. The past is always dead, the present is life, the very source of all aliveness. The past cannot face the present so it moves into the future – both are dead, both are nonexistential. The present is life; neither can the future encounter the present, nor can the past encounter the present. And your ego, your somebodiness, is your past. Unless you are empty you cannot be here, and unless you are here you cannot be alive.

How can you know the bliss of life? It is showering on you every moment and you are bypassing it.

Says Chuang Tzu:

Such is the perfect man –
his boat is empty.

Empty of what? Empty of the *I*, empty of the ego, empty of somebody there inside.

He who rules men, lives in confusion;
he who is ruled by men lives in sorrow.

He who rules men, lives in confusion ...

Why? Because the desire to rule comes from the ego; the desire to possess, to be powerful, the desire to dominate, comes from the ego. The greater the kingdom you can dominate, the greater the ego you can achieve. With your possessions your inner somebody goes on becoming bigger and bigger and bigger. Sometimes the boat becomes so small and the ego becomes so big.

This is what is happening to politicians, to people obsessed with wealth, prestige, power. Their egos have become so big that their boats cannot contain them. Every moment they are on the point of drowning, on the verge, afraid, scared to death. And the more afraid you are the more possessive you become, because you think that through possessions, somehow security is achieved. The more afraid you are, the more you think that if your kingdom could be a little greater, you would be more secure.

He who rules men, lives in confusion ...

Really, the desire to rule comes out of your confusion; the desire to be leaders of men comes out of your confusion. When you start leading others you forget your confusion – this is a sort of escape, a trick. You are ill, but if somebody is ill and you become interested in curing that man, you forget your own illness.

I have heard ...

Once George Bernard Shaw phoned his doctor and said, "I am in much trouble and I feel that my heart is going to fail. Come immediately!"

The doctor came running. He had to climb three staircases, perspiring. He came in and without saying anything, just fell down on a chair and closed his eyes. Bernard Shaw jumped out of his bed and asked, "What has happened?"

The doctor said, "Don't say anything. It seems I am dying. It is a heart attack."

Bernard Shaw started helping him; he brought a cup of tea, some aspirin, whatsoever he could do. Within half an hour the doctor was okay. And then he said, "Now I must leave, give me my fee."

George Bernard Shaw said, "This is really something. You should pay me! I have been running around for half an hour doing things for you and you have not even asked anything about me."

But the doctor said, "I have cured you. This is a treatment and you have to pay me the fee."

When you become interested in somebody else's illness you forget your own, hence so many leaders, so many gurus, so many masters. It gives you an occupation. If you are concerned with other people, if you are a servant of people, a social worker, helping others, you will forget your own confusion, your inner turmoil – you are too occupied.

Psychiatrists never go mad – not because they are immune to it, but they are so much concerned with curing and helping other people's madness, that they forget completely that they can also go mad.

I have come to know many social workers, leaders, politicians, gurus, and they stay healthy just because they are concerned with others.

But if you lead others, dominate others, out of your confusion you will create confusion in their lives. It may be a treatment for yourself, it may be a good escape for you, but it is spreading the disease.

He who rules men, lives in confusion ...

And not only lives in confusion, he also goes on spreading confusion in others. Out of confusion only confusion is born.

If you are confused, please remember – don't help anybody, because your help is going to be poisonous. If you are confused don't get occupied with others, because you are simply creating trouble, your disease will become infectious. Don't give advice to anybody, and if you have a little clarity of thought, don't take advice from someone who is confused. Remain alert, because confused people always like to give advice. And they give it free of charge, they give it very generously. Remain alert! Out of confusion only confusion is born.

... he who is ruled by men lives in sorrow.

If you dominate men, you live in confusion; if you allow others to dominate you, you will live in sorrow, because a slave cannot be blissful.

Yao therefore desired
neither to influence others
nor be influenced by them.

Someone of the name Yao – Chuang Tzu is talking about that man.

Yao therefore desired
neither to influence others
nor be influenced by them.

You should not try to influence anybody – and you should be alert, not to be influenced by others. The ego can do both, but it cannot remain in the middle. The ego can try to influence, then it feels good dominating; but remember that the ego also feels good being dominated. The masters feel good because so many slaves are dominated, and the slaves also feel good being dominated.

There are two types of mind in the world: the mind of those who dominate – the male mind, and the mind of those who like to be dominated – the female mind. By female I don't mean women, or by male, men. There are women who have masculine minds and there are men who have feminine minds. They are not always the same.

These are the two types of mind: one which likes to dominate and one which likes to be dominated. In both ways the ego is fulfilled because whether you dominate or are dominated you are important. If someone dominates you, then too you are important, because his domination depends on you. Without you, where will he be? Without you, where will his kingdom be, his domination, his possession? Without you, he will be nobody. The ego is fulfilled at both extremes; only in the middle does the ego die. Don't be dominated and don't try to dominate.

Just think what will happen to you. You are not important in any way, not significant in any way, neither as a master nor as a slave. Masters cannot live without slaves and slaves cannot live without masters – they need each other, they are complementary. Just like man and woman they are complementary. The other is required for their fulfillment.

Don't be either. Then who are you? Then suddenly you disappear because then you are not significant at all, nobody depends on you, you are not needed.

There is a great need to be needed. Remember, you feel good whenever you are needed. Sometimes, even if it brings misery to you, even then you love to be needed.

A crippled child, always on the bed and the mother always saying: "What to do? I have to serve this child and my whole life is being wasted." But still, if this child dies, this mother will feel lost, because at least this child needs her so totally that she has become important.

If there is nobody who needs you, who are you? You create the need to be needed. Even slaves are needed.

Yao therefore desired
neither to influence others
nor be influenced by them.
The way to get clear of confusion
and free of sorrow
is to live with Tao
in the land of the void.

This middle point is the land of the void, or the door to the land of the void – as if you are not, as if nobody needs you, and you don't need anybody. You exist as if you are not. If you are not significant the ego cannot persist. That is why you go on trying to become significant in some way or other. Whenever you feel that you are needed, you feel good. But this is your misery and confusion, and this is the base of your hell.

How can you be free? Look at these two extremes. Buddha called his religion the middle path, *majjhim nikaya*. He called it the middle path because he said that mind lives in extremes. Once you remain in the middle the mind disappears. In the middle there is no mind.

Have you seen a tightrope walker? Next time you see one, observe. Whenever the tightrope walker leans toward the left, he immediately has to move towards the right to balance; and whenever he feels he is leaning too much to the right, he has to lean towards the left.

You have to go to the opposite to create balance. So it happens that masters become slaves, slaves become masters; possessors become possessed, the possessed becomes the possessor. It goes on, it is a continuous balance.

Have you observed it in your relationships? If you are a husband, are you really a husband for twenty-four hours? Then you have not observed. In twenty-four hours the change happens at least twenty-four times – sometimes the wife is the husband and the husband is the wife, sometimes the husband is again the husband and the wife is again the wife.

And this goes on changing from left to right. It is a tightrope walk. You have to balance. You cannot dominate for twenty-four hours, because then the balance will be lost and the relationship will be destroyed.

Whenever the tightrope walker comes to the middle, neither leaning to the right nor leaning to the left, then it is difficult for you to observe unless you yourself are the tightrope walker; in the middle the mind disappears. Tightrope walking has been used in Tibet as a meditation, because in the middle the mind disappears. The mind comes into existence again when you lean towards the right, then the mind comes again into being and says: "Balance it, lean towards the left."

When a problem arises, the mind arises. When there is no problem, how can the mind arise? When you are just in the middle, balanced totally, there is no mind. The equilibrium means no mind.

One mother, I have heard, was very worried about her son. He was ten years old and he had not yet spoken a single word. Every effort was made but the doctors said, "Nothing is wrong, the brain is absolutely okay. The body is fit, the child is healthy, and nothing can be done. If something were wrong, then something could be done."

But still he would not speak. Then suddenly, one day in the morning, the son spoke and he said, "This toast is burned."

The mother couldn't believe it. She looked, she got scared, she said, "What! You have spoken? And spoken so well! Then why were you always silent? We persuaded and tried and you never spoke."

The child said, "There was never anything wrong. For the first time the toast is burned."

If there is nothing wrong why should you speak?

People come to me and they say, "You go on speaking every day ... " I say, "Yes, because so many wrong people go on coming here and listening. There is so much wrong that I have to speak. If nothing is wrong then there is no need to speak. I speak because of you, because the toast is burned."

Whenever it is in the middle, between any extreme or polarity, the mind disappears. Try it. Rope walking is a beautiful exercise, and one of the very subtle methods of meditation. Nothing else is needed. You can observe the rope walker yourself, how it happens.

And remember, on a rope thinking stops because you are in such danger. You cannot think. The moment you think, you will fall. A rope walker cannot think, he has to be alert every moment. The balance has to be maintained continuously. He cannot feel safe, he is not safe; he cannot feel secure, he is not secure. The danger is always there – any moment, a slight change of balance and he will fall – and death awaits.

If you walk on a tightrope you will come to feel two things: thinking stops because there is danger, and whenever you really come to the middle, neither left nor right, just the midpoint, a great silence descends on you such as you have not known before. And this happens in every way. The whole of life is a tightrope walk.

... *Yao therefore desired* to remain in the middle – neither be dominated nor be dominating, neither be a husband nor be a wife, neither be a master nor be a slave.

> *The way to get clear of confusion*
> *and free of sorrow*
> *is to live with Tao*
> *in the land of the void.*

In the middle the door opens – the land of the void. When you are not, the whole world disappears, because the world hangs on you. The whole world that you have created around you hangs on you. If you are not there the whole world disappears.

Not that existence goes into nonexistence, no. But the world disappears and existence appears. The world is a mind creation; existence is the truth. This house will be there, but then this house will not be yours. The flower will be there but the flower will become nameless. It will be neither beautiful nor ugly. It will be there, but no concept will arise in your mind. All conceptual framework disappears. Existence: bare, naked, innocent, remains there in its pure, mirrorlike beingness. All the concepts, all the imaginations, and all the dreams disappear in the land of the void.

> *If a man is crossing a river*
> *and an empty boat collides with his own skiff,*
> *even though he be a bad-tempered man*
> *he will not become very angry.*
> *But if he sees a man in the boat,*
> *he will shout to him to steer clear.*
> *And if the shout is not heard he will shout*
> *again, and yet again, and begin cursing –*

and all because there is somebody in that boat.
Yet if the boat were empty,
he would not be shouting, and he would not be angry.

If people go on colliding with you and if people go on being angry with you, remember, they are not at fault. Your boat is not empty. They are angry because you are there. If the boat is empty they will look foolish, if they are angry they will look foolish.

Those who are very intimate with me sometimes get angry with me and they look very foolish. If the boat is empty you can even enjoy the anger of others, because there is nobody to be angry with, they have not looked at you. So remember, if people go on colliding with you, you are too much of a solid wall. Get a door, become empty, let them pass.

But even then sometimes people will be angry – they are even angry with a buddha. Because there are foolish people – if their boat collides with an empty boat, they will not look whether there is somebody in it or not. They will start shouting; they will get so messed up within themselves they will not be able to see whether there is somebody in it or not.

But even then the empty boat can enjoy it because then the anger never hits you; you are not there, so whom can it hit?

This symbol of the empty boat is really beautiful. People are angry because you are too much there, because you are too heavy there – so solid they cannot pass. And life is intertwined with everybody. If you are too much, then every-where there will be collision, anger, depression, aggression, violence – the conflict continues.

Whenever you feel that someone is angry or someone has collided with you, you always think that he is responsible. This is how ignorance concludes, inter-prets. Ignorance always says, "The other is responsible." Wisdom always says, "If somebody is responsible, then I am responsible, and the only way not to collide is not to be."

"I am responsible" doesn't mean, "I am doing something, that is why they are angry." That is not the question. You may not be doing anything, but just your being there is enough for people to get angry. It is not a question of whether you are doing good or bad. The question is that you are there.

· This is the difference between Tao and other religions. Other religions say: Be good, behave in such a way that no one gets angry with you. Tao says: Don't be.

It is not a question of whether you behave or misbehave. This is not the question. Even a good man, even a very saintly man creates anger, because he is there. Sometimes a good man creates more anger than a bad man, because a good man means a very subtle egoist. A bad man feels guilty – his boat may be filled, but he feels guilty. He is not really too spread out on the boat, his guilt helps him to shrink. A good man feels himself to be so good that he fills the boat completely, overfills it.

So whenever you come near a good man, you will always feel tortured – not that *he* is torturing you, just his presence. With so-called good men you will always feel sad, and you would like to avoid them. So-called good men are really very heavy. Whenever you come into contact with them they make you sad, they depress you, and you would like to leave them as soon as possible.

The moralists, the puritans, the virtuous, they are all heavy, and they carry a burden around them, dark shadows. Nobody likes them. They cannot be good companions, they cannot be good friends. Friendship is impossible with a good man – almost impossible, because his eyes are always condemning. The moment you come near him, he is good and you are bad. Not that he is doing anything – just his very being creates something, and you will feel angry.

Tao is totally different. Tao has a different quality, and to me Tao is the deepest religion that has existed on this earth. There is no comparison to it. There have been glimpses, there are glimpses in the sayings of Jesus, Buddha, and Krishna – but only glimpses.

Lao Tzu or Chuang Tzu's message is the purest – absolutely pure, nothing has contaminated it. And this is the message: it is all because there is somebody in the boat. This whole hell is all because there is somebody in the boat.

Yet if the boat were empty,
he would not be shouting,
and he would not be angry.

If you can empty your own boat
crossing the river of the world,
no one will oppose you,
and no one will seek to harm you.

The straight tree is the first to be cut down,
the spring of clear water is the first to be drained dry.
If you wish to improve your wisdom
and shame the ignorant,
to cultivate your character and outshine others,
a light will shine around you
as if you had swallowed the sun and the moon –
and you will not avoid calamity.

This is unique, because Chuang Tzu is saying that the halo of saintliness around you shows that you are still there. The halo ... that you are good, is sure to create calamity for you, and calamity for others also. Lao Tzu and Chuang Tzu – master and disciple – both have never been painted in pictures with halos or auras, like Jesus, Zarathustra, Krishna, Buddha, or Mahavira. They have never been painted with an aura around their head, because they say if you are really good no aura appears around your head; rather, on the contrary, the head disappears. Where to draw the aura? The head disappears.

All auras are somehow related to the ego. It is not Krishna who has made a self-portrait, it is the disciples, who cannot think of him without drawing an aura around his head – otherwise he looks ordinary. And Chuang Tzu says: "To be ordinary is to be the sage." Nobody recognizes you, nobody feels that you are somebody extraordinary. Chuang Tzu says: "You go in the crowd and you mix." Nobody knows that a buddha has entered the crowd. No one comes to feel that somebody is different, because if someone feels it then there is bound to be anger and calamity. Whenever someone feels that you are somebody, his own anger, his own ego is hurt. He starts reacting, he starts attacking you.

So Chuang Tzu says: "Character is not to be cultivated," because that too is a sort of wealth. And so-called religious people go on teaching: cultivate character, cultivate morality, be virtuous.

But why? Why be virtuous? Why be against the sinners? Your mind is dual, you are still ambitious. And if you reach paradise and you see sinners sitting there around God, you will feel very hurt – your whole life has been wasted. You cultivated virtue, you cultivated character, while these people were enjoying themselves and doing all sorts of things which are condemned – and here they are sitting around God. If you see saints and sinners together in paradise you will be very hurt, you will become very sad and miserable – because your virtue is also part of your ego. You cultivate saintliness to be superior, but the mind remains the same. How to be superior in some way or other, how to make others inferior is the motive.

If you can gather much wealth, then they are poor and you are rich. If you can become an Alexander, then you have a great kingdom and they are beggars. If you can become a great scholar, then you are knowledgeable and they are ignorant, illiterate. If you can become virtuous, religious, respectable, moral, then they are condemned, they are sinners. But the duality continues. You are fighting against others and you are trying to be superior.

Chuang Tzu says: "If you cultivate your character and outshine others, you will not avoid calamity." Don't try to outshine others, and don't try to cultivate character for this egoistic purpose.

So for Chuang Tzu there is only one character worth mentioning, and that is egolessness – all else follows it. Without it, nothing has worth. You may become godlike in your character, but if the ego is there inside, all your godliness is in the service of the Devil; all your virtue is nothing but a face and the sinner is hidden behind. And the sinner cannot be transformed through virtue or through any type of cultivation. It is only when you are not there that it disappears.

A wise man has said:
"He who is content with himself
has done worthless work.
Achievement is the beginning of failure,
fame is the beginning of disgrace."

... very paradoxical sayings, and you will have to be very alert to understand them; otherwise they can be misunderstood.

A wise man has said:
"He who is content with himself
has done worthless work."

Religious people go on teaching: Be content with yourself. But yourself remains there to be content with. Chuang Tzu says: "Don't be there," then there is no question of contentment or discontentment. This is real contentment, when you are not there. But if you feel that you are content, it is false – because you are there, and it is just an ego fulfillment. You feel that you have achieved, you feel that you have reached.

Tao says that one who feels that he has achieved has missed already. One who feels that he has reached has lost, because success is the beginning of failure. Success and failure are two parts of one circle, of one wheel. Whenever success reaches its climax the failure has already started, the wheel is already turning downward. Whenever the moon has become full there is no further progress. Now there is no further movement. The next day the downward journey starts and now every day the moon will be less and less and less.

Life moves in circles. Whenever you feel that you have achieved, at that moment the wheel has moved, you are already losing. It may take time for you to recognize this, because mind is dull. Much intelligence is needed, clarity is needed, to see things when they happen. Things happen to you and you take many days to recognize it, sometimes many months or many years. Sometimes you even take many lives to recognize what has happened.

But just think about your past. Whenever you had a feeling that you had succeeded, immediately things changed, you started falling – because the ego is part of the wheel. It succeeds because it can fail; if it cannot fail then there is no possibility of success. Success and failure are two aspects of the same coin.

Chuang Tzu says:

A wise man has said:
"He who is content with himself
has done worthless work."

... Because he is still there, the empty boat has not come into being yet, the boat is still filled. The ego is sitting there, the ego is still enthroned.

Achievement is the beginning of failure,
fame is the beginning of disgrace."
Who can free himself of achievement and fame
then descend and be lost
amid the masses of men?
He will flow like Tao ...

Be alert and attentive.

Who can free himself of achievement and fame
then descend and be lost
amid the masses of men?
He will flow like Tao, unseen,
he will go about like life itself
with no name and no home.
Simple is he, without distinction.
To all appearances he is a fool.

This is how a wise man is – a fool.

To all appearances he is a fool.
His steps leave no trace. He has no power.
He achieves nothing, he has no reputation.
Since he judges no one, no one judges him.
Such is the perfect man –
his boat is empty.

The ego cannot flow like a river. It is frozen. How can a frozen river flow? The ice must melt, only then can it flow. Frozen, you have a form – melted, the form disappears. Frozen, you are somebody, somewhere, a name – melted, the name is lost, "somebodyness" disappears. You have become nothing, formless. Only when you are not frozen do you flow, and when you flow you are like life itself because life is a movement. Only death is unmoving, only death remains where it is. Life goes on moving and moving and moving – it is a continuous flow.

If you have succeeded, you are frozen because now you are afraid to melt – because if you melt the whole success will be lost. Your success is part of your frozenness. If you have become famous you are frozen, now you are dead, now you cannot melt. You have to protect yourself, your fame, your respect, your reputation. You have to protect, and you have to remain with your past. You cannot move into the unknown future, because who knows, the unknown path may lead you to somewhere where the fame is lost, the reputation is lost. So you will move only on the trodden path, on the charted, on the known. You will move in the circle of memory, on the wheel of memory.

Life never moves on the trodden path, it always moves into the unknown. Every moment it is moving into the unknown and if you are afraid of the unknown you are frozen, you will be dead. Life will not wait for you. You have to melt and only one who has no reputation to save, no fame to protect, can move with the unknown and can move happily. He has nothing to lose. Hence, Buddha's beggars – nameless, homeless, nothing to protect, nothing to preserve. They could move anywhere, just like clouds in the sky, homeless, with no roots anywhere, floating, with no goal, no purpose, no ego.

He will flow like Tao, unseen,
he will go about like life itself
with no name and no home.

This is what a sannyasin means to me. When I initiate you into sannyas, I initiate you into this death, into namelessness, into homelessness. I am not giving you any secret key to success, I am not giving you any secret formula for how to succeed.

If I am giving you anything, it is a key to how not to succeed, how to be a failure and unworried, how to move nameless, homeless, without any goal, how to be a beggar – what Jesus calls poor in spirit. A man who is poor in spirit is egoless – he is the empty boat.

Simple is he, without distinction.

Whom do you call simple? Can you cultivate simplicity?

You see a man who eats only once a day, who wears only a few clothes or remains naked, who doesn't live in a palace, who lives under a tree – you say this man is simple. Is this simplicity? You can live under a tree and your living may be just a cultivation. You have cultivated it to be simple, you have calculated it to be simple. You may eat once a day, but you have calculated it, this is mind-manipulated. You may remain naked – that cannot make you simple. Simplicity only happens.

Simple is he, without distinction.

You feel that you are a saint because you live under a tree, and you eat once a day, and you are a vegetarian, and you live naked, you don't possess any money – you are a saint.

And then a man passes who possesses money; condemnation arises in you, and you think, "What will happen to this sinner? He will be condemned to hell." And you feel compassion for this sinner. Then you are not simple. Because distinctions have entered, you are distinct.

It makes no difference how the distinction has been created. A king lives in a palace – he is distinct from those who live in huts. A king wears clothes which you cannot wear – they are so valuable that he is distinct. Then a man lives naked on the street and you cannot live naked in the street – so he is distinct. Wherever distinction is, ego exists. When there is no distinction, ego disappears; and non-ego is simplicity.

Simple is he, without distinction.
To all appearances he is a fool.

This is the deepest saying that Chuang Tzu has uttered. It is difficult to understand because we always think that an enlightened person, a perfect man, is a man of wisdom. He says: *To all appearances he is a fool* ...

But this is how it should be. Amongst so many fools, how can a wise man be otherwise? To all appearances he will be a fool and that is the only way. How can he change this foolish world and so many fools ... toward sanity? He will have to be naked, and go under the table and crow like a rooster. Only then can he change you. He must become crazy like you, he must be a fool, he must allow you to laugh at him. Then you will not feel jealous, then you will not feel hurt, then you will not be angry with him, then you can tolerate him, then you can forget him and forgive him, then you can leave him alone to himself.

Many great mystics have behaved like fools and their contemporaries were at a loss – what to make out of their lives – and the greatest wisdom existed in them. To be wise amongst you is really foolish. That won't do; you will create much trouble. Socrates was poisoned because he didn't know Chuang Tzu. If he had known Chuang Tzu, there would have been no need for him to be poisoned. He tried to behave like a wise man amongst fools, he tried to be wise.

Chuang Tzu says: "To all appearances the wise man will be like a fool."

Chuang Tzu himself lived like a fool, laughing, singing, dancing, talking in jokes and anecdotes. Nobody thought him to be serious. And you could not find a man more sincere and serious than Chuang Tzu. But nobody thought him to be serious. People enjoyed him, people loved him, and through this love he was throwing seeds of his wisdom. He changed many, he transformed many.

But to change a madman you have to learn his language, and you have to use his language. You have to be like him, you have to come down. If you go on standing on your pedestal then there can be no communion.

This is what happened to Socrates, and it had to happen there because the Greek mind is the most rational mind in the world, and a rational mind always tries not to be foolish. Socrates angered everybody. People really had to kill him, because he would ask awkward questions and he would make everybody feel foolish. He would put everybody in a corner – you cannot answer even ordinary questions.

If somebody insists, if you believe in God, then Socrates will ask something about God: "What is the proof?" You cannot answer, you have not seen. But God is a far off thing; you cannot even prove ordinary things. You have left your wife at home – how can you prove, really, that you have left your wife at home, or that you have even got a wife? It may be just in your memory. You may have seen a dream, and when you go back there is neither house nor wife.

Socrates would ask penetrating questions, analyzing everything, and everybody in Athens became angry. This man was trying to prove that everybody is a fool. They killed him. Had he met Chuang Tzu – and at that time Chuang Tzu was alive in China, they were contemporaries – then Chuang Tzu would have told him the secret: "Don't try to prove that anybody is foolish because fools don't like this. Don't try to prove to a madman that he is mad, because no madman likes it. He will get angry, arrogant, aggressive. He will kill you if you prove too much. If you come to the point where it can be proved, he will take revenge."

Chuang Tzu would have said, "It is better to be foolish yourself, then people enjoy you, and then by a very subtle methodology you can help them change. Then they are not against you."

That's why in the East, particularly in India, China and Japan, such an ugly phenomenon never happened as happened in Greece – Socrates was poisoned and killed. It happened in Jerusalem – Jesus was killed, crucified. It happened in Iran, in Egypt, in other countries – many wise men were killed, murdered. It never happened in India, China, or Japan, because in these three countries people came to realize that to behave as a wise man is to invite calamity.

Behave like a fool, like a madman, just be mad. That is the first step of the wise man – to make you at ease so you are not afraid of him. This is why I told you that story.

The prince became friendly with this man. He was afraid of others, doctors, learned experts, because they were trying to change him, cure him, and he was not mad. He did not think that he was mad, no madman ever thinks that he is mad. If a madman ever comes to realize that he is mad, madness has disappeared. He is no longer mad.

All those wise men who were trying to cure the prince were foolish, only this old sage was wise. He behaved foolishly. The court laughed, the king laughed, the queen laughed. They said, "What? How is this man going to change the prince? He himself is crazy and seems to be deeper in madness than the prince."

Even the prince was shocked. He said, "What are you doing? What do you mean?" But this man must have been an enlightened sage.

Chuang Tzu is talking about this type of phenomenon, this phenomenal man.

To all appearances he is a fool.
His steps leave no trace.

You cannot follow him. You cannot follow an enlightened man – no, never – because he leaves no trace, there are no footprints. He is like a bird in the sky, he moves and no trace is left.

Why does a wise man not leave traces? So that you should not be able to follow. No wise man likes you to follow him because when you follow you become imitators. He is always moving in such a zigzag way that you cannot follow. If you try to follow him, you will miss. Can you follow me? It is impossible, because you don't know what I am going to be tomorrow. You cannot predict. If you can predict, you can plan. Then you know where I am going, then you know the direction, then you know my steps. You know my past, you can infer my future. But I am illogical.

If I am logical you can conclude what I am going to say tomorrow. Just by looking at whatsoever I have said in my yesterdays you can conclude logically what I am going to say tomorrow. But that is not possible. I may contradict myself completely. My every tomorrow will contradict my every yesterday, so how are you going to follow me? You will go crazy if you try to follow.

Sooner or later you will have to realize that you have to be yourself, you cannot imitate.

His steps leave no trace.

He is not consistent. He is not logical. He is illogical. He is like a madman.

He has no power.

This will be very difficult to follow because we think that the sage has power, that he is the most powerful of men. He will touch your blind eyes and they will open and you will be able to see; you are dead and he will touch you and you will be resurrected. To us a sage is a miracle worker.

But Chuang Tzu says: *He has no power* – because to use power is always part of the ego. The ego wants to be powerful. You cannot persuade a wise man to use his power, it is impossible. If you can persuade him, it means some ego was left which can be persuaded. He will never use his power because there is no one to use and manipulate it. The ego, the manipulator, is no longer there, the boat is empty. Who will direct this boat? There is nobody.

A sage *is* power, but he has no power; a sage is powerful, but he has no power – because the controller is no longer there. He is energy – overflowing, unaddressed, undirected – there is no one who can direct it. You may be cured in his presence, your eyes may open, but he has not opened them, he has not touched them, he has not cured you. If he thinks that he has cured you, he himself has become ill. This *I* – "I have cured" – is a greater illness, it is a greater blindness.

He has no power.
He achieves nothing, he has no reputation.
Since he judges no one,
no one judges him.
Such is the perfect man –
his boat is empty.

And this is going to be your path. Empty your boat. Go on throwing out whatsoever you find in the boat, until everything is thrown out and nothing is left, even *you* are thrown out, nothing is left, your being has become just empty.

The last thing and the first thing is to be empty; once you are empty you will be filled. The all will descend on you when you are empty – only emptiness can receive the all, nothing less will do, because to receive all you have to be so empty, boundlessly empty. Only then can the all be received. Your minds are so small they cannot receive the divine. Your rooms are so small you cannot invite the divine. Destroy this house completely because only the sky, space, total space, can receive.

Emptiness is going to be the path, the goal, everything. From tomorrow morning try to empty yourself of all that you find within: your misery, your anger, your ego, jealousies, sufferings, your pain, your pleasures — whatsoever you find, just throw it out. Without any distinction, without any choice, empty yourself. And the moment you are totally empty, suddenly you will see that you are the whole, the all. Through voidness, the whole is achieved.

Meditation is nothing but emptying, becoming nobody.

In this camp move as a nobody. If you create anger in somebody and you collide, remember, you must be there in the boat, that's why it is happening. Soon, when your boat is empty, you will not collide, there will be no conflict, no anger, no violence — nothing.

This nothing is the benediction, this nothing is the blessing. For this nothing you have been searching and searching. But unless the searcher is lost, there can be no fulfillment.

And now that you have come, don't go back filled with yourself. Go empty. Move in this wide world as an empty boat, and all the blessings of life, all the blessings that are possible in existence will be yours. Claim them but you can claim them only when you are not. This is the problem — how not to be. And I say to you it can be solved. I have solved it, that's why I say it.

It will be difficult for you to meet Chuang Tzu. But I am here. You can look in me, you will find the same empty boat. I'm talking to you, but nobody is talking to you. And I'm not claiming any wisdom, I'm not claiming anything. I have no powers to cure you, no miracles will happen here, because I'm interested only in the ultimate miracle — when somebody becomes ordinary. That is the ultimate miracle. Meditate on it, pray for it, make all efforts for it. And remember only one thing — you have to become the empty boat.

Enough for today.

Chapter 2

The Man of Tao

The man in whom Tao
Acts without impediment
Harms no other being
By his actions
Yet he does not know himself
To be "kind," and "gentle."

He does not struggle to make money
And does not make a virtue of poverty.
He goes his way
Without relying on others.
And does not pride himself
On walking alone.

"The man of Tao
Remains unknown
Perfect virtue
Produces nothing
'No-Self' is 'True-Self.'
And the greatest man
Is Nobody."

The most difficult thing, almost impossible for the mind, is to remain in the middle, is to remain balanced. To move from one thing to its opposite is the easiest. To move from one polarity to the opposite polarity is the nature of the mind. This has to be understood very deeply, because unless you understand this, nothing can lead you into meditation.

Mind's nature is to move from one extreme to another. It depends on imbalance. If you are balanced, mind disappears. Mind is like a disease: when you are imbalanced it is there, when you are balanced, it is not there.

That is why it is easy for a person who overeats to go on a fast. It looks illogical, because we think that a person who is obsessed with food cannot go on a fast. You are wrong. Only a person who is obsessed with food can go on a fast, because fasting is the same obsession in the opposite direction. It is not really changing yourself. You are again obsessed with food. Before you were overeating; now you are remaining hungry – but the mind remains focused on food from the opposite extreme.

A man who has been overindulging in sex can become a celibate very easily. There is no problem. But it is difficult for the mind to come to the right diet, difficult for the mind to stay in the middle.

Why is it difficult to stay in the middle? It is just like the pendulum of a clock. The pendulum goes to the right, then it moves to the left, then again to the right, then again to the left; the whole clock depends on this movement. If the pendulum stays in the middle, the clock stops. And when the pendulum is going to the right, you think it is only going to the right, but at the same time it is gathering momentum to go to the left. The more it moves to the right, the more energy it gathers to move to the left, to the opposite. When it is moving to the left it is again gathering momentum to move to the right.

Whenever you are overeating you are gathering momentum to go on a fast. Whenever you overindulge in sex, sooner or later, *brahmacharya* will appeal to you, celibacy will appeal to you.

And the same is happening from the opposite pole. Go and ask your so-called *sadhus*, your *bhikkus*, sannyasins. They have made it a point to remain celibate, now their minds are gathering momentum to move into sex. They have made it a point to remain more and more hungry, starving, and their minds are constantly thinking about food. When you are thinking about food too much it shows that you are gathering momentum for it. Thinking means momentum. The mind starts arranging for the opposite.

One thing: whenever you move, you are also moving to the opposite. The opposite is hidden, it is not apparent.

When you love a person you are gathering momentum to hate him. That's why only friends can become enemies. You cannot suddenly become an enemy unless you have first become a friend. Lovers quarrel, fight. Only lovers can quarrel and fight, because unless you love, how can you hate? Unless you have moved to the far extreme, to the left, how can you move to the right? Modern research says that so-called love is a relationship of intimate enmity. Your wife is your intimate enemy, your husband is your intimate enemy – both intimate and inimical. They appear opposites, illogical, because we think: one who is intimate, how can he be the enemy? One who is a friend, how can he also be the foe?

Logic is superficial, life goes deeper, and in life all opposites are joined together, they exist together. Remember this, because then meditation becomes balancing.

Buddha taught eight disciplines, and with each discipline he used the word *right*. He said: "Right effort," because it is very easy to move from action to inaction, from waking to sleep, but to remain in the middle is difficult. When Buddha used the word *right* he was saying: "Don't move to the opposite, just remain in the middle. Right food" – he never said to fast. Don't indulge in too much eating and don't indulge in fasting. He said: "Right food." Right food means standing in the middle.

When you are standing in the middle you are not gathering any momentum. And this is the beauty – a man who is not gathering any momentum to move anywhere, can be at ease with himself, can be at home.

You can never be at home, because whatsoever you do you will immediately have to do the opposite to balance. And the opposite never balances, it simply gives you the idea that maybe you are becoming balanced, but you will have to move to the opposite again.

A buddha is neither a friend to anyone nor an enemy. He has simply stopped in the middle – the clock is not functioning.

It is said about one Hasid mystic, a *magid* – that when he attained enlightenment suddenly his clock on the wall stopped. It may have happened, it may not have happened, because it is possible, but the symbolism is clear: when your mind stops, time stops; when the pendulum stops, the clock stops. From then on the clock never moved, from then on it always showed the same time.

Time is created by the movement of the mind, just like the movement of the pendulum. Mind moves, you feel time. When mind is nonmoving, how can you feel time? When there is no movement, time cannot be felt. So scientists and mystics agree on this point: that movement creates the phenomenon of time. If you are not moving, if you are still, time disappears, eternity comes into existence. Your clock is moving fast, and the mechanism moves from one extreme to another.

The second thing to be understood about mind is that the mind always longs for the distant, never for the near. The near gives you boredom, you are fed up with it; the distant gives you dreams, hopes, possibility of pleasure. So the mind always thinks of the distant. It is always somebody else's wife who is attractive, beautiful; it is always somebody else's house which obsesses you; it is always somebody else's car which fascinates you. It is always the distant. You are blind to the near. The mind cannot see that which is very near. It can only see that which is very far.

And what is very far, the most distant? The opposite is the most distant. You love a person – now hatred is the most distant phenomenon; you are overeating – now fasting is the most distant phenomenon; you are celibate – now sex is the most distant phenomenon; you are a king – now to be a monk is the most distant phenomenon.

The most distant is the most dreamy. It attracts, it obsesses, it goes on calling, inviting you, and then when you have reached the other pole, this place from where you have traveled will become beautiful again. Divorce your wife, and after a few years the wife has gained beauty again.

A film actress came to me. She had divorced her husband fifteen years ago. Now she is old, less beautiful than she was when she and her husband were separated. Their son was married last year, so at the marriage she met her husband again, and they had to travel together. The husband fell in love with her again, so she came to me and asked, "What should I do? Because now he is proposing again, he wants to get married to me again."

She was also fascinated. She was just waiting for me to say yes. I said, "But you lived together, there was always conflict and nothing else. I know the whole story — how you were fighting, quarreling, how you were creating hell and misery for each other. Now again ... ?"

The distant always becomes fascinating. You can move into the same rut and then again you will start thinking of the opposite. Remember, mind always thinks of the opposite, is always fascinated with the opposite. So if you are rich you will have a fascination for poverty. All rich people think that poverty has such a freedom no rich man can enjoy. Whenever a king passes and he looks at a beggar sleeping under a tree — the traffic moves but he is not disturbed, he can sleep even in the market, what beautiful sleep — and the king feels jealous. Kings are always jealous of beggars, and kings always dream that they have become monks, sannyasins.

It is not a coincidence that Mahavira, Buddha, all the *tirthankaras* of Jainas were kings. They came from the palaces, they had left their kingdoms. For a king, the beggar is always the attraction. This country has been the country of kings and beggars, both. At the one extreme kings have existed, at the other extreme the beggars. And we have raised beggars to the highest peak of glory. Buddha called his sannyasins *bhikkus* — beggars. He was a king. He was fed up with all that being a king implies. He was fascinated with the simple life, the innocent life of a beggar.

But ask some beggar ... he is not happy. If kings are not happy how can beggars be happy? He is unhappy and he is just waiting for the chance when he can also become a king. Go into his dreams and you will find him always becoming an emperor. Beggars dream of kingdoms, kings dream of becoming sannyasins, renouncing everything. Beggars dream of possessing the whole world, kings dream of not possessing anything at all.

For the mind the opposite is magnetic, and unless you transcend this through understanding, the mind will go on moving from left to right, from right to left, and the clock will continue.

It has continued for many lives, and this is how you have been deceiving yourself — because you don't understand the mechanism. Again the distant becomes appealing, again you start traveling. The moment you reach, that which was with you is now distant, has appeal, it becomes a star, something worthwhile.

I was reading about a pilot. He was flying over California with a friend. He told the friend, "Look down at that beautiful lake. I was born near it, that is my village."

He pointed to a small village just perched in the hills near the lake, and he said, "I was born there. When I was a child I used to sit near the lake and fish; fishing was my hobby. But at that time, when I was a child fishing near the lake, airplanes always used to pass in the sky, and I would think of the day when I would become a pilot myself, I would be piloting an airplane. That was my only dream. Now it is fulfilled, and what misery! Now I am continuously looking down at the lake and thinking about when I will retire and go fishing again. That lake is so beautiful ... "

This is how things are happening. This is how things are happening to you. In childhood, you long to grow up fast because older people are more powerful, young men more powerful. A child just longs to grow up immediately. Old people are wise, and the child feels that whatsoever he is doing is always wrong. Then ask the old man — he always thinks that when childhood was lost, everything was lost; paradise was there in childhood. And all the old men die thinking of childhood, the innocence, the beauty, the dreamland.

Whatsoever you have looks useless, whatsoever you don't have looks useful. Remember this, otherwise meditation cannot happen, because meditation means this — understanding the mind, the working of the mind, the very process of the mind.

Mind is dialectical, it makes you move again and again towards the opposite. And this is an infinite process, it never ends unless you suddenly drop out of it, unless you suddenly become aware of the game, unless you suddenly become aware of the trick of the mind, and you stop in the middle.

Stopping in the middle is meditation.

Thirdly, because mind consists of polarities, you are never whole. The mind cannot be whole; it is always half. When you love someone have you observed that you are suppressing your hatred? The love is not total, it is not whole; just behind it all the dark forces are hidden and they may erupt any moment. You are sitting on a volcano.

When you love someone, you simply forget that you have anger, you have hate, you have jealousy. You simply drop them as if they never existed. But how can you drop them? You can simply hide them in the unconscious. Just on the surface you can become loving, deep down the turmoil is hidden. Sooner or later when you are fed up, when the beloved has become familiar – and they say familiarity breeds contempt ... It is not that familiarity breeds contempt – familiarity makes you bored, contempt has always been there, hidden. It comes up, it was waiting for the right moment, the seed was there.

The mind always has the opposite within it, and that opposite goes into the unconscious and waits for its moment to come up. If you observe minutely, you will feel it every moment. When you say to someone, "I love you," close your eyes, be meditative, and feel – is there any hatred hidden? You will feel it. But because you want to deceive yourself, because the truth is so ugly – that you hate a person that you love – you don't want to face it. You want to escape from the facticity, so you hide it. But hiding won't help, because it is not deceiving somebody else, it is deceiving yourself.

So whenever you feel something, just close the eyes and go into yourself to find the opposite somewhere. It is there. And if you can see the opposite, that will give you a balance, then you will not say, "I love you." If you are truthful you will say, "My relationship with you is one of love and hate."

All relationships are love/hate relationships. No relationship is of pure love, and no relationship is of pure hate. It is both love and hate. If you are truthful you will be in difficulty. If you say to a girl, "My relationship with you is one of both love and hate; I love you as I have never loved anybody and I hate you as I have never hated anybody," it will be difficult to get married unless you find a meditative girl who can understand the reality; unless you can find a friend who can understand the complexity of the mind.

Mind is not a simple mechanism, it is very complex, and through mind you can never become simple because mind goes on creating deceptions. To be meditative means to be aware of the fact that mind is hiding something from you; you are closing your eyes to some facts which are disturbing. Then sooner or later those disturbing facts will erupt, overpower you, and you will move to the opposite. And the opposite is not there in a distant, faraway place, in some star; the opposite is hidden behind you, in you, in your mind, in the very functioning of the mind. If you can understand this, you will stop in the middle.

If you can see – I love and I hate – suddenly both will disappear, because both cannot exist together in the consciousness. You have to create a barrier: one has to exist in the unconscious and one in the conscious. Both cannot exist in the conscious; if both exist they will negate each other. The love will destroy hate, the hate will destroy love; they will balance each other, and they will simply disappear. The same amount of hate and the same amount of love will negate each other. Suddenly they will evaporate – you will be there, but no love and no hate. Then you are balanced.

When you are balanced, mind is not there – then you are whole. When you are whole, you are holy, but mind is not there. So meditation is a state of no-mind. Through mind it is not achieved. Through mind, whatsoever you do, it can never be achieved. Then what are you doing when you are meditating?

Because you have created so much tension in your life, now you are meditating. But this is the opposite of tension, not real meditation. You are so tense that meditation has become attractive. That is why in the West meditation appeals more than in the East, because more tension exists there than in the East. The East is still relaxed, people are not so tense, they don't go mad so easily, they don't commit suicide so easily. They are not so violent, not so aggressive, not so scared, not so fearful – no, they are not so tense. They are not living at such a mad speed where nothing but tension is accumulated.

So if Mahesh Yogi comes to India, nobody listens. But in America, people are mad about him. When there is much tension, meditation will appeal. But this appeal is again falling into the same trap. This is not real meditation, this is again a trick. Then you meditate for a few days, you become relaxed; when you become relaxed, again activity arises, and the mind starts thinking of doing something, of moving. You get bored with it.

People come to me and say, "We meditated for a few years, then it became boring, then there was no more fun."

Just the other day a girl came and she was saying, "Now meditation is no longer fun, what should I do?"

Now the mind is seeking something else, now it is enough! Now that she is at ease, the mind is asking for more tensions – something to get disturbed about. When she says that now meditation is no longer fun, she means that now the tension is not there, so how can the meditation be fun? She will have to move into tension again, then meditation will again become something worthwhile.

Look at the absurdity of the mind: you have to go away to come near, you have to become tense to be meditative. But this is not meditation, again this is a trick of the same mind; on a new level the same game continues.

When I say meditation, I mean going beyond the game of the polar opposites, dropping out of the whole game, looking at the absurdity of it and transcending it. The very understanding becomes transcendence.

Mind will force you to move to the opposite – don't move to the opposite. Stop in the middle and see that this has always been the trick of the mind. This is how mind has dominated you – through the opposite. Have you felt it?

Whenever you make love to a woman, after it you suddenly start thinking of *brahmacharya*, and *brahmacharya* has such an alluring fascination at that moment that you feel as if there is nothing else to achieve. You feel frustrated, deceived, you feel that there was nothing in this sex, only *brahmacharya* has the bliss. But after twenty-four hours, sex becomes important again, significant, and again you have to move into it.

What is the mind doing? After the sex act it started thinking about the opposite, which again creates the taste for sex.

A violent man starts thinking about nonviolence, then he can easily be violent again. A man who gets angry again and again always thinks of non-anger, always decides not to be angry again. This decision helps him to be angry again.

If you really want not to be angry again don't decide against anger. Just look into the anger and just look at the shadow of the anger which you think is non-anger. Look into sex, and at the shadow of sex, which you think is *brahmacharya*, celibacy. It is just negativity, absence. Look at overeating, and the shadow of it, fasting, which always follows overeating. Overindulgence is always followed by vows of celibacy; tension is always followed by some meditation techniques. Look at them together, feel how they are related; they are part of one process.

If you can understand this, meditation will happen to you. It is not really something to be done, it is a point of understanding. It is not an effort, it is nothing to be cultivated. It is something to be deeply understood.

Understanding gives freedom. Knowledge of the whole mechanism of the mind is transformation. Then suddenly the clock stops, time disappears – and with the stopping of the clock, there is no mind. With the stopping of time, where are you? The boat is empty.

Now we will enter this sutra of Chuang Tzu:

The man of Tao
acts without impediment,
harms no other being
by his actions,
yet he does not know himself
to be kind and gentle.

The man of Tao acts without impediment ... You act always with impediment, the opposite is always there creating the impediment; you are not a flow.

If you love, the hate is always there as an impediment. If you move, something is holding you back; you never move totally, something is always left, the movement is not total. You move with one leg but the other leg is not moving. How can you move? The impediment is there.

And this impediment, this continuous moving of the half and nonmoving of the other half, is your anguish, your anxiety. Why are you in so much anguish? What creates so much anxiety in you? Whatsoever you do, why is bliss not happening through it?

Bliss can happen only to the whole, never to the part.

When the whole moves without any impediment the very movement is bliss. Bliss is not something that comes from outside, it is the feeling that comes when your whole being moves, the very movement of the whole is bliss. It is not something happening to you, it arises out of you, it is a harmony in your being.

If you are divided – and you are always divided: half-moving, half-withholding, half saying yes, half saying no, half in love, half in hate, you are a divided kingdom – there is constant conflict in you. You say something but you never mean it, because the opposite is there impeding, creating a hindrance.

Baal Shem used to say – his disciples used to write down whatsoever he said, and he used to say: "I know that whatsoever you are writing is not what has been said by me. You have heard something, I have said something else, and you are writing still something else. And if you look at the meaning, the meaning is something else again. You will never do what you have written, you will do something else – fragments, not an integrated being." Why are these fragments there?

Have you heard the story about the centipede? A centipede was walking – a centipede has one hundred legs – that's why he is called a centipede. It is a miracle to walk with a hundred feet, even to manage two is so difficult. To manage one · hundred legs is really impossible, almost impossible. But the centipede has been managing it.

One fox became curious – and foxes are curious. In folklore the fox is the symbol of the mind, of the intellect, of logic. Foxes are great logicians. The fox looked, she observed, she analyzed, she couldn't believe it. She said, "Wait, one question! How do you manage, how do you know which foot has to follow which? One hundred legs! How does this harmony happen, that you walk so smoothly?"

The centipede said, "I have been walking but I have never thought about it. Give me a little time."

So he closed his eyes. For the first time he became divided: the mind as observer, and himself as the observed. For the first time the centipede became two. He had been living and walking, but his life had been one whole; there was no observer standing looking at himself, he was never divided; he had been an integrated being. For the first time division arose. He was looking at his own self, thinking. He had become subject and object, he had become two, and then he started walking. It was difficult, almost impossible. He fell down – how do you manage one hundred legs?

The fox laughed and he said, "I knew it must be difficult, I knew it beforehand."

The centipede started crying and weeping, tears came to his eyes. He said, "It has never been difficult, but you have created the problem. Now I will never be able to walk again."

The mind has come into being; mind comes when you are divided. The mind feeds on division. Hence, Krishnamurti goes on saying that when the observer has become the observed you are in meditation.

The opposite happened to the centipede. The wholeness was lost, he became two: the observer and the observed, divided; the subject and the object, the thinker and the thought. Then everything was disturbed, then bliss was lost then the flow stopped. Then he became frozen.

Whenever the mind comes in, it comes as a controlling force, a manager. It is not the master, it is the manager. And you cannot get to the master unless this manager is put aside. The manager won't allow you to reach the master, the manager will always be standing in the doorway managing. And all managers only mismanage – mind has done such a great job of mismanaging.

Poor centipede, he had always been happy. There had been no problem at all. He had lived, he had moved, he had loved, everything; no problems at all, because there was no mind. Mind came in with the problem, with the question, with the inquiry. And there are many foxes around you. Beware of them – philosophers, theologians, logicians, professors all around – foxes. They ask you questions and they create a disturbance.

Chuang Tzu's master, Lao Tzu, said: "When there was not a single philosopher, everything was solved, there were no questions, and all answers were available. When philosophers arose, questions came and answers disappeared." Whenever there is a question the answer is very far away. Whenever you ask, you will never get the answer, but when you stop asking, the answer has always been there.

I do not know what happened to this centipede. If he was as foolish as human beings, he would be somewhere in a hospital, crippled, paralyzed forever. But I don't think that centipedes are so foolish. He must have thrown the question out. He must have told the fox, "Keep your questions to yourself, let me walk." He must have come to know that division wouldn't allow him to live, because division creates death. Undivided you are life, divided you become dead – the more divided, the more dead.

What is bliss? Bliss is the feeling that comes to you when the observer has become the observed. Bliss is the feeling that comes to you when you are in harmony, not fragmented; one, not disintegrated, not divided, undivided, one. Feeling is not something that happens from the outside. It is the melody that arises out of your inner harmoniousness.

Says Chuang Tzu:

The man of Tao
acts without impediment ...

... Because he is not divided, so who is there to impede? What is there to function as an impediment? He is alone, he moves with his wholeness. This movement in wholeness is the greatest beauty that can happen, that is possible. Sometimes you have glimpses of it. Sometimes when you are suddenly whole, when the mind is not functioning, it happens.

The sun is rising ... and suddenly you look, and the observer is not there. The sun is not there and you are not there, there is no observer and no observed. The sun is simply rising and your mind is not there to manage. You don't see it and say, "The sun is beautiful." The moment you say it the bliss is lost. Then there is no bliss, it has already become the past, it is already gone.

Suddenly you see the sun rising, and the seer is not there, it has not come into being yet, it has not become a thought. You have not looked, you have not analyzed, you have not observed. The sun is rising and there is no one, the boat is empty; there is bliss, a glimpse. But the mind immediately comes in, and says, "The sun is beautiful, this sunrise is so beautiful." The comparison has come in and the beauty is lost.

Those who know say that whenever you say to a person, "I love you," the love is lost. When the love has already gone it is always said – because the lover has come in, how can the love exist? The division has already come in, the manager has come in? The mind says, "I love you," because in love there is no *I* and no *thou*. In love there are no individuals. Love is a melting, a merging, they are not two.

Love exists, not lovers. In love, love exists, not the lovers, but the mind comes in and says, "I am in love, I love you." When *I* comes, doubt enters; division comes in and love is no longer there.

You will come many times to such glimpses in your meditation. Remember, whenever you feel such a glimpse, don't say, "How beautiful!" don't say, "How lovely!" because this is how you will lose it. Whenever the glimpse comes, let the glimpse be there. Don't do what the centipede did – don't raise any question, don't make any observation, don't analyze, don't allow the mind to come in. Walk with a hundred legs, but don't think about how you are walking.

When in meditation you have the glimpse of some ecstasy, let it happen, let it go deep. Don't divide yourself. Don't make any statement, otherwise the contact is lost.

Sometimes you have glimpses, but you have become so efficient at losing your contact with those glimpses that you cannot understand how they come and how you lose them again. They come when you are not, you lose them when you come again. When you are, they are not. When the boat is empty, bliss is always happening. It is not an accident, it is the very nature of existence. It doesn't depend on anything – it is a showering, it is the very breath of life.

It is really a miracle how you have managed to be so miserable, so thirsty, when it is raining all over. You have really done the impossible! Everywhere it is light and you live in darkness. Death is nowhere and you are constantly dying; life is a benediction and you are in hell.

How have you managed it? Through division, through thinking – thinking depends on division, analysis. Meditation is when there is no analysis, no division, when everything has become synthesized, when everything has become one.

Says Chuang Tzu:

The man of Tao
acts without impediment,
harms no other being
by his actions,

How can he do harm? You can harm others only when you have already harmed yourself. Remember this; this is the secret. If you harm yourself, you will harm others. And you will harm even when you think you are doing good to others. Nothing can happen through you but harm, because one who lives with wounds, one who lives in anguish and misery, whatsoever he does will create more misery and anguish for others. You can give only that which you have got.

I have heard ...

It happened in a synagogue, a beggar came and he told the rabbi, "I am a great musician, and I have heard that the musician who belonged to this synagogue is dead, and you are searching. So I offer myself."

The rabbi was happy, the congregation was happy because they were really missing their music. Then the man played – it was horrible! It was more musical without his music. He created a hell. It was impossible to feel any silence in that synagogue that morning. He had to be stopped, because most of the congregation started to leave. People escaped as fast as they could because his music was just anarchic, it was like madness, and it started to affect people.

When the rabbi heard that everybody was already leaving, he went to the man and stopped him. The man said, "If you don't want me, you can pay for this morning and then I will go."

The rabbi said, "It is impossible to pay you, we have never experienced such a horrible thing."

Then the man said, the musician said, "Okay, then keep it as a contribution from me."

The rabbi said, "But how can you contribute what you don't already have? You don't have any music at all – how can you contribute? You can contribute only when you have it. This is not music; rather, on the contrary, it is something like antimusic. Please take it with you, don't contribute it to us, otherwise it will go on haunting us."

You give only that which you have. You always give your being really. If you are dead within, you cannot help life; wherever you go you will kill. Knowingly, unknowingly, that is not the point – you may think that you are helping others to live, but still you will kill.

A great psychoanalyst, Wilhelm Reich, was asked once – because he was studying children, their problems – he was asked, "What is the most basic problem with children? What do you find at the root of all their misery, their problems, abnormalities?"

He said, "The mothers."

No mother can agree with this, because every mother is just helping her children without any selfishness on her part. She is living and dying for the child. And yet psychoanalysts say mothers are the problem. Unknowingly they are killing, crippling; knowingly they think they are loving.

If you are crippled within, you will cripple your children. You cannot do anything else, you can't help it, because you give out of your being – there is no other way to give.

Says Chuang Tzu: *The man of Tao … harms no other being by his actions.* Not that he cultivates nonviolence, not that he cultivates compassion, not that he lives a good life, not that he behaves in a saintly way – no. He cannot harm because he has stopped harming himself. He has no wounds. He is so blissful that from his actions or inactions only bliss flows. Even if it may appear sometimes that he is doing something wrong, he cannot.

It is just the opposite with you. Sometimes it appears that you are doing something good – you cannot. The man of Tao cannot do harm, it is impossible. There is no way to do it, it is inconceivable – because he is without divisions, fragments. He is not a crowd, he is not *polypsychic*. He is a universe now and nothing other than melody is happening inside. Only this music goes on spreading.

The man of Tao is not one of much action – he is not a man of action, the least possible action happens through him. He is really a man of inaction, he is not much occupied with activity.

But you are occupied with activity just to escape from yourself. You cannot tolerate yourself, you cannot tolerate the company of yourself. You go on looking for somebody as an escape, some occupation wherein you can forget yourself, where you can get involved. You are so bored with yourself.

A man of Tao, a man who has attained the inner nature, a man who is really religious, is not a man of much activity. Only the necessary will happen. The unnecessary is cut out completely, because he can be at ease without activity, he can be at home without doing anything, he can relax, he can be company for himself, he can be with his self.

You cannot be with yourself, hence the constant urge to seek company. Go to a club, go to a meeting, go to a party, a rally, move into the crowd, where you are not alone. You are so afraid of yourself that if you are left alone you will go mad. In just three weeks if you are left absolutely alone without any activity, you will go mad. And this is not something said by religious people, now psychologists agree with it. For only three weeks, if all activity is taken away from you, all company taken away, if you are left in a room – within three weeks you will be mad – because all your activity is just to throw out your madness, it is a catharsis.

What will you do when you are alone? For three or four days you will dream and talk within, an inner chattering. Then this will become boring. After the first week you will start talking aloud because at least you can hear your own voice. If it happens that you are passing along a dark street in the night you start whistling. Why? How is this whistling going to give you courage? How is this whistling going to help you? Just listening to it you feel that you are not alone, somebody is whistling. The illusion of two is created.

After the first week you will start talking aloud because then you can also listen. You are not alone, you are talking and you are listening as if somebody else is talking to you. After the second week you will start answering yourself. You will not only talk, you will answer – you are divided. Now you are two; one who questions, one who answers. Now there is a dialogue – you have gone completely crazy.

A man was asking his psychiatrist, "I am very worried, I talk to myself. What should I do? Can you help me?"

The psychiatrist said, "This is nothing to be worried about. Everybody talks to himself. Only when you start answering, then come to me, then I can be of help."

But the difference is only of degree; it is not of kind, it is only of quantity. If you start talking to yourself, sooner or later you will start answering also, because how can one go on simply talking? The answer is needed, otherwise you will feel foolish. By the third week you start answering – you have gone crazy.

This world, the world of activity, business and occupation, saves you from the madhouse. If you are occupied, energy moves out; then you need not care about the inward, the inner world, you can forget it.

A man of Tao is not a man of much activity – only the essential activity. It is said of Chuang Tzu that if he could stand, he would not walk, if he could sit, he would not stand, if he could fall asleep, he would not sit. Only the essential, the most essential, would he do, because there is no madness in it.

You do the nonessential, you go on doing the nonessential. Look at your activities: ninety-nine percent are nonessential. You can drop them, you can save much energy, you can save much time. But you cannot drop them because you are afraid, you are scared of yourself. If there is no radio, no television, no newspaper, nobody to talk to, what will you do?

I have heard …

One man, a priest, died. Of course, he expected to go to paradise, to heaven. And he reached, and everything was beautiful. The house he entered was one of the most wonderful ever dreamed of, palatial. And the moment a desire came, immediately a servant appeared. If he was hungry, a servant was there with the food, the most delicious he had ever tasted. If he was feeling thirsty, the desire was there – even before the desire had become a thought, just the feeling – and a man will appear with drinks.

So it continued, he was very happy for two or three days, and then he began to feel uneasy because a man has to do something, you cannot just sit in a chair. Only a man of Tao can just sit in a chair and go on sitting and sitting and sitting. You cannot sit in a chair …

The man became uneasy. For two or three days it was okay as a holiday, as a rest. And he had been in so much activity – so much public service, mission, church, giving sermons. He was a priest and he was so much involved with the society and the community, so he rested. But how much can you rest? Unless your being is at rest, sooner or later the holiday ends, and you have to come back to the world. Uneasiness arose; he started feeling discomfort.

Suddenly the servant appeared and asked, "What do you want? This is not a want; you are neither thirsty nor hungry, just uneasy. So what should I do?"

The man said, "I cannot sit here forever and forever, for eternity, I want some activity."

The servant said, "That is impossible. All your desires will be fulfilled. What is the need of any activity when every desire is to be fulfilled by us? For what do you need activity? It is not provided here."

The priest became very uneasy and he said, "What type of heaven is this?"

The man said, "Who said this is heaven? This is hell. Who told you this is heaven?"

And this really was hell. Now he understood: without activity, this was hell. He must have gone mad sooner or later. No communication or talk, no social service to be done, no pagans to be converted to Christianity, no foolish people to be made wise – what could he do?

Only a man of Tao could have changed that hell into a heaven. A man of Tao, wherever he is, is at peace, at ease. Only the essential is done, and if you can do the essential for him, he is happy. The nonessential is dropped.

You cannot drop the nonessential. Really, ninety-nine percent of your energy is wasted on the nonessential. The essential is not enough, and the mind always hankers for the nonessential, because the essential is so little, so small, it can be fulfilled easily. Then what will you do?

People are not much interested in having good food. They are more interested in having a big car because good food can be obtained very easily. Then what? People are not interested in having good healthy bodies. That can be attained very easily. They are interested in something which cannot be attained so easily, something impossible, and the nonessential is always the impossible. There are bigger houses, bigger cars, they go on getting bigger and bigger and you are never allowed to rest.

The whole world is trying to fulfill the nonessential. If you look at industry, ninety percent of industry is involved with the nonessential. Fifty percent of human labor is just wasted on that which is not useful in any way. Rather, fifty percent of industry is devoted to the feminine mind, the feminine body: designing new dresses every three months, designing new houses, clothes, powders, soaps, creams; fifty percent of industry is devoted to such nonsense. And humanity is starving, people are dying without food, and half of humanity is interested in something absolutely nonessential.

To reach the moon is absolutely nonessential. If we were a little wiser we would not think about it. It is absolutely foolish wasting as much money as could feed the whole earth. Wars are nonessential, but humanity is mad, and it needs wars more than food. It needs to go to the moon more than food, more than clothes, more than the essential, because the essential is not enough.

And now science has created the greatest horror, and that horror is that the essential can be fulfilled very easily. Within ten years, all the needs of humanity can be fulfilled; as far as the necessities are concerned this whole earth can be satisfied. Then what? Then what will you do? You will feel in the same position in which the priest found himself. He was thinking he was in heaven, and then he found that it was hell. Within ten years the whole earth can become a hell.

The nonessential is needed for your madness to remain engaged. So moons are not enough, we will have to go further, we will have to go on creating the useless. It is needed. To be occupied, it is needed.

A man of Tao is not a man of much activity. His actions are the most essential – those which cannot be avoided. That which can be avoided, he avoids. He is so happy with himself there is no need to move in actions. His activity is like inactivity; he does without there being anybody who is doing..

He is an empty boat, moving on the sea, not going anywhere.

Yet he does not know himself
to be kind and gentle.

Allow this point to penetrate deep into your heart. *Yet he does not know himself to be kind and gentle* – because if you know, you have missed the point; if you know that you are a simple man, you are not. This knowledge makes it complex. If you know that you are a man of religion, you are not, because this cunning mind which knows is still there.

When you are gentle, and you don't know, when you are simple, and you are not aware of it, it has become your nature. Then you are not aware of it. When something is imposed you are aware of it. When something is alien, you are aware of it. When something is really natural you are not aware of it. Look – somebody becomes rich, and newly rich, then he is aware of his house, of his swimming pool, of his riches, and you can see that he is not an aristocrat, because he is showing it so much.

A newly rich man ordered three swimming pools for his garden. They were made, and he was showing them to a friend. The friend was a little puzzled. He said, "Three swimming pools? For what? One will do."

The newly rich man said, "No, how can one do? One is for hot baths, one for cold baths."

The man asked, "And the third?"

He said, "For those who cannot swim. The third is going to remain empty."

You can see if a man has newly acquired wealth – he will be showing it. A real aristocrat is one who has forgotten that he is rich. A man of Tao is the aristocrat of the inner world.

If a person shows his religion he is not yet really religious. The religion is still like a thorn, it is not natural, it hurts, he is eager to show it. If you want to show your simplicity what type of simplicity is this? If you exhibit your gentleness, then it is simply cunning, nothing gentle exists in it.

A man of Tao is an aristocrat of the inner world. He is so attuned to it, there is no exhibition — not only to you, he himself is not aware of it. He does not know that he is wise, he does not know that he is innocent — how can you know if you are innocent? Your knowledge will disturb the innocence.

It is said, once it happened: A follower of Hazrat Mohammed went with him to the mosque for a prayer, the early morning prayer. And when they were returning, many people ... it was summertime, early morning, and many people were still asleep in their houses or just on the street, a summer morning and many people were still asleep ...

The man very arrogantly said to Hazrat Mohammed, "What will happen to these sinners? They have not been to the morning prayer."

And this man has gone only for the first time. Yesterday he was also asleep like these sinners. A newly rich man wanted to exhibit, to show off, even to Mohammed: "Hazrat, what will happen to these sinners? They have not been to the morning prayer, they are still lazy and asleep."

Mohammed stopped and said, "You go home, I will have to go back to the mosque again."

The man said, "Why?"

He replied, "My morning prayer is wasted because of you; keeping company with you has destroyed everything. I will have to do my prayer again. And you remember please, never to come again — better that you were asleep like the others; at least then they were not sinners. Your prayer has done only one thing — it has given you the key to condemn others."

The so-called religious person is only religious so as to look at you with a condemning eye, so he can say that you are sinners. Go to your saints, your so-called saints, and look into their eyes. You will not find the innocence that should be there. You will find a calculating mind looking at you and thinking about hell: "You will be thrown in hell and I will be in heaven, because I have been praying so much, five times a day, and I have been fasting so much." As if you can purchase heaven ... ! These are the coins — fasting, prayer — these are the coins he is trying to bargain with.

If you see condemnation in the eyes of a saint, know well that he is a newly rich man; he is no aristocrat of the inner world, he has not yet become one with it. He knows it — but you know something only when it is separate from you.

One thing has to be remembered here: because of this, self-knowledge is impossible. You cannot know the self, because whenever you know it, it is not the self, it is something else, something separate from you. The self is always the knower, never the known, so how can you know it? You cannot reduce it to an object.

I can see you. How can I see myself? Then who will be the seer and who will be the seen? No, the self cannot be known in the same way that other things are known.

Self-knowledge is not possible in the ordinary sense, because the knower always transcends, always goes beyond. Whatsoever it knows, it is not that. The Upanishads say: *neti neti* – not this, not that. They say: Whatsoever you know, you are not this; whatsoever you don't know, you are not that either. You are the one who knows, and this knower cannot be reduced to a known object.

Self-knowledge is not possible. If your innocence comes out of your inner source you cannot know it. If you have imposed it from the outside you can know it; if it is just like a dress you have put on you know it, but it is not the very breath of your life. That innocence is cultivated, and a cultivated innocence is an ugly thing.

A man of Tao does not know himself to be kind and gentle. He *is* gentle, but he doesn't know; he is kind, but he doesn't know; he is love, but he doesn't know – because the lover and the knower are not two, the gentleness, the kindness, the compassion and the knower, are not two. No, they cannot be divided into the known and the knower. This is the inner aristocracy, when you have become so rich you are not aware of it. When you are so rich, there is no need to exhibit it.

I have heard …

It happened once, Henry Ford came to England. At the airport inquiry office he asked, he inquired about the cheapest hotel in town. The man at the office looked – the face was famous. Henry Ford was known all over the world. Just the day before there were big pictures of him in the newspapers saying that he was coming. And he was, asking for the cheapest hotel, and his coat looked as old as he himself.

So the man at the inquiry office asked, "If I am not mistaken, you are Mr. Henry Ford. I remember well, I have seen your picture."

The man said, "Yes."

The clerk was very puzzled, and he said, "And you are asking for the cheapest hotel, and your coat looks as old as you yourself. I have also seen your son coming here, and he always inquires about the best hotel, and he comes in the best of clothes."

Henry Ford is reported to have said, "Yes, my son's behavior is exhibitionist, he is not yet attuned. There is no need for me to stay in a costly hotel; wherever I stay I am Henry Ford. Even in the cheapest hotel I am Henry Ford, it makes no difference. My son is still new, afraid of what people will think if he stays in a cheap hotel. And this coat, yes, this belonged to my father – but it makes no difference, I don't need new clothes. I am Henry Ford, whatsoever the dress; even if I am standing naked, I am Henry Ford. It makes no difference at all."

When you are really attuned, really rich in the inner world, you are not concerned with exhibition. When you first go to a temple, your prayer is a little louder than others. It has to be. You want to show off.

Showmanship is part of the ego, what you show is not the problem. You show, you exhibit, then the ego is there, the boat is not empty – and a man of Tao is an empty boat. He is gentle, not aware; he is innocent, not knowing; he is wise, that's why he can move as a fool, not worried. Whatsoever he does makes no difference, his wisdom is intact, he can afford to be foolish. You cannot.

You are always afraid that somebody may think you a fool. You are afraid, if others think you to be a fool, you will start suspecting it. If so many people think you a fool your self-confidence will be lost. And if everybody goes on repeating that you are a fool, sooner or later you will come to believe it. Only a wise man cannot be deceived, he can appear as a fool.

I have heard about one wise man who was known as The Madman. Nobody knew anything else about him, his name or anything, he was just known as The Madman. He was a Jew, and Jews have created a few really wise men, they have something of the inner source. That is why Jesus could be born amongst them.

This madman behaved in such a foolish way that the whole community became disturbed because nobody knew what he was going to do. On the religious days, Yom Kippur or other festivals, the whole community was afraid, because it could not be predicted what this rabbi would do, how he would appear there, how he would behave. His prayers were also mad.

Once he called the court, the Jewish court, all the ten judges of the court. The court came, because the rabbi had called, and he said, "I have a case against God, so you decide how to punish this fellow, God. And I will give all the arguments which prove that God is unjust and a criminal."

The judges, the people, became very afraid, but they had to listen because he was the rabbi, the chief of the temple. And he gave all the arguments like a lawyer in court.

He said, "You created the world, and now you send messengers telling us how to renounce it. What foolishness! You gave us desires and now all your teachers go on coming and saying: "Be desireless." So what do you think you are doing? If we have committed any sins it is really *you* who are the culprit, otherwise why did you create desire?"

What should the court have decided? He was right, but the court decided that this man had gone completely mad. So the court decided to expel this madman from the temple.

But this man is really saying a fact. He loves God so much – it is an I/thou relationship, so intimate. He asks, "What are you doing? Enough now, stop, no more fooling." He must have loved the divine so much that he could behave in that way.

And it is said, in the story, that God immediately stopped when he called. He had to listen to this man.

It is said that the angels asked, "Suddenly you stopped, what happened?"

God said, "That madman, he is praying. I have to listen, because whatsoever he says is true, and he loves me so much that there is no need to follow any manners." In love, in hate, everything is permitted, everything is allowed.

This madman was passing and a woman came to him. She asked, "I have been longing and longing for a child for forty years now. And if within three or four years a child does not come, then it will not be possible. So help me."

The madman said, "I can help, because my mother was in the same trouble. She waited and waited for forty years and no child came. Then she went to Baal Shem, a mystic; she told him, and he intervened. My mother gave him a beautiful cap. Baal Shem put the cap on his head, looked up and said to God, 'What are you doing? This is unjust. There is nothing wrong in the demand of this woman, so give her a child.' And after nine months, I was born."

So the woman said, beaming, happy, she said "I will go home and I will bring you such a cap, more beautiful than you have ever seen. Then will the child be born to me?"

The madman said, "You have missed. My mother never knew the story. Your cap won't do, you have missed. You cannot imitate religion, you cannot imitate prayer. Once you imitate you have missed." So whenever people came to this madman, he would say, "Don't imitate, throw away all the scriptures."

When this madman died he had all the books that had been written about him burned. And the last thing he did, he said to his disciples, "Go around the house and have a search, and tell me that nothing is left, not even a single letter written by me, so that I can die at ease. Otherwise people will start following, and when you follow, you miss." So everything was gathered and burned. When everything was burned he said, "Now I can die easily, I am not leaving any traces behind."

This type of wise man is not afraid. How can a wise man be afraid of anybody? What he says is meaningless. He can to all appearances be a fool, he need not exhibit his wisdom.

Have you observed yourself? You are always trying to exhibit your wisdom, in search of a victim to whom you can show your knowledge, ability, just searching, hunting for somebody weaker than you – then you will jump in and you will show your wisdom.

A wise man need not be an exhibitionist. Whatsoever is, is. He is not aware of it, he is not in any hurry to show it. If you want to find it, you will have to make effort. If you want to know whether he is gentle or not, that is going to be your discovery.

He does not struggle to make money,
and he does not make a virtue of poverty.

Remember this. It is very easy to make money and it is also very easy to make a virtue out of poverty. But these two types are not different. A man goes on making money, and then suddenly he gets frustrated. He has achieved, and nothing is gained – so he renounces. Then poverty becomes the virtue, then he lives the life of a poor man and then he says: "This is the only real life, this is religious life." This man is the same, nothing has changed. The pendulum moved to the left but has now gone to the other extreme.

He does not struggle to make money ...

This you will understand; the other part is more difficult.

... he does not make a virtue of poverty.

He is neither poor nor rich. He is not making any effort for money, he is not making any effort to be poor – whatever happens he allows it to happen. If a palace happens, he will be in the palace; if the palace disappears, he will not look for it. Whatever is happening, he will be with it, his bliss cannot be disturbed. He is not struggling for money, he is not struggling for poverty.

He goes his way
without relying on others ...

This you can understand easily.

He goes his way
without relying on others,
and does not pride himself
on walking alone.

The opposite has to be dropped immediately. You depend on others, your wife, your children, your father, mother, friends, society; then suddenly you drop – and you escape to the Himalayas. Then you start priding yourself: "I live alone, I don't need anybody, I am free of that world."

Even then you are still not alone because your aloneness still depends on the world. How could you be alone if there was not a world to leave? How could you be alone if there was not a society to renounce? How could you be alone if there was not a wife, children, a family to leave behind? Your aloneness depends on them. How could you be poor if there was no money to be left? Your poverty depends on your riches.

No, a perfect man, a man who is really a sage, the man of Tao, he goes his way without relying on others. Because if you rely on others you will suffer, if you rely on others, you will always be in bondage. If you rely on others, you will become dependent and weak. But that doesn't mean that you pride yourself that you walk alone. Walk alone, but don't take pride in it. Then you can move in the world without being a part of it. Then you can live in a family without being a member of it. Then you can be a husband without being a husband. Then you can possess without being possessed by your possessions. Then the world is there outside, but not within. Then you are there, but not corrupted by it.

This is true loneliness – moving in the world without being touched by it. But if you are proud, you have missed. If you think, "I have become somebody," the boat is not empty, and again you have fallen victim to the ego.

The man of Tao
remains unknown.
Perfect virtue
produces nothing.
No self is true self.
And the greatest man
is nobody.

Listen ... The man of Tao remains unknown. Not that nobody will know him, but it is up to you to discover him. He is not making any effort to be known. Any effort to be known comes from the ego, because ego cannot exist when you are unknown, it exists only when you are known. It exists, feeds, when people look at you, when they pay attention to you, when you are somebody important, significant.

But how can you be significant if nobody knows you? When the whole world knows you, then you are significant. That is why people are after fame so much, and if fame cannot be achieved then they will settle for being notorious – but not for being unknown. If people cannot praise you then you will settle for being condemned, but they should not be indifferent to you.

I have heard about a politician. He had a great following once, many followers, many who appreciated him when he was not in power, because in politics everything is momentary. When you are not in power, you look very innocent because when there is no power, what can you do, how can you harm? So your real nature comes only to be known when you get power.

Look at the Gandhians in India before independence – so saintly. And now everything has gone to the opposite extreme. Now they are the most corrupted. What happened? A simple law: when they were not in power they were like doves, innocent; when power came they became like serpents, cunning, corrupted, exploiting.

Your real nature is known only when you have power. When you can harm, then it is known whether you will harm or not.

Lord Acton has said: "Power corrupts, and absolute power corrupts absolutely." No, that is not right. Power never corrupts, it only brings corruption out. How can power corrupt? You were already corrupt but there was no opportunity. You were already ugly but you were standing in darkness. Now you are standing in light, so will you say that light makes you ugly? No, light only reveals.

... This politician was very much appreciated, loved, he had a charismatic personality. Then he came to power and everybody was against him. Then he was thrown out of power, his name became notorious, he was condemned everywhere, so he had to leave his town because people would not allow him to live there, he had done such harm.

So with his wife he was looking for a new residence in a new town. He traveled to many towns just to look and see where he should stay. In one town people started throwing stones at him. He said, "This will be the right place, we should choose this town."

The wife said, "Are you mad? Have you gone crazy? The people are throwing stones."

The politician said, "At least they are not indifferent."

Indifference hurts you most because the ego cannot exist in indifference. Either for me or against me, the ego can exist, but don't be indifferent to me because then how can I exist, how can the ego exist? The man of Tao remains unknown. That means that he is not seeking people who should know him. If they want to know, they should seek him.

Perfect virtue
produces nothing.

This is one of the basics of Taoist life.

Perfect virtue produces nothing, because when you are perfectly virtuous nothing is needed. When you are perfectly virtuous there is no desire, there is no motivation. You are perfect. How can perfection move? Only imperfection moves. Only imperfection desires to produce something. So a perfect artist never paints a picture, and a perfect musician throws away his sitar. A perfect archer breaks his bow and throws it away, and a perfect man like Buddha is absolutely useless. What has Buddha produced – poetry, a sculpture, a painting, a society? What has Buddha produced? He seems to be absolutely unproductive, he has done nothing.

Perfect virtue produces nothing, because it needs nothing. Production comes out of desire, production comes because you are imperfect. You create something as a substitute because you feel unfulfilled. When you are absolutely fulfilled, why should you create, how can you create? Then you yourself have become a glorious creation, then the inner being itself is so perfect, nothing is needed.

Perfect virtue produces nothing. If the world is virtuous, all utilitarian goals will be lost. If the world is really virtuous there will be play and no production. Then the whole thing will just become a game. You enjoy it, but you don't need it. A perfect sage is absolutely useless.

No self is true self.

When you feel that you are not, for the first time you are, because the self is nothing but a synonym for the ego. That is why Buddha, Lao Tzu, Chuang Tzu, they all say there is no self, no atman. Not that there is not – they say there is no atman, there is no self, because your ego is so cunning it can hide behind it. You can say, "*Aham brahmasmi*, I am brahman, *Ana'l haq*, I am God," and the ego can hide behind it.

Buddha says there is nobody to claim, there is no self within you. Buddha says you are like the onion: you peel, you go on peeling the layers, and finally nothing remains. Your mind is like an onion, go on peeling. This is what meditation is – go on peeling, go on peeling, and a moment comes when nothing is left. That nothingness is your true self.

No self is true self. When the boat is empty then only for the first time you are in the boat.

And the greatest man
is nobody.

It happened: Buddha renounced the kingdom. Then he was searching from one forest to another, from one ashram to another, from one master to another, walking. He had never walked without shoes but now he was just a beggar. He was passing a river, walking by the side of the river, on the sand, and his footprints were left.

While he was resting in the shade of a tree one astrologer saw him. He was coming back from Kashi, from the seat of learning. He had become proficient in astrology, he had become perfect, he had become a great doctor of astrology, and he was coming back to his home town to practice.

He looked at the footprints on the wet sand. He became disturbed because these footprints could not belong to a man who walks on the sand without shoes in such a hot summer, at noon. These feet belong to a great emperor, a *chakravartin*. A *chakravartin* is an emperor who rules the whole world. All the symbols were there, that this man was a *chakravartin*, an emperor of the whole world, of the six continents. But why should a *chakravartin* walk on the sand with naked feet, without any shoes, on such a hot summer afternoon? It was impossible!

He was carrying his most valuable books. He thought, "If this is possible I should throw these books in the river and forget astrology forever, because this is absurd. It is very, very difficult to find a man who has the feet of a *chakravartin*. Once in millions of years a man becomes a *chakravartin* and what is this *chakravartin* doing here?"

So he followed the footprints and he reached Buddha. He looked at him sitting, resting under a tree with closed eyes. He became more disturbed, this astrologer, he became absolutely disturbed because the face was also the face of a *chakravartin*. But the man looked like a beggar, with his begging bowl just there by his side, with torn clothes. But the face looked like that of a *chakravartin*, so what to do?

He asked, he said, "I am very disturbed, put me at ease. I have only one question to ask. I have seen and studied your footprints. They should belong to a *chakravartin*, to a great emperor who rules over all the world, the whole earth is his kingdom – and you are a beggar. So what should I do? Should I throw away all my astrology books? My twelve years of effort in Kashi have been wasted and those people there are fools. I have wasted the most important part of my life, so put me at ease. Tell me, what should I do?"

Buddha said, "You need not worry. This will not happen again. You take your books, go to the town, start your practice, don't bother about me. I was born to be a *chakravartin*. These footprints carry my past."

All footprints carry your past – the lines on your hand, your palm, carry your past. That is why astrology and palmistry are always true about the past, never so true about the future, and absolutely untrue about a buddha, because one who throws off his whole past moves into the unknown – you cannot predict his future.

Buddha said, "You will not come across such a troublesome man again. Don't worry, this will not happen again, take it as an exception."

But the astrologer said, "A few more questions. I would like to know who you are. Am I really seeing a dream? A *chakravartin* sitting like a beggar? Who are you? Are you an emperor in disguise?"

Buddha said, "No."

Then the astrologer asked, "But your face looks so beautiful, so calm, so filled with inner silence. Who are you? Are you an angel from paradise?"

Buddha said, "No."

The astrologer asked one more question: "It is not good manners to ask, but you have created the desire, the urge. Are you a human being? If you are not an emperor, a *chakravartin*, if you are not a *deva* from paradise, then are you a human being?"

And Buddha said, "No, I am nobody. I don't belong to any form, to any name."

The astrologer said, "You have disturbed me more now. What do you mean?"

This is what Buddha meant:

And the greatest man
is nobody.

You can be somebody, but you cannot be the greatest. There is always someone greater somewhere in the world. And who is somebody? You are the measure. You say that this man is great – but who is the measure? You.

The spoon is the measure of the ocean. You say, "This man is great." You say, and many like you say, "This man is great" – and he becomes great because of you.

No. In this world, whosoever is somebody cannot be the greatest, because the ocean cannot be measured by spoons. And you are all teaspoons measuring the ocean. No, it is not possible.

So the really greatest will be nobody amongst you. What does it mean when Chuang Tzu says, "The greatest will be nobody"? It means it will be immeasurable. You cannot measure, you cannot label, you cannot categorize, you cannot say, "Who is this?" He simply escapes measurement. He simply goes beyond and beyond and beyond and the teaspoon falls on the ground – immeasurable.

God must be nobody. He cannot be somebody because who will make him somebody? You? – then you have measured. Then you have become greater than

God, then the teaspoon has become greater than the ocean. No, God cannot be measured. He will remain a nobody.

I'm reminded of this madman again, this Jew. He used to say in his prayers, "God, you and I are two strangers in this world."

So one day a disciple heard his prayer that he was saying: "God, you and I are two strangers in this world."

The disciple asked, "What do you mean? God and you, strangers?"

He said, "He's nobody and I'm also nobody – immeasurable – neither can you measure him nor can you measure me."

Somebody means you are measured. You are labeled, categorized. You are known. *Nobody* means you remain unknowable. Howsoever you know, whatsoever you know, your knowledge will not exhaust him. You will know that this is not the boundary. And the more intimate you become, the greater he becomes, the more immeasurable. A moment comes and you simply throw your teaspoon, you simply stop the effort to measure. And only then are you intimate with the great man, the man of Tao.

Enough for today.

Chapter 3

The Owl and the Phoenix

Hui Tzu was Prime Minister of Liang. He had what he believed to
be inside information that Chuang Tzu coveted his post and was
intriguing to supplant him. In fact, when Chuang Tzu came to visit
Liang, the Prime Minister sent out the police to apprehend him. The
police searched for him three days and three nights, but meanwhile
Chuang Tzu presented himself before Hui Tzu of his own accord, and
said:

"Have you heard about the bird
That lives in the south
The Phoenix that never grows old?

"This undying Phoenix
Rises out of the South Sea
And flies to the Sea of the North,
Never alighting
Except on certain sacred trees.
He will touch no food
But the most exquisite
Rare fruit,
Drinks only
From clearest springs.

"Once an owl
Chewing a dead rat
Already half-decayed,
Saw the Phoenix fly over,
Looked up,
And screeched with alarm,
Clutching the rat to himself
In fear and dismay.

"Why are you so frantic
Clinging to your ministry
And screeching at me
In dismay?"

The religious mind is basically nonambitious. If there is any sort of ambition, then to be religious is impossible, because only a superior man can become religious. Ambition implies inferiority. Try to understand this because it is one of the basic laws. Without understanding it you can go to temples, you can go to the Himalayas, you can pray and you can meditate, but everything will be in vain. You will be simply wasting your life if you have not understood the nature of the mind – whether it is ambitious or nonambitious. Your whole search will be futile, because ambition can never lead to the divine. Only non-ambition can become the door.

Modern psychology also agrees with Chuang Tzu, with Lao Tzu, with Buddha, with all those who have known that inferiority creates ambition. Hence politicians come from the worst stuff in humanity. All politicians are sudras, untouchables. It cannot be otherwise, because whenever the mind feels the inferiority complex it tries to become superior – the opposite is born. When you feel ugly, you try to be beautiful. If you are beautiful, then there is no effort.

So look at ugly women and you will come to know the nature of the politician. An ugly woman is always trying to hide the ugliness, always trying to be beautiful. At least the face, the painted face, the clothes, the ornaments, they all belong to the ugly. The ugliness has somehow to be overcome and you have to create the opposite to hide it, to escape from it. A really beautiful woman will not worry, she will not even be conscious of her beauty. And only an unconscious beauty is beautiful. When you become conscious, the ugliness has entered.

When you feel that you are inferior, when you compare yourself and you see that others are superior to you, what will you do? The ego feels hurt – you are inferior. You just cannot accept it, so you have to deceive yourself and others.

How do you deceive? There are two ways. One is to go mad. Then you can declare that you are an Alexander, a Hitler, a Nixon. Then you can declare easily because then you don't bother what others say. Go to the madhouses all over the world and there you will find all the great people of history still present.

When Pandit Jawaharlal Nehru was alive, at least one dozen people in India believed that they were Pandit Jawaharlal Nehru. Once he came to a madhouse to inaugurate some new department. And the authorities of that madhouse had arranged for a few people to be released by him, because now they had become healthy and normal. The first person was brought to Nehru, and introduced, so Nehru introduced himself to the madman who had become more normal and said, "I am Pandit Jawaharlal Nehru, prime minister of India."

The madman laughed and said, "Don't worry. Be here for three years and you will become as normal as I have become. Three years ago when I first came to this madhouse this is what I believed – I was Pandit Jawaharlal Nehru, prime minister of India. But they have cured me completely, so don't worry."

This has happened in many ways. Lloyd George was prime minister of England. In the war days, at six o'clock in the evening there used to be a blackout and nobody could move outside their houses. All traffic stopped, and everybody had to go in some shelter. No light, no electricity was allowed. Lloyd George was on his routine evening walk. He forgot.

Suddenly the siren … It was six o'clock and his house was far away and he had to walk at least a mile. So he knocked on the nearest door and said to the man who opened it, "Let me rest here for the night; otherwise the police will catch me. I am Lloyd George, the prime minister."

The man suddenly grabbed him and said, "Come in. This is the right place for you. We have three Lloyd Georges already!" It was a madhouse.

Lloyd George tried to convince the man, but he said, "Don't try, they all try to convince; you just come in, or I will beat you."

So Lloyd George had to keep quiet for the whole night, or he would have been beaten. How could he convince them? There were already three Lloyd Georges and they had all tried to prove it.

One way is to go mad – then you suddenly declare that you are superior, the most superior. Another way is to go politician. Either go mad or go politician. Through politics you cannot suddenly declare – you have to prove that you really are the prime minister or you are the president. So it is a long way. Madness is the shortcut to fame, politics is the long way. But they reach the same goal.

And if the world is to become a sane, normal world, then two types of people have to be cured: madmen and politicians. Both are ill. One has taken the long route, one has taken the shortcut. And remember well that the madman is less harmful than the politician, because he simply declares, he never bothers to prove it; the politician bothers to prove it – and the proof is very costly.

What was Hitler trying to prove? That he was the most superior, the supreme-most Aryan. It would have been better for the world if he had gone mad, and declared through the shortcut; then there would have been no Second World War.

Politicians are more dangerous because they are madmen with proofs. They are madmen working, reaching, achieving a goal, just to hide the inferiority in them. Whenever somebody feels inferior, he has to prove it, or simply hypnotize himself – that he is not inferior. You cannot be religious if you are mad, in this sense. Not mad in the way a Saint Francis is mad – that madness comes through ecstasy, this madness comes through inferiority. The madness of a Saint Francis or a Chuang Tzu comes out of superiority, comes out of the heart, comes from the original source. This other madness comes out of the ego, comes out of inferiority. The soul is always superior and the ego is always inferior.

So an egotist has to become a politician somehow or other. Whichever profession he chooses, through that profession he will be a politician.

What do I mean when I say politics? I mean the conflict between egos, the struggle to survive. Between the egos — your ego and my ego in conflict — then we are politicians. When I am not in conflict with anybody's ego, I am a religious man. When I don't try to be superior, I am superior. But this superiority is not opposite to inferiority, it is an absence of the feeling of inferiority.

This distinction has to be remembered. There are two types of superiority. In one you have just hidden the inferiority, covered it, you are using a mask — the inferiority is there behind the mask. Your superiority is just superficial; deep down you remain inferior, and because you go on feeling that inferiority, you have to carry this mask of superiority, of beauty. Because you are aware that you are ugly you have to manage to be beautiful, you have to exhibit, you have to have a false face. This is one type of superiority; it is not real.

There is another type of superiority, and that superiority is the absence of inferiority, not opposite to it. You simply don't compare. When you don't compare, how can you be inferior? Look, if you are the only one on earth and there is nobody else, will you be inferior? To whom? With whom will you compare yourself? Relative to what? If you are alone what will you be, inferior or superior? You will be neither. You cannot be inferior because there is no one ahead of you; you cannot declare yourself superior because there is no one behind you. You will be neither superior nor inferior — and I say to you that this is the superiority of the soul. It never compares. Compare, and the inferiority arises. Don't compare, and you simply are — unique.

A religious man is superior in the sense that the inferiority has disappeared. A politician is superior in the sense that he has overcome his inferiority. It is hidden there, it is still inside. He is just using the garb, the face, the mask of a superior man.

When you compare, you miss; then you will always look to others. And no two persons are the same, they cannot be. Every individual is unique and every individual is superior, but this superiority is not comparable. You are superior because you cannot be anything else. Superiority is just your nature. The tree is superior, the rock is also superior because the whole of existence is divine. How can anything be inferior here? It is existence, overflowing in millions of ways. Somewhere existence has become a tree, somewhere existence has become a rock, somewhere existence has become a bird, somewhere existence has become you. Only godliness exists, so there is no comparison. And existence is superior, but not to anything – because only godliness is, and there cannot be any inferiority.

A religious man comes to experience his uniqueness, comes to experience his divineness, and through his experience of divineness he comes to realize the divineness of all. This is nonpolitical because now there is no ambition, you have nothing to prove, you are already proved; you have nothing to declare, you are already declared. Your very being is the proof. You are ... it is enough. Nothing else is needed.

Hence, remember this as the basic law: if in religion you also go on comparing, you are in politics, you are not in religion. That is why all religions have become political. They use religious terminology, but hidden behind is politics. What is Islam, what is Christianity, what is Hinduism now? – all political groups, political organizations doing politics in the name of religion.

When you go to the temple to pray, do you simply pray or do you compare? If somebody is there praying, does comparison arise in your mind? Is he praying better than you, or are you doing better than him? Then the temple is no longer there. The temple has disappeared, it has become politics.

In religion comparison is not possible; you simply pray, and prayerfulness becomes your inner being. It is not something outward to be compared. This incomparable prayerfulness, incomparable meditation, will lead you to the intrinsic superiority of all existence.

Buddha says: Don't be ambitious, because through ambition you will always remain inferior. Be non-ambitious and attain to your intrinsic superiority. It is intrinsic, it is nothing to be proved or achieved, you already have it, you have got it. It is already there – it has always been with you and it will always remain with you. Your very being is superior but you don't know what being is there. You don't know who you are – hence so much effort in seeking your identity, in searching, in proving that you are superior to others. You don't know who you are.

Once you know, then there is no problem. You are already superior. And it is not only you that is superior – everything is superior. The whole of existence is superior without anything being inferior, because existence is one. Neither the inferior nor the superior can exist. The non-ambitious mind comes to realize this.

Now, we shall take Chuang Tzu's sentences, this beautiful incident which really happened. Chuang Tzu was coming to the capital and the prime minister became afraid. He must have heard the news that Chuang Tzu was coming through the secret police, the CID. And politicians are always afraid, because everybody is their enemy, even friends are enemies, one has to protect oneself from friends because they too are trying to push or pull you down.

Remember, nobody is a friend. In politics, everybody is an enemy. Friendship is just a façade. In religion there is no one who is an enemy. In religion there cannot be any enemy; in politics there cannot be any friend.

The prime minister became afraid – Chuang Tzu was coming. And Chuang Tzu's superiority was such that the prime minister thought that he might try to become prime minister. It was dangerous, and of course Chuang Tzu *was* superior; not superior in comparison to anybody else, he was simply superior. It was intrinsic.

When a man like Chuang Tzu moves, he is king; whether he is living like a beggar or not, it doesn't make any difference. He is a king wherever he moves. A kingdom is not something external to him, it is something internal.

One beggar, a monk from India, went to America at the beginning of this century; his name was Ramateertha. He used to call himself "The Emperor." The president of America came to see him; he looked around – he was just a beggar! The president asked, "I cannot understand. Why do you go on calling yourself The Emperor? You live like a beggar. You have even written a book – Why?" He had written a book: *Six Orders of Emperor Ram*.

Ramateertha laughed and said, "Look within me, my kingdom belongs to the inner world. Look in me. I *am* an emperor. My kingdom is not of this world."

Because of this, Jesus was crucified. He was always talking of the kingdom. He was always saying, "I am the king." He was misunderstood. The man who was the king, Herod, became alert. The viceroy, Pontius Pilate, thought this man dangerous, because he talked about the kingdom and the king, and he had declared, "I am the *king of the Jews*." He was misunderstood. He was talking of a different type of kingdom, which is not of this world.

When he was being crucified the soldiers poked fun at him, threw stones and shoes at him, and just to mock him, put a crown of thorns on his head with the words, King of the Jews, written on it And when they were throwing stones and shoes at him they were saying, "Now, tell us something about the kingdom, tell us something, you king of the Jews!"

He was talking of some other kingdom, not of this world; that kingdom is not without, that kingdom is within. But whenever a man like Jesus walks, he is the emperor. He cannot help it. He is not in competition with anybody, he is not hankering for any crown of this world, but wherever he moves ambitious people become afraid, politicians become afraid. This man is dangerous, because the very face, the eyes, the way he walks, he looks like an emperor. He need not prove it, he is the proof. He need not utter it, need not say it.

When the prime minister heard through the secret police that Chuang Tzu was coming, he thought he must be coming to the capital to supplant him;

otherwise, why come? People only came to the capital for that. One never goes to Delhi for anything else. People come to the capitals in search of ambition, in search of ego, identity. Why should he come – a fakir, a beggar? What is the need for him to come to the capital?

"He must be coming to take my seat, my chair. He must be coming to the king to say, 'I am the right man. Make me prime minister and I will put every wrong right. I will solve all your problems.'"

And the man had a glory around him, a charisma. The prime minister became afraid. Prime ministers are always inferior. Deep down the inferiority complex is there, like a disease, like a worm eating the heart, always afraid of the superior.

Hui Tzu was Prime Minister of Liang. He had what he believed to be inside information that Chuang Tzu coveted his post, and was plotting to supplant him.

Politicians cannot think otherwise. The first thing to be understood: you think of others according to what you are. Your desires, your own ambitions give you the pattern. If you are after money you think that everybody is after money. If you are a thief, you are always checking your pocket, again and again. That is how you show that you are a thief. Your inner desire is the language of your understanding. Politicians always think in terms of plots, conspiracies – "Somebody is going to supplant me; somebody is going to throw me out." Because that is what they have done; plotting is what they have been doing all their lives. Politicians are conspirators; that is their language. And you look at others through your mind, you project onto others things which are hidden deep within you.

Hui Tzu thought, "This Chuang Tzu is plotting to supplant me."

When Chuang Tzu came to visit Liang the Prime Minister sent out police to arrest him, but although they searched for three days and nights they could not find him.

This is beautiful!

The police can only find thieves – they understand each other. The mind of the policeman and the mind of a thief are not different – thieves in the service of the government are the police. Their mind, their way of thinking is the same, only their masters are different. A thief is in his own service, a policeman is in the service of the state – but both are thieves. That is why policemen can catch thieves. If you send a sadhu to find a thief, he won't find him, because he will look at others through his mind.

A rabbi was passing. A young man was standing there, it was a religious day and he was smoking, and smoking was forbidden on that day. So the rabbi stopped and asked the young man "Don't you know, young man, that this is a religious day, and you should not be smoking?"

The young man said, "Yes, I know that this is a religious day." Still he continued smoking – not only that, he was blowing smoke in the rabbi's face.

The rabbi asked, "And don't you know that smoking is forbidden?"

The young man said arrogantly, "Yes, I know it is forbidden." And he continued.

The rabbi looked at the sky and said, "Father, this young man is beautiful. He may be breaking the law, but nobody can force him to lie. He is a truthful man. He says, 'Yes, I know this is a religious day, and yes, I know it is forbidden.' Remember this on the day of last judgment, that this young man could not be forced to lie."

This is a beautiful rabbi. This is the mind of a sadhu. He cannot see wrong, he always sees right.

The police could not find Chuang Tzu. They could have found him if he had been an ambitious man, if he had been plotting, if he were thinking in terms of politics – then he could have been caught. The police must have looked in places where he was not, and their paths must have crossed many times. He was a beggar; the police must not have noticed that he was a beggar, a non-ambitious man. He was not plotting. He had no mind for plots, he was like the breeze. The police searched and searched for many days and couldn't find him.

You can find only that which you are. You always find yourself in others, because others are just mirrors. To catch Chuang Tzu, a Lao Tzu was needed. Nobody else could catch him, because who could understand him? A buddha was needed; Buddha would have caught hold of him immediately: "Here he is!" But a policeman? – impossible! Only if he were a thief would it be possible. Look at the policeman, the way he is, the way he talks, the dirty, vulgar language he uses; it is even more vulgar than thieves use. The policeman has to be more vulgar, otherwise thieves would win.

I have heard ...

A man was caught, and the magistrate asked, "Tell me, when you were caught, what did this policeman say to you?"

The man said, "Can I use the vulgar language that he used, here in court? Will you not feel offended?"

The magistrate said, "Leave out the vulgar language and say what he said."

The man thought and said, "Then ... he said nothing."

The police came back to Hui Tzu and reported: "This man cannot be found, there is no such man." They must have had a picture, they must have been given a picture, some way of identifying this man Chuang Tzu, how he is to be found, how he is to be caught, what type of man he was.

But Chuang Tzu has no identity, he has no face. Moment to moment he is a flow, a liquidity. Moment to moment he reflects, responds to existence. He has no fixed abode, he is homeless, faceless. He has no name. He is not a past, he is always a present, and all photographs belong to the past.

It looks absurd, but it is said, and it is beautiful and meaningful, that whenever there is a man like Buddha, you cannot photograph him. Not that you cannot photograph him – but the moment the photograph is there, Buddha has moved. So it is always of the past and never of the present. You cannot catch Buddha's present face. The moment you catch it, it has passed. The moment you understand, it is already gone.

One of the names of Buddha is *Tathagata*. This word is really wonderful, it means: just like the wind he came and he is gone, thus came like the wind and thus gone. You cannot photograph a wind, a breeze. Before you have caught it, it has already gone, it is there no longer.

Chuang Tzu could not be found because the police were searching for his past and he lived in the present. He was a being, not a mind. Mind can be caught but being cannot be caught. There are no nets. The being cannot be caught. Mind can be caught very easily, and you are all caught in some way or other. Because you have a mind, a wife, a husband will catch you; a shop, a treasure, a position, anything will catch you. There are nets, millions of nets. And you cannot be free unless you are free of the mind. You will be caught again and again. If you leave this wife, another woman will catch you immediately. You cannot escape. You can escape this woman, but you cannot escape women. You can escape this man but where will you go? Before you have left one, another has come. You can leave this town, but where will you go? Another town will catch you. You can leave this desire, another will become the bondage. Because mind is always in bondage, it is already caught. When you drop the mind, then the police cannot catch you.

This Chuang Tzu was without mind. He was a mindless beggar, or an emperor, it means the same. He could not be caught.

When Chuang Tzu came to visit Liang the Prime Minister sent the police out to arrest him, but although they searched for three days and nights, they could not find him. Meanwhile, Chuang Tzu presented himself to Hui Tzu of his own accord, and said ...

Suddenly on the third day or the fourth day Chuang Tzu appeared of his own accord. This type of man, this manner of man, Chuang Tzu, cannot be caught. He always appears of his own accord. It is his freedom. You cannot catch him, you can only invite him. It is his freedom to appear or not.

When there is mind, you are always caught. The mind forces you, you are its prisoner. When there is no mind you are free. You can appear, you can disappear of your own accord. It is your own freedom.

If I am speaking to you it is not that you have asked a question, it is of my own accord. If I am working with you it is not because of you, it is on my own accord. When there is no mind there is freedom. Mind is the basis of all slavery.

Chuang Tzu appeared of his own accord and told a beautiful parable. Listen from the deepest core of your heart.

"Have you heard about the bird
That lives in the south
The Phoenix ...

a mythical bird ...

... that never grows old?"

A Chinese myth, beautiful, and carries much meaning. Myth is not truth, but truer than any truth. Myth is a parable, it indicates something which cannot be indicated otherwise. Only through a parable, through poetry, can it be said. Myth is poetry, it is not a description. It indicates the truth, not an event in the outer world; it belongs to the inner.

"Have you heard about the bird that lives in the south?" In China, India is the south, and that bird lives here. It is said that when Lao Tzu disappeared, he disappeared into the south. They don't know when he died — he never died. Such people never die, they simply go to the south — they disappear into India.

It is said that Bodhidharma came from the south. He left India, and then he waited nine years for a disciple to whom he was to transmit the treasure of Buddha. He transmitted it, and it is said that then he disappeared again into the south. India is the south for China. Really, India is the source of all myth; there exists not a single myth all over the world which has not arisen here.

Science arose out of the Greek mind, myth arose out of the Indian mind. And there are only two ways of looking at the world: one is science, the other is religion. If you look at the world, one day through science, another day through religion ...

If you look at the world through science, it is looking through analysis, mathematics, logic. Athens, the Greek mind, gave science to the world, the Socratic method of analysis, logic and doubt. Religion is a totally different pattern of looking at the world. It looks at the world through poetry, through myth, through love. Of course, it is romantic. It cannot give you facts, it will only give you fictions. But I say fictions are more factual than any facts, because they give you the innermost core, they are not concerned with the outer event. Hence, India has no history. It has only myth, *puranas*; no *itihas*, no history, just mythology.

Rama is not an historical person. He may have been, he may not have been. You cannot prove it; nobody can say anything, whether he was, or not. Krishna is a myth, not an historical fact. Maybe he was, maybe he was not. But India is not bothered whether Krishna and Rama are historical. They are meaningful, they are great poetry, epics. And history is meaningless for India because history contains only bare facts, the innermost core is never revealed. We are concerned with the innermost core, the center of the wheel. The wheel keeps on moving, that is history, but the center of the wheel, which never moves, is the myth.

Said Chuang Tzu: "*Have you heard about the bird that lives in the south – the phoenix that never grows old?*" All that is born grows old. History cannot believe in this bird, because history means the beginning and the end, history means birth and death. The span between birth and death is history, and the span between the birthless and the deathless is myth.

Rama is never born and never dies. Krishna is never born and never dies. They are always there. Myth is not concerned with time, it is concerned with eternity. History goes on changing, myth always remains relevant. There is not, and there can never be, a myth which will become out of date. Newspaper is history, yesterday's newspaper is already out of date. Rama is not part of the newspaper, he is not news, and he will never be out of date. He is always in the present, always meaningful, relevant. History goes on changing; Rama remains there at the center of the wheel, unmoving.

Says Chuang Tzu: "*... that lives in the south – the phoenix that never grows old?*"

Have you ever seen a picture of Rama or Krishna which belongs to their old age? They are always young, without even a beard or mustache. Have you ever seen any picture of Rama with a beard? Unless there was some hormonal defect, if he was really a man – and he was a man – then the beard must have grown. If Rama was historical, then the beard must have been there; but he was beardless, we have pictured him beardless, because the moment the beard grows you have already started becoming old. Sooner or later it will turn white. Death is coming near and we cannot think that Rama dies so we have washed his face completely clean of any sign of death. And this is not only so with Rama; the twenty-four *tirthankaras* of the Jainas are all beardless, no mustaches. Buddha and all the avatars of the Hindus had no beards, no mustaches – just to indicate their eternal youth, the eternity, the timelessness, the foreverness.

"*... the phoenix that never grows old.*" There is time – in time everything changes – and there is eternity. In eternity nothing changes. History belongs to time, myth belongs to eternity. Science belongs to time, religion belongs to the nontemporal, the eternal.

In you also, both exist – time and eternity. On your surface the wheel, time – you were born, you will die, but this is only on the surface. You are young, you will become old. You are healthy, you will be ill. Now you are full of life, sooner or later everything will ebb, death will penetrate you. But this is only on the surface, the wheel of history. Deep down right now, eternity exists in you, the timeless exists. There nothing grows old – the phoenix, the south, the India, the eternal. Where nothing grows old, nothing changes, everything is unmoving. That south is within you.

That is why I go on saying that India is not part of geography, it is not part of history, it is part of an inner map. It doesn't exist in Delhi, it never existed there. Politicians don't belong to it; it doesn't belong to politics. It is the inner. It exists everywhere.

Wherever a man comes deep down into himself he reaches India. That is the reason for the eternal attraction, the magnetism of India. Whenever a person becomes uneasy with his life, he moves towards India. This is just symbolic. Through physical movement you will not find India. A different movement is needed, where you start moving from the outer to the inner, to the south, to the land of myth, and the deathless, " *... the phoenix that never grows old.*"

> "This undying phoenix
> rises out of the south sea
> and flies to the seas of the north,
> never alighting
> except on certain sacred trees.
> He will touch no food
> but the most exquisite
> rare fruit,
> and he drinks only
> from the clearest springs."

This soul, this innermost core of your being, " *... never alighting except on certain sacred trees,*" this inner bird, this is your being. It alights only on certain sacred trees.

He will touch no food
but the most exquisite
rare fruit,
and he drinks only
from the clearest springs.

"Once an owl
chewing an already half-decayed
dead rat
saw the phoenix fly over.
Looking up
he screeched with alarm
and clutched the dead rat to himself
in fear and dismay."

Chuang Tzu is saying: "I am the phoenix, and you are just an owl with an already dead rat, chewing it. And you are alarmed that I am coming to supplant you. Your position, your power is nothing but a dead rat to me. This is no food for me. Ambition is not a way for life, it is only for those who are already dead. I have looked into ambition, and I have found it useless."

Once it happened: a woman came crying and weeping to a rabbi, but the rabbi was at his prayer. So she said to the secretary, "Go in, and even if his prayer has to be interrupted, interrupt. My husband has left me. The rabbi should pray for me, that my husband comes back."

The secretary went in and interrupted the prayer. The rabbi sent the secretary back to the woman, saying, "Don't worry, the husband will come back soon."

The secretary went back to the woman and said, "Don't worry, don't be sad. The rabbi says that your husband will come back soon. Go home and be at ease."

Happy, the woman left, saying, "God will reward your rabbi a million times over, he is so kind."

When the woman left, the secretary became sad, and told someone who was standing there that this was not going to help: "Her husband cannot come back, poor woman, and she left here so happy."

The bystander said, "But why? Don't you believe in your rabbi and his prayer?"

The secretary said, "Of course I believe in my rabbi and I believe in his prayer. But he has only heard the petition of the woman, and I have seen her face. Her husband cannot *ever* come back."

One who has seen the face of ambition, one who has seen the face of desire, one who has seen the face of lust, will never come back to desire, to lust, to ambition. It is impossible, the face is so ugly.

Chuang Tzu has seen the face of ambition. That is why he says: "Your post, your power, your prime-ministership, is just a dead rat to me. Don't screech, and don't get dismayed."

> *"This undying phoenix*
> *rises out of the south sea*
> *and flies to the seas of the north,*
> *never alighting except on certain sacred trees.*
> *He will touch no food*
> *but the most exquisite*
> *rare fruit,*
> *and he drinks only*
> *from the clearest springs."*

> *"Once an owl*
> *chewing an already half-decayed*
> *dead rat*
> *saw the phoenix fly over.*
> *Looking up*
> *he screeched with alarm*
> *and clutched the dead rat to himself*
> *in fear and dismay."*

> *"Prime minister,*
> *why are you so frantic,*
> *clinging to your ministry*
> *and screeching at me in dismay?"*

This is the fact, but only once you know it, only then. Listening to a Buddha, or to a Jesus, or to a Zarathustra, you have always heard: "Drop desiring and bliss will be yours." But you cannot drop it, you cannot understand how bliss can happen when you drop desire, because you have tasted only desire. It may be poisonous, but it has been your only food. You have been drinking from poisoned sources, and when someone says, "Drop it," you think, "then I will die, thirsty." You don't know that there are clear springs, and you don't know that there are trees with rare fruit. You look only through your desire, so you cannot see those fruits and those trees.

When your eyes are filled with desire they see only dead rats. Ramakrishna used to say that there are people who cannot see anything else than the objects of their lust. This owl can sit at the top of a high tree, but he is only looking for dead rats. Whenever a dead rat appears on the street, the owl becomes excited. He will not become so excited, he will not even see, if you throw him a beautiful fruit. He will not see, he will not become aware; the information never reaches him because the desires work like a screen. Continuously, only that which your desires allow enters you. Your desires are just like a watchman standing at the door of your being. They allow only that which appeals to them.

Change this watchman; otherwise you will always live on dead rats. You will remain an owl, and that is the misery, because deep within you the phoenix is hidden and you are behaving like an owl. That is the discontent. That is why you can never feel at ease, that is why you can never feel blissful. You cannot feel — how can a phoenix feel blissful with a dead rat? He is always a stranger, this is not the right food for him.

And this you have felt many times. Making love to a woman or to a man, you have felt many times that this is not for you. The phoenix asserts itself but the owl is much noisier. The phoenix cannot be heard, the voice is very subtle, silent, not aggressive. In moments of peace and meditation the phoenix says, "What are you doing? This is not for you. What are you eating? This is not for you. What are you drinking? This is not for you."

But the owl is very noisy and you have believed in the owl for so long that you go on following it just like a habit. It has become a dead habit. You simply follow it, because there is the least resistance. The rut is there. You don't have to do anything. You simply run on the track, and go on running — the same desires, the same lusts, the same ambitions, and you go on running in a circle. No wonder you live in anguish, you live in a nightmare.

Let the inner Chuang Tzu assert himself, let the inner phoenix assert itself. Listen to it, it is a still, small voice. You will have to calm down, you will have to put this owl to sleep; only then will you be able to listen. This owl is the ego, the mind; the phoenix is the soul. It is born in the south, out of the sea. It is not a part of the land, it is not part of the mud — out of the vast sea it is born. It never grows old, it never dies. It alights only on rare, holy, sacred trees, eats only exquisite rare fruit, drinks only from the clearest of springs. Those springs are there, those holy trees are there. You have been missing them because of the owl, and the owl has become the leader.

All meditation is nothing but an effort to make this owl silent so that the still small voice can be heard. Then you will see what you have been doing — chewing a dead rat.

Chuang Tzu is right. The prime minister was unnecessarily in dismay. When you, your inner phoenix, comes to live its life, the owl, the prime minister, will be in very much dismay in the beginning. Your mind will create every type of hindrance to meditation because the mind is afraid, the prime minister is afraid – this Chuang Tzu, this meditativeness, is coming to supplant him.

Your mind will catch hold of the dead rat, and will scream, scared, as if somebody is going to take that food away from you. In the beginning it will happen – and you have to be alert and aware of it. By and by only your awareness will help.

Whenever one starts meditating, the mind becomes rebellious. It starts all types of arguments: "What are you doing, why are you wasting time? Use this time! Much can be done in it, much can be achieved. That desire has been waiting for so long and there has been no time, and you are wasting time in meditation? Forget it. Those who say that meditation is possible are deceiving you. These Buddhas, these Chuang Tzus, don't believe them. Believe in the mind" – says the mind. It creates all kinds of doubts about everybody, but it never creates any doubt about itself.

I have heard ...

One man was talking to his small child. The child had written a letter as part of his homework and was showing it to his father. There were as many spelling mistakes as there were words, even more. So the father said, "Your spelling is awful. Why don't you look in the dictionary? When you feel in doubt, look in the dictionary."

The child said, "But, Dad, I never feel in doubt."

This is what your mind is doing. It says to Buddha, "But Dad, I never feel in doubt."

Mind never doubts itself, that is the problem. It doubts everybody – it will doubt even a Buddha. If Krishna knocks at your door, it will doubt; if Jesus comes it will doubt. It has always been so, you have been doing it continuously.

You doubt me but you never doubt yourself, because once the mind starts doubting itself it is already going out of existence. Once self-doubt arises the base is broken, the mind has lost its confidence. Once you start doubting the mind, sooner or later you will fall into the abyss of meditation.

Baal Shem, a mystic, died. His son, Hertz, was a very sleepy person, very unconscious. When Baal Shem was dying he was fast asleep, and Baal Shem had said, "This night is going to be my last."

But Hertz had said, "Nobody can know when death will come." He doubted. Baal Shem was his father, and thousands believed that he was the messiah, the man who would lead millions to salvation. But the son doubted, he fell asleep.

He was awakened at midnight. His father was dead. He started crying, weeping. He had missed a great opportunity, and now there would be no possibility of a meeting. But he never doubted his mind, he doubted Baal Shem.

Then in dismay and despair, he started crying. He closed his eyes and for the first time in his life, when the father was dead, he started talking to him. His father had called him many times: "Hertz, come to me." And he would say, "Yes, I will come, but there are other, more important things to do first."

This is what your mind is saying. I go on calling you: "Come to me." You say, "There are other more important things right now. I will come later on; wait!"

But death had broken the bridge. So Hertz cried and started talking to his father, and he said, "What should I do now? I am lost. I am in darkness. Now how can I drop this mind which has deceived me? I never doubted it, and I doubted you. Now it makes me very sad."

Baal Shem appeared inside Hertz and said, "Look at me. Do the same." As if in a dream Hertz was seeing Baal Shem go to the top of a hill and drop himself into the abyss. And he said, "Do the same."

Said Hertz, "I cannot understand." Really, doubt arose again: "What is this man saying? This will be suicide."

Baal Shem laughed, and said, "You are still doubting me, not doubting yourself. Then do this." In his vision Hertz saw a big mountain, all aflame, like a volcano, fire all over, rocks splitting, and the whole mountain breaking into fragments. Said Baal Shem, "Or do like this. Let the mind be thrown into an abyss, let the mind be burnt up completely."

And the story goes that Hertz said, "I will think it over."

Whenever you say, "I will think it over," you have started doubting. Doubt thinks, not you. And when there is no doubt, faith acts, not you. Doubt thinks, faith acts. Through doubt you can become a great philosopher; through faith you will become a Chuang Tzu, a phoenix which never grows old, which is undying. Through doubt you can penetrate the mysteries of time; through faith you will enter the door of eternity.

I have heard ...

Two men were once lost in a forest. It was very dangerous, the forest was so dense, it was night, darkness and wild animals all around. One man was a philosopher and the other was a mystic – one a man of doubt, the other a man of faith. Suddenly, there was a storm, a crashing of the clouds, and great lightning.

The philosopher looked at the sky, the mystic looked at the path. In that moment of lightning, the path was before him, illuminated. The philosopher looked at the lightning, and started wondering, "What is happening?" and missed the path.

You are lost in a forest denser than that in the story. The night is darker. Sometimes lightning comes. Look at the path.

A Chuang Tzu is lightning, a Buddha is lightning, I am lightning. Don't look at me, look at the path. If you look at me, you have already missed, because the lightning will not continue. It lasts only for a moment, and the moment is rare when eternity penetrates time; it is just like lightning.

If you look at the lightning, if you look at a buddha – and a buddha is beautiful, the face fascinates, the eyes are magnetic – if you look at the buddha, you have missed the path.

Look at the path, forget the buddha. Look at the path. But that look happens only when there is no doubt, when there is faith; when there is no thinking, no mind.

Chuang Tzu has not to be thought about. Don't think about him. Just let this story penetrate you, and forget it. Through this story the path is illuminated. Look at the path, and do something. Follow the path, act. Only action will lead you, not thinking, because thinking goes on in the head, it can never become total. Only when you act, it is total.

Enough for today.

Chapter 4

Apologies

If a man steps on a stranger's foot
In the marketplace,
He makes a polite apology
And offers an explanation
"This place is so terribly
Crowded!"

If an elder brother
Steps on his younger brother's foot,
He says, "Sorry!"
And that is that.

If a parent
Treads on his child's foot
Nothing is said at all.

The greatest politeness
Is free of all formality.
Perfect conduct
Is free of concern.
Perfect wisdom
Is unplanned.
Perfect love
Is without demonstrations.
Perfect sincerity offers
No guarantee.

All that is great, all that is beautiful, all that is true and real, is always spontaneous. You cannot plan it. The moment you plan it, everything goes wrong. The moment planning enters, everything becomes unreal.

But this has happened to humanity. Your love, your sincerity, your truth, everything has gone wrong because you have planned it, because you have been taught not to be spontaneous. You have been taught to manipulate yourself, to control, to manage, and not to be a natural flow. You have become rigid, frozen, dead.

Life knows no planning. It is itself enough. Do the trees plan how to grow, how to mature, how to come to flower? They simply grow without even being conscious of the growth. There is no self-consciousness, there is no separation.

Whenever you start planning you have divided yourself, you have become two – the one who is controlling and the one who is controlled. A conflict has arisen, now you will never be at peace. You may succeed in controlling but there will be no peace, or you may not succeed in controlling, then too there will be no peace. Whether you succeed or fail, ultimately you will come to realize that you have failed. Your failure will be a failure, your success will also be a failure. Whatsoever you do, your life will be miserable.

This division creates ugliness, you are not one, and beauty belongs to oneness, beauty belongs to a harmonious whole. All culture, all civilization, all societies, make you ugly. All morality makes you ugly because it is based on division, on control.

I have heard ...

Once Baal Shem was traveling in a beautiful coach with three horses. But he was wondering continuously. For three days he had been traveling, but not even once had any of the horses neighed. What had happened to the horses? Then suddenly on the fourth day, a passing peasant shouted at him to relax control. He relaxed, and suddenly all three horses started neighing, they came alive. For three days continuously they had been dead, dying.

This has happened to you all, to the whole of humanity. You cannot neigh, and unless a horse neighs the horse is dead, because neighing means he is enjoying, there is an overflowing. But you cannot neigh, you are dead. Your life is not an overflowing song in any way, a dance that happens when the energy is too much.

Flowering is always a luxury, it is not a necessity. No tree needs flowers as a necessity, roots are enough. Flowering is always luxurious. Flowers come only when the tree has too much, it needs to give, it needs to share.

Whenever you have too much, life becomes a dance, a celebration. But society doesn't allow you to dance, to celebrate, so society has to see that you never have more energy than necessary. You are only allowed to live at starvation level. You are not allowed to be too much, because once you are too much you cannot be controlled, and society wants to control you. It is a very subtle domination.

Every child is born overflowing. Then we have to cut the energy source, we have to prune the child from here and there so that he becomes controllable. And the root of all control is to divide the child in two. Then you need not bother, he himself will do the controlling. Then you need not bother, he himself will be the enemy of his own self.

So they tell the child, "This is wrong. Don't do this." Suddenly the child is divided, now he knows what is wrong, now he knows what part of his being is wrong, and his head becomes the controller.

Through division intellect has become the controller, the master. If you are undivided, you will not have any head. Not that the head will disappear or the head will fall off, but you will not be head-oriented – your total being will be you.

Right now you are only the head, the rest of the body is just to sustain the head. The head has become the exploiter, the dictator. And this has come through conflict, the creation of conflict in you. You have been taught that this is good and that is bad. The intellect learns it and then the intellect goes on condemning you.

Remember, if you condemn yourself you will condemn everybody – you will condemn the whole. And a person who condemns himself cannot love. A person who condemns himself cannot pray. A person who condemns himself, for him there is no God, there cannot be. A condemning mind can never enter the divine temple. Only when you dance, only when you are ecstatic, not condemning, only when you are overflowing, with nobody sitting in control, nobody managing, does life become a let-go. It is not formal, it is natural. Then you enter, then everywhere is the door. Then you can reach the temple from anywhere.

But right now, as you are, you are schizophrenic. You are not only schizophrenic when a psychoanalyst says that you are. There is no need for any psychoanalyst to analyze you. Society creates schizophrenics; division is schizophrenia. You are not one. You are born one but immediately society starts working, great surgery is to be done, you are operated upon continuously, to be divided. Then society is at ease because you are fighting with yourself, your energy is dissipated in the inner fight, it is never an overflowing. Then you are not dangerous.

Overflowing energy becomes rebellion. Overflowing energy is always rebel-lious, overflowing energy is always in revolution. It is just like a river in flood – it doesn't believe in the banks, in the rules, in the laws, it simply goes on overflowing towards the sea. It knows only one goal – to become the sea, to become the infinite.

Overflowing energy is always moving towards godliness. This is missing in our world, not because of science, not because of atheists. It is because of the so-called religious people. They have divided you so much that the river goes on fighting with itself. Nothing is left to move, no energy is left; you are so tired fighting with yourself, how can you move towards the sea?

One of the basic laws of Tao, of Lao Tzu, of Chuang Tzu, is that if you are spontaneous it is the highest prayerfulness; you cannot miss God, whatsoever you do you will reach him. So Chuang Tzu never talks about God; talk is irrelevant, it isn't needed. He talks only of how to bring out the wholeness in you. The holy is irrelevant. When you become whole, you become holy. When your fragments dissolve into one, your life has become prayerfulness. Men of Tao never talk about prayer, it is not needed.

Spontaneity, living as a whole ... But if you want to live as a whole, you cannot plan. Who will plan? You cannot decide for tomorrow, you can live only here and now. Who will decide? If you decide, division has entered, then you will have to manipulate. Who will plan? The future is unknown, and how can you plan for the unknown? If you plan for the unknown the planning will come from the past. That means that the dead will control the living. The past is dead, and the past goes on controlling the future, hence you are so bored. It is natural, it has to happen. Boredom comes from the past, because the past is dead and the past is trying to control the future.

The future is always an adventure, but you don't allow it to be an adventure. You plan it. Once planned, your life is running on a track. It is not a river.

When you run on a track you know where you are going, what is happening. Everything is just a repetition. Who will plan? If mind plans, mind is always of the past. Life cannot be planned, because through planning you are committing suicide.

Life can only be unplanned, moving moment to moment into the unknown. But what is the fear? You will be there to respond; whatsoever the situation, you will be there to respond. What is your fear? Why plan it?

The fear comes because you are not certain of whether you will be there or not. You are so unconscious, that is the uncertainty. You are not alert.

You are going to an interview for a job, so you go on planning in the mind what to answer, how to answer, how to enter the office, how to stand, how to sit. But why? You will be there, you can respond.

But you are not certain about yourself, you are so unalert, you are so unconscious, you don't know — if you don't plan, something may go wrong. If you are alert, then there is no question. You will be there, so whatever the situation demands, you will respond.

And remember, this planning is not going to help, because if you cannot be conscious, cannot be aware in a situation when you are planning, then that planning is also being done in sleep. But you can repeat it so many times it becomes mechanical, then when the question is asked you can answer. The answer is ready-made, you are not needed. It is a fixed pattern, you simply repeat it; you become a mechanical device, you need not be there at all. The answer can be given, it comes from the memory; if you have repeated it so many times you know you can rely on it.

Through planning life becomes more and more unconscious, and the more unconscious you are, the more you need planning. Before really dying, you are dead. Alive means responding, sensitive. Alive means: whatsoever comes, I will be there to respond, and the response will come from me, not from the memory. I will not prepare it.

See the difference: a Christian missionary or a Christian minister, a priest, prepares his sermon ...

I once visited a theological college. There they prepare their ministers, their priests — five years' training. So I asked them where Jesus was prepared and trained, who taught him how to speak.

Of course these Christian priests are dead, everything about them is planned. When you say this, that gesture is to be made — even the gesture is not allowed to be spontaneous. When you say that, you have to look this way, even the eyes are not allowed to be spontaneous. How you have to stand, when you have to be loud, and when you have to whisper, when you have to hammer the table and when not — everything is planned.

I asked them where Jesus was trained. He was not a minister at all, he was not a priest. He never went to any theological college, he was the son of a carpenter.

For two thousand years Christian priests have been trained, but they have not produced a single Jesus, and they will never produce one again because Jesus cannot be produced. You cannot produce Jesus in a factory. And these are factories, these theological colleges, where you produce priests, and these priests are just boring, dead, a burden — it is obvious that it is going to be so.

There are two types of religion. One is of the mind — it is dead. That religion is known as theology. There is another type of religion — the real, the spontaneous. It is not theological, it is mystical. And remember, Hindus have one theology, Mohammedans a different one, Christians again another, but religion, the mystical religion, is the same; it cannot be different.

Buddha and Jesus and Chuang Tzu and Lao Tzu, they are the same because they are not theologians. They are not talking from the head, they are simply pouring from their heart. They are not logicians, they are poets. They are not saying something from the scriptures, they are not trained for it, they are simply responding to a necessity in you. Their words are not ready-made, their manners not fixed, their behavior not planned.

Now we will enter Chuang Tzu's sutra:

If a man steps on a stranger's foot
in the marketplace,

he makes a polite apology
and offers an explanation:
"This place is
so crowded."

Apology is needed because there is no relationship, the other is a stranger. Explanation is needed because there is no love. If there is love then there is no need for an explanation, the other will understand. If there is love, there is no need for apology, the other will understand – love always understands.

So there is no higher morality than love, there cannot be. Love is the highest law, but if it is not there then substitutes are needed. Stepping on a stranger's foot in the marketplace, apology is needed, and an explanation also:

"This place is
so crowded."

In reference to this, one thing has to be understood. In the West even a husband will offer an apology, a wife will offer an explanation. It means that love has disappeared. It means that everybody has become a stranger, that there is no home, that every place has become a marketplace. In the East it is impossible to conceive of this, but Westerners think that Easterners are rude. A husband will never give an explanation – no need, because we are not strangers and the other can understand. When the other cannot understand, only then apology is needed. And if love cannot understand, what good is apology going to do?

If the world becomes a home, all apologies will disappear, all explanations will disappear. You give explanations because you are not certain about the other. Explanation is a trick to avoid conflict, apology is a device to avoid conflict. But the conflict is there, and you are afraid of it.

This is a civilized way to get out of the conflict! You have stepped on a stranger's foot, you look – violence is in his eyes – he has become aggressive, he will hit you. Apology is needed, his anger will subside with an apology – it is a trick. You need not be authentic in your apology, it is just a social device, it works as a lubricant. Then you give an explanation just to say, "I am not responsible, the place is so crowded, it is a marketplace, nothing can be done, it had to happen." Explanation says that you are not responsible.

Love is always responsible, whether the place is crowded or not, because love is always aware and alert. You cannot shift the responsibility to the situation, *you* are responsible.

Look at this phenomenon – apology is a device, just like a lubricant, to avoid conflict, and explanation is shifting the responsibility onto something else. You don't say, "I was unconscious, unaware, that is why I stepped on your foot." You say, "The place is so crowded!"

A religious person cannot do this, and if you go on doing this you will never become religious, because religion means taking all the responsibility that is there, not avoiding, not escaping. The more responsible you are, the more awareness will arise out of it; the less you feel responsible, the more and more unconscious you will become. Whenever you feel that you are not responsible you will go to sleep. And this has happened — not only in individual relationships, on all levels of society this has happened.

Marxism says that society is responsible for everything. If a man is poor society is responsible, if a man is a thief, society is responsible. You are not responsible, no individual is responsible. That is why communism is anti-religious — not because it denies God, not because it says there is no soul, but because of this. It shifts the whole responsibility onto society; you are not responsible.

Look at the religious attitude, which is totally different, qualitatively different. A religious man thinks himself responsible: If someone is begging, if a beggar is there, I am responsible. The beggar may be at the other end of the earth, I may not know him, I may not come across his path, but if the beggar is there, I am responsible. If a war goes on anywhere, in Israel, in Vietnam, anywhere, I am not participating in it in any visible way, but I am responsible. I am here. I cannot shift the responsibility onto society.

What do you mean when you say society? Where is this society? This is one of the greatest escapes — only individuals exist — you will never come across society. You will never be able to pinpoint it; this is society. Everywhere the individual is in existence, and society is just a word.

Where is society? Ancient civilizations played a trick. They said: God is responsible, fate is responsible. Now communism plays the same game saying that society is responsible. But where is society? God may be somewhere, society is nowhere; there are only individuals. Religion says: You are, rather, I am responsible. No explanation is needed to avoid this.

And remember one thing more: whenever you feel that you are responsible for all the ugliness, for all the mess, anarchy, war, violence, aggression, suddenly you become alert. Responsibility penetrates your heart and makes you aware. When you say, "This place is much too crowded," you can go on walking sleepily. Really, you step on the stranger's foot not because the place is crowded, but because you are unconscious. You are walking like a somnambulist, a man walking in his sleep. When you step on his foot, you suddenly became aware because now there is danger. You make the apology, you fall asleep, and again you say, "The place is crowded!" You start moving again.

I have heard about one simple villager, who had come to the city for the first time. On the platform at the station someone stepped on his foot and said, "Sorry." Then he went into a hotel, someone again clashed with him and said, "Sorry!" Then he went into a theater and someone almost knocked him down, and he said, "Sorry."

The villager said, "This is beautiful, we never knew this trick. Do whatever you want to do to anybody and say sorry!" So he hit hard a man who was passing and said, "Sorry!"

What are you really doing when you say sorry? Your sleep is broken, you were walking in a dream — you must have been dreaming, imagining, something was going on in the mind — and then you stepped on someone. Not that the place was crowded — you would have stumbled even if no one were there, even then you would have stepped on someone.

It is you, your unconsciousness, your unconscious behavior. A buddha cannot stumble even if it is a marketplace, because he moves with full consciousness. Whatsoever he is doing, he is doing it knowingly. And if he steps on your foot it means he has stepped knowingly; there must be some purpose in it. It may be just to help you wake up; just to make you awake he may have stepped on your foot, but he will not say that the place is crowded, he will not give any explanation.

Explanations are always deceptive. They look logical, but they are false. You give explanations only when you have to hide something. You can watch and observe this in your own life. This is not a theory, this is a simple fact of everybody's experience — you give explanations only when you want to hide something.

Truth needs no explanation. The more you lie, the more explanations are needed. There are so many scriptures because man has lied so much, then explanations are needed to hide the lies. You have to give an explanation, then this explanation will need further explanation, and it goes on and on. It is an infinite regression. And even with the last explanation nothing is explained, the basic lie remains a lie — you cannot convert a lie into a truth just by explaining it. You may think so, but nothing is explained by explanations.

Once it happened: Mulla Nasruddin went on his first air trip, and he was afraid but he didn't want anybody to know. It happens to everybody on their first air trip. Nobody wants this to be their first. He wanted to behave nonchalantly, so he walked very bravely. That bravery was an explanation: "I always travel by air." Then he sat down in his seat and he wanted to say something just to make himself at ease, because whenever you start talking, you become brave; through talk, you feel less fear.

So Nasruddin spoke to the passenger next to him. He looked out of the window and said, "Look, what a height! People look like ants."

The other man said, "Sir, we have not taken off yet. Those *are* ants."

Explanations cannot hide anything. Rather, on the contrary, they reveal. If you can look, if you have eyes, every explanation is transparent. It would have been better if he had been silent. But don't try silence as an explanation. As an explanation it is of no use. Your silence will be revealing, and your words will reveal – it is better not to be a liar! Then you need not give any explanations. It is better to be truthful – the easiest thing is to be true and authentic. If you are afraid, it is better to say, "I am afraid," and accepting the fact, your fear will disappear.

Acceptance is such a miracle. When you accept that you are afraid and say, "This is my first trip," suddenly you will feel a change coming over you. The basic fear is not fear, the basic fear is the fear of the fear – no one should know that I am afraid. No one should know that I am a coward. But everybody is a coward in a new situation, and in a new situation to be brave will be foolish. To be cowardly only means that the situation is so new that your mind cannot supply any answers, the past cannot give the answers, so you are trembling. But this is good! Why try to supply an answer from the mind? Tremble, and let the answer come from your present consciousness. You are sensitive, that is all; don't kill this sensitivity through explanations.

Next time you try to give an explanation, be alert. What are you doing? Trying to hide something? Trying to explain away something? Nothing like this will be of any help.

A man who had become newly rich went to a beach, the most costly, expensive, the most exclusive, and he was spending madly just to influence the people around him. The next day, while swimming, his wife drowned. She was carried to the shore, a crowd gathered, so he asked, "What are you doing?"

One man said, "We are going to give air to your wife, artificial respiration."

The man said, "Nothing doing, give her the real thing. I can pay for it."

Whatsoever you do, whatsoever you don't do, whatsoever you say, whatsoever you don't say, reveals you. Everywhere mirrors are all around you. Every other person is a mirror, every situation is a mirror – and whom do you think you are deceiving? And if it becomes a habit to deceive, ultimately you will have deceived yourself and no one else. It is your life that you are wasting in deceptions.

Chuang Tzu says: explanations show that you are not true, you are not authentic.

If an elder brother
steps on his younger brother's foot
he says, "Sorry!"
and that is that.

Two brothers ... When the relationship is more intimate, the other is not a stranger. Then no explanation is needed, the brother simply says sorry. He accepts the blame. He says, "I have been unconscious." He is not shifting the responsibility onto somebody else, he accepts it and that is that. The relationship is closer.

If a parent
treads on his child's foot
nothing is said at all.

There is no need, the relationship is even closer, more intimate. There is love, and that love will do. No substitute is needed, no explanation, no apology.

The greatest politeness
is free of all formality.
Perfect conduct
is free of concern.
Perfect wisdom
is unplanned.
Perfect love
is without demonstrations.
Perfect sincerity offers
no guarantee.

But all these perfections need one thing – and that is spontaneous awareness; otherwise you will always have false coins, you will always have false faces. You can be sincere, but if you have to make any effort then that sincerity is just formal.

You can be loving, but if your love needs effort, if your love is of the type which Dale Carnegie talks about in *How to Win Friends and Influence People*, if that type of love is there, it cannot be real. You have been manipulating it. Then even friendship is a business.

Beware of Dale Carnegies; these are dangerous people, they destroy all that is real and authentic. They show you how to win friends, they teach you tricks, techniques, they make you efficient, they give you the knowhow.

But love has no knowhow, it cannot have. Love needs no training, and friendship is not something which you have to learn. A learned friendship will not be a friendship, it will just be exploitation – you are exploiting the other and deceiving him. You are not true, this is a business relationship.

But in America everything has become business, friendship and love also – and Dale Carnegie's books have sold millions of copies, hundreds of editions, next only to the Bible.

Nobody knows how to be a friend, it has to be learned. Sooner or later there will be colleges for love, training courses, even by post, lessons you can learn and apply. And the problem is that if you succeed then you are lost forever, because the real will never happen to you, the door is completely closed. Once you become efficient in a certain thing, the mind resists. The mind says: This is the short cut, and you know it well, so why choose another path?

Mind is always for the least resistance. That is why clever people are never able to love. They are so clever they start manipulating. They will not say what is in their heart, they will say what will appeal. They will look at the other person and see what he wants to be said. They will not speak their heart, they will just create a situation in which the other is deceived.

Husbands deceiving wives, wives deceiving husbands, friends deceiving friends ... The whole world has become just a crowd of enemies. There are only two types of enemies: those you have not been able to deceive and those you have been able to deceive. This is the only difference. Then how can there be ecstasy in your life?

So this is not a learning ... Authenticity cannot come through schooling, authenticity comes through awareness – if you are aware, if you live in a conscious way. Look at the difference: to live consciously means to live openly, not to hide, not to play games. To be alert means to be vulnerable, and whatsoever happens, happens. You accept it, but you never compromise, you never purchase anything by giving up your consciousness. Even if you are left totally alone, you will accept being left alone, but you will want to be consciously alert. Only in this alertness does real religion start happening.

I will tell you a story:

It happened once, in ancient times: there was a king who was also an astrologer. He had a very deep interest in studying the stars. Suddenly there was panic in his heart because he became aware that the coming year's harvest was going to be dangerous. Whoever will eat the coming year's harvest will go mad. So he called his prime minister, his adviser and counselor, and told him that this was going to happen, that it was a certainty. "The stars are clear. The combination of cosmic rays is such that this year's harvest is going to be poisonous. It happens rarely, in thousands of years, but this is going to happen this year and anybody who will eat will go mad. So what should we do? The prime minister said, "It is impossible to provide for everybody from last year's harvest, but one thing can be done. You and I can both live on last year's harvest. Last year's harvest can be gathered, requisitioned. There is no problem, for you and me it will be enough."

The king said, "This doesn't appeal to me. Then all my devoted people will go mad – women, saints and sages, devoted servants, all my subjects, even children, and it doesn't appeal to me to be an outsider. It would not be worth saving myself and you; that will not do. I would rather be mad with everybody else. But I have another suggestion. I will mark your head with the seal of madness and you will mark my head with the seal of madness."

"But," the prime minister said, "How is this going to help anybody?"

The king said, "I have heard: it is one of the ancient pillars of wisdom, so let us try it. After everybody has gone mad, after we have gone mad, whenever I look at your forehead I will remember that I am mad. And whenever you look at my forehead, remember that you are mad."

The prime minister was still puzzled; he said, "But what will it do?"

The king said, "I have heard from wise men that if you can remember that you are mad, you are mad no longer."

A madman cannot remember that he is mad. An ignorant man cannot remember that he is ignorant. A man who is in a dream cannot remember that he is dreaming. If, in your dreams, you become alert and know that you are dreaming, the dream has stopped, you are fully awake. If you can understand that you are ignorant, ignorance drops. Ignorant people go on believing that they are wise, and mad people think that they are the only really sane ones. When someone becomes really wise, he becomes so by recognizing his ignorance. So the king said, "This we are going to do."

I don't know what happened, the story ends here, but the story is meaningful.

Only alertness can help when the whole world is mad, nothing else. Keeping yourself outside, going to the Himalayas, will not be of much help. When everyone is mad, you are going to be mad, because you are part and parcel of everybody; it is a totality, an organic totality.

How can you separate yourself? How can you go to the Himalayas? Deep down you remain part of the whole. Even living in the Himalayas you will remember your friends. They will knock in your dreams, you will think of them, you will wonder what they are thinking of you – you go on being related.

You cannot go out of the world. There is no place outside the world, the world is one continent. Nobody can be an island – even islands are joined with the continent deep down. You can just think superficially that you are separate, but nobody can be separate.

The king was really wise. He said, "It is not going to help. I am not going to be an outsider, I will be an insider, and this is what I will do. I will try to remember that I am mad, because when you forget that you are mad, then you are really mad. This is what is to be done."

Wherever you are, remember yourself, that you are; this consciousness that you are should become a continuity. Not your name, your caste, your nationality, those are futile things, absolutely useless. Just remember that I am; this must not be forgotten. This is what Hindus call self-remembrance, what the Buddha called right-mindfulness, what Gurdjieff used to call self-remembering, what Krishnamurti calls awareness.

This is the most substantial part of meditation, to remember that I am. Walking, sitting, eating, talking, remember that: I am. Never forget this. It will be difficult, very arduous. In the beginning you will keep forgetting; there will be only single moments when you will feel illuminated, then it will be lost. But don't get miserable; even single moments are much. Go on, whenever you can remember, remember again, catch hold of the thread again. When you forget, don't worry — remember again, again catch hold of the thread, and by and by the gaps will lessen, the intervals will start dropping, a continuity will arise.

And whenever your consciousness becomes continuous, you need not use the mind. Then there is no planning, then you act out of your consciousness, not out of your mind. Then there is no need for any apology, no need to give any explanation. Then you are whatsoever you are, there is nothing to hide. Whatsoever you are, you are. You cannot do anything else. You can only be in a state of continuous remembrance. Through this remembrance, this mindfulness, comes the authentic religion, comes the authentic morality.

The greatest politeness
is free of all formality.

If you are not formal, then nobody is a stranger. Whether you move in the marketplace or in a crowded street, nobody is a stranger, everybody is a friend. Not only a friend, really, everybody is just an extension of you. Then formality is not needed. If I step on my own foot — which is difficult — I will not say sorry, and I will not say to myself, "The place is very crowded!" When I step on your foot, I am stepping on my foot.

A mind which is fully alert knows that consciousness is one, life is one, being is one, existence is one, it is not fragmented. The tree flowering there is me in a different form; the rock lying there on the ground is me in a different form. Then the whole of existence becomes an organic unity — organic, life flowing through it, not mechanical. A mechanical unity is a different thing — it is dead.

A car is a mechanical unity, there is no life in it, and that is why you can replace one part with another. Every part is replaceable. But can you replace a man? Impossible! When a man dies, a unique phenomenon disappears; disappears completely, you cannot replace it. When your wife dies or your husband dies, now how can you replace them? You may get another wife, but this will be another wife, not a replacement. And the shadow of the first will always be there; the first cannot be forgotten, it will always be there. It may become a shadow, but even shadows of love are very substantial.

You cannot replace a person, there is no way. If it is a mechanical unity then wives are replaceable parts, you can even have spare wives. You can keep them in your storeroom and whenever your wife dies, you replace her.

This is what is happening in the West. They have started to think in terms of mechanism. So now they say nothing is a problem – one wife dies you get another, one husband is no more, you get another replacement. Marriage in the West is a mechanical unity, that's why divorce is possible. The East denies divorce because marriage is an organic unity. How can you replace a live person? It will never happen again, that person has simply disappeared into the ultimate mystery.

Life is an organic unity. I say you cannot replace a plant because every plant is unique, you cannot find another, the same cannot be found. Life has a quality of uniqueness. Even a small rock is unique – you can go all over the world to find a similar rock and you will not be able to. How can you replace it? This is the difference between organic unity and mechanical unity. Mechanical unity depends on the parts; the parts are replaceable, they are not unique. Organic unity depends on the whole, not on the parts. Parts are not really parts, they are not separate from the whole – they are one, they cannot be replaced.

When you become alert to the inner flame of your inner being, suddenly you become alert that you are not an island, it is a vast continent, an infinite continent. There are no boundaries separating you from it. All boundaries are false, make-believe. All boundaries are in the mind; in existence there are no boundaries.

Then who is a stranger? When you step on somebody, it is you; you have stepped on your own foot. No apology is needed, no explanation is needed. There is no one else, there is only one. Then your life becomes real, authentic, spontaneous; then it is not formal, then you do not follow any rules. You have come to know the ultimate law. Now no rules are needed. You have become the law – there is no need to remember the rules now.

The greatest politeness
is free of all formality.

Have you looked at people who are polite? You will not find more egoistic people than these. Look at a polite person, the very way he stands, the way he talks, the way he looks, walks; he has managed everything to look, to appear, polite, but inside the ego is manipulating.

Look at the so-called humble people. They say they are nobodies, but when they say it, look into their eyes, at the ego asserting. And this is a very cunning ego, because if you say, "I am somebody," everybody will be against you, and everybody will try to put you in your place. If you say, "I am nobody," everybody is for you, nobody is against you.

Polite people are very cunning, clever. They know what to say, what to do, so that they can exploit you. If they say, "I am somebody," everybody is against them. Then conflict arises because everybody thinks that he is an egoist. It will be difficult to exploit people then because everybody is closed, against you. If you say, "I am nobody, I am just dust on your feet," then the doors are open and you can exploit. All etiquette, culture, is a type of sophisticated cunningness, you are exploiting.

The greatest politeness
is free of all formality.

It happened that Confucius came to see Lao Tzu, Chuang Tzu's master. And Confucius was the image of formal politeness. He was the greatest formalist in the world, the world has never known such a great formalist. He was simply manners, formality, culture, etiquette. He came to see Lao Tzu, the polar opposite.

Confucius was very old, Lao Tzu was not so old. So to be formal when Confucius came in, Lao Tzu should have stood up to receive him. But he remained sitting. It was impossible for Confucius to believe that such a great master, known all over the country for his humbleness, should be so impolite. He had to talk about it.

Immediately he said, "This is not good. I am older than you."

Lao Tzu laughed loudly and said, "Nobody is older than me. I existed before everything came into existence. Confucius, we are of the same age, everything is of the same age. From eternity we have been in existence, so don't carry this burden of old age. Sit down."

Confucius had come to ask some questions. He said, "How should a religious man behave?"

Lao Tzu said, "When the *how* comes in, there is no religion. *How* is not a question for a religious man. The *how* shows that you are not religious but that you want to behave like a religious man – that is why you ask how."

Does a lover ask how one should love? He loves! Really, it is only later on that he becomes aware that he has been in love. It may be that when the lover has gone he becomes aware that he has been in love. He simply loves. It happens. It is a happening, not a doing.

Whatsoever Confucius asked, Lao Tzu replied in such a way that Confucius became very disturbed: "This man is dangerous!"

He went back; his disciples asked, "What happened, what manner of man is this Lao Tzu?"

Confucius said, "Don't go near him. You may have seen dangerous snakes, but nothing compares with this man. You may have heard about ferocious lions, they are nothing before this man. This man is a dragon walking on the earth, he can swim in the sea, he can go to the very end of the sky — very dangerous. He is not for us little people, we are too small. He is dangerous, vast like an abyss. Don't go near him, otherwise you will feel dizzy and you may fall. Even I felt dizzy. I couldn't understand what he said, he is beyond understanding."

Lao Tzu is bound to be beyond understanding if you try to understand him through formality; otherwise he is simple. But for Confucius he is difficult, almost impossible to understand, because he sees through forms and Lao Tzu has no form and no formality. Nameless, without any form, he lives in the infinite.

The greatest politeness
is free of all formality.

Lao Tzu was sitting, Confucius was waiting for him to stand up. Who was really polite? Confucius waiting for Lao Tzu to stand up and welcome him and receive him because he is older, is just egoistic. Now the ego has taken the form of age, seniority.

But Confucius could not look directly into the eyes of Lao Tzu, because Lao Tzu was right. He was saying: We are of the same age. Really, we are the same. The same life flows in you that flows in me. You are not superior to me, I am not superior to you. There is no question of superiority and inferiority, and there is no question of seniority and juniority. There is no question, we are one.

If Confucius could have looked into the eyes, and seen that those eyes were divine. But a man whose own eyes are filled with laws, rules, regulations, formalities, is almost blind, he cannot see.

Perfect conduct
is free of concern.

You conduct yourself well because you are concerned. You behave well because you are concerned.

Just the other day a man came to me. He said, "I would like to take the jump, I would like to become a sannyasin, but there is my family, my children are studying at college and I have a great responsibility toward them."

He is concerned. He has a duty to fulfill, but no love. Duty is concern; it thinks in terms of something that has to be done because it is expected, because "What will people say if I leave?" Who thinks about what people will say? The ego. "What will people say? So first let me fulfill my duties."

I never tell anybody to leave, I never tell anybody to renounce, but I insist that one should not be in some relationship because of duty — because then the whole relationship is ugly. One should be in a relationship because of love. Then this man would not say, "I have a duty to fulfill." He would say, "I cannot come right now. My children are growing, and I love them, and I am happy working for them."

Then this will be a happiness. Now it is not a happiness, it is a burden. When you carry a burden, when you even turn your love into a burden, you cannot be happy. And if you have turned your love into a burden, your prayer will also become a burden, your meditation will also become a burden. Then you will say, "Because of this guru, this master, I am caught, and now I have to do this." It will not come out of you, out of your totality; it will not be overflowing.

Why be worried? If there is love, wherever you are, there is no burden. And if you love your children, even if you leave them, they will understand. And if you don't love your children, and you go on serving them, they will never understand, and they will know that these are just false things.

This is happening. People come to see me and they say, "I have worked my whole life and nobody even feels thankful towards me." How can anybody feel thankful towards you? You were carrying them like a burden. Even small children understand well when love is there, and they understand well when you are just doing as a duty. Duty is ugly, duty is violent; it shows your concern but doesn't show your spontaneity.

Says Chuang Tzu:

Perfect conduct
is free of concern.

Whatsoever is done, is done out of love — then you are not honest because honesty pays, you are honest because honesty is lovely.

Even businessmen are honest if honesty pays. They say: Honesty is the best policy. How can you destroy a beautiful thing like honesty and turn it into a best policy? Policy is politics, honesty is religion.

One old man was on his deathbed, dying. He called his son and said, "Now I am dying I must tell you my secret. Always remember two things – this is how I succeeded. First, whenever you make a promise, fulfill it. Whatsoever the cost, be honest and fulfill it. This has been my basis, this is why I succeeded. And the second thing, never make any promises."

For a businessman even religion is a policy, for a politician even religion is a policy – everything is a policy, even love is a policy. Kings and queens never marry ordinary, common people. Why? It is part of politics. Kings marry other princesses, queens, and the concern is about which relationship will be more profitable for the kingdom. If two kingdoms become related, they will become friends, they will not be antagonistic. So with whom should the marriage be made?

In India, in olden days, a king would marry many women, hundreds, even thousands. It was part of politics, so he would marry the daughter of anybody who had some power, so that he could create a network of power relationships. The person whose daughter you have married will become your friend, he will help you.

In Buddha's time India had two thousand kingdoms. So the most successful king was the one who had two thousand wives, one wife from every kingdom. Then he could live in peace, now there was no one antagonistic, inimical towards him. Now the whole country became like a family. But how can love exist in such a concern? Love never thinks of consequences, never hankers for results. It is enough unto itself.

Perfect conduct
is free of concern.
Perfect wisdom
is unplanned.

A wise man lives moment to moment, never planning. Only ignorant people plan, and when ignorant people plan, what can they plan? They plan out of their ignorance. Unplanned they would have been better off, because out of ignorance only ignorance arises; out of confusion, only greater confusion is born.

A wise man lives moment to moment, he has no planning. His life is just free like a cloud floating in the sky, not going to some goal, not determined. He has no map for the future, he lives without a map, he moves without a map – because the real thing is not the goal, the real thing is the beauty of the movement. The real thing is not reaching, the real thing is the journey. Remember, the real thing is the journey, the very traveling. It is so beautiful, why bother about the goal? If you are too bothered about the goal, you will miss the journey, and the journey is life – the goal can only be death.

The journey is life and it is an infinite journey. You have been on the move from the very beginning – if there was any beginning. Those who know say there was no beginning, so from no beginning you have been on the move, to the no end you will be on the move – and if you are goal-oriented, you will miss. The whole is the journey, the path, the endless path, never beginning, never ending. There really is no goal – goal is created by the cunning mind. Where is this whole existence moving? Where? It is not going anywhere. It is simply going, and the going is so beautiful, that is why existence is unburdened. There is no plan, no goal, and no purpose. It is not a business, it is a play, a *leela*. Every moment is the goal.

Perfect wisdom
is unplanned.
Perfect love
is without demonstrations.

Demonstration is needed because love is not there. And the less you love, the more you demonstrate – when it is there, you don't demonstrate. Whenever a husband comes home with some present for the wife she will know that something is wrong. He must have stepped out of line, he must have met another woman. Now this is the explanation, this is a substitute; otherwise love is such a present, no other present is needed. Not that love will not give presents, but love itself is such a present. What else can you give? What else is possible?

But whenever the husband feels that something is wrong, he has to put it right. Everything has to be rearranged, balanced. And this is the problem – women are so intuitive that they know immediately, your present cannot deceive them. It is impossible, because women still live with their intuition, with their illogical mind. They jump immediately, and they will understand that something has gone wrong, otherwise why this present?

Whenever you demonstrate, you demonstrate your inner poverty. If your sannyas becomes a demonstration you are not a sannyasin. If your meditation becomes a demonstration you are not meditative, because whenever the real exists, it is such a light – no need to demonstrate it. When your house is lighted, when there is a flame, you do not go to the neighbors and tell them, "Look, our house has a lamp." It is there. But when your house is in darkness you try to convince your neighbors that the light is there. Convincing them, you try to convince yourself that this is the real. Why do you want to demonstrate? Because if the other is convinced, his conviction, her conviction, will help you to be convinced.

I have heard …

Once Mulla Nasruddin had a beautiful house, but he got bored, as everybody gets bored. Whether it was beautiful or not made no difference; living in the same house every day, he got bored. The house was beautiful, with a big garden, acres of green land, swimming pool, everything. But he got bored, so he called a real estate agent and told him, "I want to sell it. I am fed up, this house has become a hell."

The next day an advertisement appeared in the morning papers; the real estate agent had put in a beautiful advertisement. Mulla Nasruddin read it again and again and he was so convinced that he phoned the agent: "Wait, I don't want to sell it. Your advertisement has convinced me so deeply that now I know that for my whole life I have been wanting this house, looking for this very house."

When you can convince others of your love, you yourself become convinced. But if you have love, there is no need, you know.

When you have wisdom, there is no need to demonstrate it. But when you have only knowledge, you demonstrate, you convince others, and when they are convinced, you are convinced that you are a man of knowledge. When you have wisdom, there is no need. If not a single person is convinced, even then you are convinced, you alone are enough proof.

Perfect sincerity
offers no guarantee.

All guarantees are because of insincerity. You guarantee, you promise, you say: "This is the guarantee, I will do this." While you are giving the guarantee, at that very moment the insincerity is there.

Perfect sincerity offers no guarantee because perfect sincerity is so aware, aware of so many things. First, the future is unknown. How can you make a guarantee? Life changes every moment, how can you promise? All guarantees, all promises, can be only for this moment, not for the next. For the next moment nothing can be done. You will have to wait.

If you are really sincere and you love a woman you cannot say, "I will love you for my whole life." If you say this, you are a liar. This guarantee is false. But if you love, this moment is enough. The woman will not ask for your whole life. If love is there this moment, it is so fulfilling that one moment is enough for many lives. A single moment of love is eternity; she will not ask. But she is always asking because in this moment there is no love. So she asks, "What is the guarantee? Will you love me always?"

This moment there is no love and she is asking for a guarantee. This moment there is no love and you guarantee for the future — because only through that guarantee can you deceive in this moment. You can create a beautiful picture of the future and you can hide the ugly picture of the present. You say, "Yes, I will love you forever and forever. Even death will not part us." What nonsense! What insincerity! How can you do this?

You can do this and you do it so easily because you are not aware of what you are saying. The next moment is unknown; where it will lead, no one knows, what will happen, no one knows, no one can know it.

Unknowability is part of the future game. How can you guarantee? At the most you can say, "I love you this moment and this moment I feel – this is a feeling of this moment – that even death cannot part us. But this is a feeling of this moment. This is not a guarantee. This moment I feel like saying that I will love you always and always, but this is a feeling of this moment, this is no guarantee. What will happen in the future nobody knows. We never knew about this moment so how can we know about other moments? We will have to wait. We will have to be prayerful that it happens, that I love you for ever and ever, but this is not a guarantee."

Perfect sincerity cannot give any guarantee. Perfect sincerity is so sincere that it cannot promise. It gives whatsoever it can give here and now. Perfect sincerity lives in the present, it has no idea of the future.

Mind moves in the future, being lives here and now. And perfect sincerity belongs to the being, not to the mind. Love, truth, meditation, sincerity, simplicity, innocence, all belong to the being. The opposites belong to the mind and to hide the opposites the mind creates false coins: false sincerity, which guarantees, promises; false love, which is just a name for duty; false beauty, which is just a face for inner ugliness. Mind creates false coins, and nobody is deceived, remember, except yourself.

Enough for today.

Chapter 5

Three in the Morning

What is this "three in the morning?"

A monkey trainer went to his monkeys and told them:
"As regards your chestnuts: you are going to have three measures in
the morning and four in the afternoon."

At this they all became angry. So he said: "All right, in that case I will
give you four in the morning and three in the afternoon." This time
they were satisfied.

The two arrangements were the same in that the number of
chestnuts did not change. But in one case the animals were
displeased, and in the other case they were satisfied. The keeper had
been willing to change his personal arrangement in order to meet
objective conditions. He lost nothing by it!

The truly wise man, considering both sides of the question without
partiality, sees them both in the light of Tao.

This is called following two courses at once.

The law of the three in the morning: Chuang Tzu loved this story very much. He often repeated it. It is beautiful, with many layers of meaning. Obviously very simple, but still very deeply indicative of the human mind.

The first thing to be understood is: the human mind is monkeyish. It was not Darwin who discovered that man comes from monkeys. It has been a long-standing observation that the human mind behaves in the same patterns as the mind of the monkey. Only rarely does it happen that you transcend your monkeyishness. When mind becomes still, when mind becomes silent, when there is really no mind at all, you transcend the monkeyish pattern.

What is the monkeyish pattern? For one thing, it is never still. And unless you are still, you cannot see the truth. You are wavering, trembling so much that nothing can be seen. Clear perception is impossible. While meditating what are you doing? You are putting the monkey in a position of stillness, hence all the difficulties of meditation. The more you try to make the mind still, the more it revolts, the more it starts getting into turmoil, the more restless it becomes.

Have you ever seen a monkey sitting still and silent? Impossible! The monkey is always eating something, doing something, swaying, chattering. This is what you are doing. Man has invented many things. If there is nothing to do he will chew gum; if there is nothing to do he will smoke. These are just foolish occupations, monkeyish occupations. Something has to be done continuously so that you remain occupied.

You are so restless that your restlessness needs to be busy somehow or other. That is why, whatsoever is said against smoking, it cannot be stopped. Only in a meditative world can smoking stop — otherwise not. Even if there is danger of death, of cancer, of tuberculosis, it cannot be stopped, because it is not a question of just smoking, it is a question of how to release the restlessness.

People who chant mantras can stop smoking because they have found a substitute. You can keep chanting Ram, Ram, Ram, and this becomes a sort of smoking. Your lips are working, your mouth is moving, your restlessness is being released. So *japa* can become a sort of smoking, a better sort, with less harm to the health.

But basically it remains the same, that your mind cannot be left at rest. The mind has to do something, not only while you are awake but even when you are asleep. Watch your wife or your husband sleeping some day, just sit for two or three hours silently and watch the face. You will see the monkey not the man. Even in sleep much goes on. The mind is engaged. This sleep cannot be deep, it cannot be really relaxing, because work is going on. By day it continues, there is no discontinuity; the mind goes on functioning in the same way. There is constant inner chatter, you go on talking with yourself, an inner monologue, and there is no wonder you get bored. You are boring yourself. Everybody looks bored.

Mulla Nasruddin was telling a story to his disciples — it must have been a day like this. Suddenly the rain started, and a passer-by, just to protect himself, came under the shed where Nasruddin was talking to his disciples. He was just waiting for the rain to stop but he couldn't help listening.

Nasruddin was telling tall stories. Many times the man found it almost impossible to resist interrupting, because he was saying such absurd things. But he thought again and again, "It is none of my business. I am just here under the shed because of the rain, and as soon as the rain stops I will go. I need not interfere." But at one point he couldn't help it, he couldn't contain himself. He interrupted, "Enough is enough. Excuse me, this is none of my business, but now you have overdone it!"

I must first tell you the story and the point where this man could not contain himself ...

Nasruddin was saying, "Once it happened, in my younger days I was traveling in the forests of Africa, the Dark Continent. One day a lion suddenly jumped out just fifteen feet away from me, and I was without any arms, without any protection, alone in the forest. That lion stared at me and started walking towards me."

The disciples became very excited. Nasruddin stopped for a moment and looked at their faces. Then one disciple said, "Now don't make us wait, what happened?"

Nasruddin said, "The lion came nearer and nearer, just five feet away."

Another disciple said, "No more waiting. Tell us what happened."

Nasruddin said, "It is so simple, it is so logical, you can conclude it yourself. The lion jumped, killed me and ate me!"

At this point, the stranger couldn't contain himself. He said, "Enough is enough. What are you saying? The lion killed you and ate you, and you are sitting here alive?"

Nasruddin looked at the man, stared at him and said, "Ha ha, do you call this being alive?"

Look at people's faces and you will understand what he meant. Do you call this being alive? So bored to death, dragging ...

Once it happened, a man asked Nasruddin, "I am very poor. It is almost impossible, seems almost impossible to survive now. I have six children and a wife, my widowed sister and old father and mother, a big family and relatives. It is getting more and more difficult. Can you suggest something? Should we commit suicide?"

Nasruddin said, "You can do two things and both will be helpful. One, start baking bread, because people have to live and they have to eat, you will always have business."

The man asked, "And the other?"

Nasruddin said, "Start making shrouds for the dead, because when people are alive, they will die. And this business also will always continue. These two businesses are good – bread, and shrouds for the dead."

After a month the man came back. He looked even more in despair, very sad, and he said, "Nothing seems to help. I have put whatever I have into the business, as you suggested, but everything seems to be against me."

Nasruddin said, "How can that happen? People have to eat bread while they are alive, and when they die their relatives have to purchase shrouds."

The man said, "But you don't understand. In this village no one is alive and no one ever dies. They are simply dragging along."

Everybody is just dragging himself, nobody is alive and nobody ever dies because to die one must first be alive. People are just dragging along. Look at their faces – there is no need to look at others' faces, just look in the mirror and you will find out what dragging means – neither alive nor dead. Life is so beautiful, death is also beautiful – dragging is ugly.

But why do you look so burdened? Because the constant chattering of the mind dissipates energy. Constant chattering of the mind is a constant leakage in your being. Energy is dissipated. You never have enough energy to make you feel alive, young, fresh, and if you are not young and fresh and alive your death is also going to be a very dull affair.

One who lives intensely dies intensely, and when death is intense, it has a beauty of its own. One who lives totally, dies totally, and wherever there is totality there is beauty. Death is not ugly because of death but because you have never lived rightly. If you have never been alive, you have not earned a beautiful death. It has to be earned. One has to live in such a way, so totally and so whole, that one can die totally, not in fragments. You live in fragments, so you die in fragments. One part dies, then another, then another, and you take many years to die. The whole thing becomes ugly. Death would be beautiful if people were alive. This inner monkey doesn't allow you to be alive, and this inner monkey will not allow you to die beautifully. This constant chattering has to be stopped.

And what is the chattering, what is the subject matter? The subject matter is the three in the morning that goes on in the mind. What are you doing inside the mind? Continuously making arrangements: to do this, not to do that, to build this house, to destroy that house; to move from this business to another because there will be more profit; to change this wife, this husband. What are you doing? Just changing arrangements.

Chuang Tzu says that finally, ultimately, if you can look at the total, the total is always the same. It is seven. Whether you are given three measures of chestnuts in the morning and four measures in the evening, or the other way around – four measures in the morning and three measures in the evening – the total is seven. This is one of the most secret of laws – the total is always the same.

You may not be able to comprehend it, but when a beggar or an emperor dies, their total is the same. The beggar lived on the streets, the emperor lived in the palaces, but the total is the same. A rich man, a poor man, a successful man and a failure, the total is the same. If you can look at the total in life, then you will come to know what Chuang Tzu means by the three in the morning.

What happens? Life is not impartial, life is not partial, life is absolutely indifferent to your arrangements – it doesn't bother about the arrangements you make. Life is a gift. If you change the arrangement, the total is not changed.

A rich man has found better food, but the hunger is lost; he cannot really feel the intensity of being hungry. The proportion is always the same. He has found a beautiful bed, but with the bed comes insomnia, he cannot sleep. He has better arrangements for sleeping. He should be falling asleep into *sushupti* – what Hindus call unconscious samadhi – but that is not happening. He cannot fall asleep. He has changed the arrangements.

A beggar is asleep just outside there in the street. Traffic is passing and the beggar is asleep. He has no bed. The place where he is sleeping is uneven, hard and uncomfortable, but he is asleep. The beggar cannot get good food, it is impossible, because he has to beg. But he has a good appetite. The total result is the same. The total result is seven.

A successful man is not only successful, for with success come all sorts of calamities. A failure is not just a failure, for with failure come many sorts of blessings. The total is always the same, but the total has to be penetrated and looked at, a clear perspective is needed. Eyes are needed to look at the total because mind can look only at the fragment. If the mind looks at the morning, it cannot look at the evening; if the mind looks at the evening, the morning is forgotten. Mind cannot look at the total day, mind is fragmentary.

Only a meditative consciousness can look at the whole, from birth to death – and then the total is always seven. That is why wise men never try to change the arrangements. That is why in the East no revolution has ever happened – because revolution means changing the arrangements.

Look what happened in Soviet Russia. In 1917 the greatest revolution happened on earth. The arrangement was changed. But I think Lenin, Stalin and Trotsky had never heard about this story of three in the morning. They could have learned much from Chuang Tzu. But then there would have been no revolution. What happened? The capitalists disappeared, now nobody was rich, nobody was poor. The old classes were no more. But only names changed. New classes have come into being. Now it is the manager and the managed. Before, it was the rich man and the poor man, the capitalist and the proletariat – now the manager and the managed. But the distinction remains the same, the gap remains the same. Nothing has changed. Only now you call the capitalist the manager.

Those who have studied the Russian revolution say that this is not a socialist revolution, it is a managerial revolution. The same gap, the same distance remains between the two classes, and a classless society has not come into being.

Chuang Tzu would have laughed. He would have related this story. What have you done? The manager has become powerful, the managed have remained powerless.

Hindus say there are people who will always be managers and there are people who will always be managed. There are sudras and *kshatriyas*; and these are not just labels, these are types of people. Hindus have divided society into

four classes and they say that society can never be classless. It is not a question of social arrangement – four types exist. Unless you change the type, no revolution is of much help.

They say there is a type, the sudra, who is a laborer, who will always be managed. If nobody manages him, he will be at a loss, he will not be happy. He needs somebody to order him, he needs somebody whom he can obey, he needs somebody who can take the whole responsibility. He is not ready to take the responsibility on his own. That is a type. If the manager is around only then will that type of person work. If the manager is not there, he will simply sit.

The manager can be a subtle phenomenon, it may even be invisible. For example, in a capitalist society the profit motive manages. A sudra works, not because he loves working, not because work is his hobby, not because he is creative, but he only works because he has to feed himself and his family. If he does not work, who will feed him? It is the profit motive, hunger, body, the stomach that manages.

In a communist country this motive is not the manager. There they have to put visible managers. It is said that in Stalin's Russia there was one policeman for each citizen. Otherwise it is difficult to manage because the profit motive is no longer there. Then one has to force, one has to order, one has to be constantly nagging, only then will the sudra work.

There is always a businessman type who enjoys money, wealth, accumulation. He will do that – it makes no difference how he does it. If money is available, he will collect money; if money is not available, then he will collect postage stamps. But he will do it, he will collect. If postage stamps are not available he will collect followers – but he will collect. He has to do something with numbers. When he says he has ten thousand, twenty thousand followers, one million followers – that is just the same as saying that he has one million rupees.

Go to your sadhus – the greater the number of followers, the greater they are. So followers are just nothing but bank balances. If nobody follows you, you are nobody – then you are a poor guru. If many people follow you then you are a rich guru. Whatsoever happens, the businessman will collect. He will count. The matter is immaterial.

There is the warrior who will fight – any excuse will do. He will fight, fighting is in his blood, in his bones. Because of this type the world cannot live in peace. It is impossible. Once every ten years there is bound to be a big war. And if you want to avoid big wars, then have many small wars, but the total will remain the same. Because of the atomic and hydrogen bombs, now a great war has become almost impossible. That is why there are so many small wars all over the world: in Vietnam, in Kashmir, in Bangladesh, in Israel, many small wars, but the total will be the same. In five thousand years man has fought fifteen thousand wars, three wars per year.

This type exists who has to fight. You can change the type, but the change will be superficial. If this warrior is not allowed to fight in war, he will fight in other ways. He will fight an election, or he may become a sportsman – he may fight in cricket or football. But he will fight, he will compete, he needs somebody to challenge. Somewhere or other fighting has to be done to satisfy him. That is why, as civilization grows, people have to be supplied with more and more games. If games are not given to the warrior type, what will he do?

Go and look when a cricket, or football, or hockey match is on – how people get mad, as if something very serious is going on, as if a real war is happening. And those who are fighting, those who are playing, they are serious, and the fans around them go mad. Fights break out, riots happen. It is dangerous, the playing field is always dangerous because the type that gathers there is the warrior type. Any moment anything can go wrong.

There is a brahmin type, who always lives in words, in scriptures. In the West there is no such type as the brahmin; the name is not important, but the brahmin exists everywhere. Your scientists, your professors, the universities are filled with them. They go on working with words, symbols, creating theories, defending, arguing. They go on and on, sometimes in the name of science, sometimes in the name of religion, sometimes in the name of literature. The names change, but the brahmin goes on.

These are the four types. You cannot create a classless society. These four will persist and the total arrangement will be the same. Fragments can change. In the morning you can do one thing, in the evening something else, but the total day will remain the same.

I have heard about one scientist – his father was against his scientific research. The father always thought it useless: "Don't waste your time. It is better to become a doctor, that will be more practical and helpful to people. Just theories, abstract theories of physics, are of no help." Finally, he persuaded his son and he became a doctor.

The first man who came to him was suffering from severe pneumonia. He looked in his books – because he was an abstract thinker, a brahmin. He looked into his books, he tried and tried. The patient became impatient; he said, "How long do I have to wait?"

The scientist, who was now practicing as a doctor said, "I don't think that there is any hope. You will have to die. There is no treatment; the illness has gone beyond cure." The patient was a tailor, he went home.

Two or three weeks later the doctor was passing and he saw the tailor working, and he was healthy and full of energy. So he said, "What, you are still alive? You should be dead. I looked in the books and this is impossible. How can you be alive?"

The tailor said, "You told me that within a week I would have to die, so I thought: Then why not live? Just one week left … Potato pancakes are my weakness, so I left your office and went directly to a hotel and ate thirty-two potato pancakes. Immediately I felt a lot of energy coming over me. And now I am absolutely okay."

The doctor immediately noted down in his diary that thirty-two potato pancakes is a sure cure for serious cases of pneumonia.

The next patient by chance also had pneumonia. He was a shoemaker. The doctor said, "Don't worry. Now the cure has been discovered. Go immediately and eat thirty-two potato pancakes, not less than thirty-two, and you will be okay; otherwise, you are going to die within a week."

After a week, the doctor knocked at the shoemaker's door. It was locked. The neighbor said, "He is dead. Your potato pancakes killed him." Immediately he noted in his diary that thirty-two potato pancakes cure tailors, kill shoemakers.

This is the abstract mind. He cannot be practical, the brahmin.

You can change surfaces, you can paint faces, but the inner type remains the same. Hence the East has not troubled itself with revolutions. The East is waiting; and those in the East who are wise, they look at the West, and they know that you are playing with toys. All your revolutions are toys. Sooner or later you will come to realize the law of three in the morning.

Now to the sutra. A disciple must have asked Chuang Tzu, "What is this three in the morning?" Because whenever somebody mentioned revolution or change, Chuang Tzu would laugh and say, "The law of the three in the morning." So a disciple must have asked, "What is this three in the morning you are always talking about?"

Said Chuang Tzu:

It is about a monkey trainer who went to his monkeys and told them:
"As regards your chestnuts, you are going to have three measures in
the morning, and four in the afternoon."

On hearing this all the monkeys became angry.

Because in the past they had been getting four measures in the morning and three in the evening. Obviously they got angry: "What do you mean? We were always getting four measures of chestnuts in the morning and now you say three. We cannot tolerate this."

So the keeper said: "All right then, I will change it to four in the
morning, and three in the afternoon." The animals were satisfied.

The total remained the same – but monkeys cannot look at the total. It was morning, so they could only see the morning. Every morning it was routine to get four measures and they were waiting for four measures, and now this man says, "Three measures in the morning." He is cutting one measure. It cannot be tolerated. They became angry, they revolted.

This monkey trainer must have been a wise man; otherwise it would be difficult to become a monkey trainer. I know it from my own experience. I am a monkey trainer.

The monkey trainer said, "Okay, then don't get disturbed. I will follow the old pattern. You will get four measures in the morning and three in the evening." The monkeys were happy. Poor monkeys – they can be happy or unhappy without any reason for either. But this man had a bigger perspective. He could see, he could add four plus three. It was still the same – seven measures were to be given to them. How they took it, in what arrangement, didn't matter. The two arrangements were the same, the number of chestnuts didn't change, but in one case the monkeys were displeased and in the other case they were satisfied.

This is how your mind goes on working, you just keep changing the arrangement. With one arrangement you feel satisfied, with another you feel dissatisfied – and the total remains the same. But you never look at the total. The mind cannot see the total. Only meditation can see the total. Mind looks at the fragment, it is near-sighted, it is very near-sighted. That is why, whenever you feel any pleasure, you jump into the pleasure immediately; you never look at the evening. This has been your experience but you have not become aware of it – that whenever there is pleasure there is pain hidden in it. But the pain will come in the evening and pleasure is here in the morning.

You never look into that which is hidden, into that which is invisible, into that which is latent. You just look at the surface, and you go mad. You do this all your life. A fragment catches you. Many people come to me and say, "In the beginning when I married this woman, everything was very beautiful. But within days everything was lost. Now it has all become ugly, now it is misery."

Once it happened – there was a car accident. The car turned upside down in a ditch by the side of the road. The man was lying on the ground completely crippled, almost unconscious. A policeman came and he started to fill in his diary. He asked the man, "Are you married?"

The man said, "I am not married. This is the biggest mess I have ever been in."

It is said that those who know will never marry. But how can you know what happens in marriage without getting married? You look at a person, at the fragment, and in the end sometimes when you think about it the fragment will look very foolish.

The color of the eyes – what foolishness! How can your life depend on the color of your eyes or somebody else's eyes? How can your life become beautiful just because of the color of the eyes? – a small pigment, three or four pennies' worth. But you get romantic: Oh, the eyes, the color of the eyes. Then you go mad and you think, "If I am not married to this woman life is lost, I will commit suicide."

But you don't see what you are doing. One cannot live by the color of the eyes forever. Within two days you will become acquainted with those eyes and you will forget them. Then there is the whole life, the totality of it, and then misery starts. Before the honeymoon is finished, misery begins; the total person was never taken into account – the mind cannot see the total. It just looks at the surface, at the figure, the face, the hair, the color of the eyes, the way the woman walks, the way she talks, the sound of her voice. These are the parts, but where is the total person?

The mind cannot see the total. The mind looks at fragments, and with fragments you get hooked. Once you are hooked, the total comes in – the total is not far away. Eyes don't exist as separate phenomena, they are part of a whole. If you are hooked by the eyes, you are hooked with the whole person. And when this whole emerges, everything becomes ugly.

Who is responsible? You should have taken account of the whole. But when it is morning the mind looks at the morning and forgets the evening completely. Remember well – in every morning the evening is hidden. The morning is constantly turning into evening and nothing can be done about it, you cannot stop it.

Says Chuang Tzu:

The two arrangements were the same – the number of chestnuts did not change, but in one case the monkeys were displeased, and in the other case they were satisfied.

Monkeys are your minds; they cannot penetrate the whole. This is the misery. You always miss, you always miss because of the fragment. If you can see the whole and then act, your life will never be a hell. And then you will not be bothered about superficial arrangements, about morning and evening, because then you can count – it is always seven. Whether you get four in the morning or three makes no difference – the total is seven.

I have heard ...

A small boy came home puzzled. His mother asked, "Why do you look so puzzled?"

The boy said, "I am in a fix. My teacher seems to have gone crazy. Yesterday she said that four plus one make five and today she told me three plus two make five. She seems to have gone mad, because if four plus one is already five, how can three plus two be five?"

The child cannot see that five can come out of many arrangements – there is not only one arrangement in which the total will be five. There can be millions of arrangements in which the total will be five.

Howsoever you arrange your life the religious man will always look to the total and the worldly man will always look to the fragment. That is the difference. The worldly will look to whatever is near, but the far is hidden there. The far is not really far, it will come, it will become near. The distant is not very distant, it will happen soon. The evening is coming.

Can you have a perspective in which the total life is seen? It is believed, and I think it is true also, that if a man is drowning, suddenly his whole life, the total, is remembered. But when you are dying, drowning in a river, no time is left, and suddenly in your mind's eye your whole life is revealed from beginning to end. It is as if the whole film passes across the screen of the mind. But what use is it, now that you are dying?

A religious man looks at the total every moment. The whole life is there, and then he acts out of that perspective of the whole. He will never repent, as you will always do. There is no possibility for you *not* to repent. Whatsoever you do you will repent.

Once it happened. A king went to visit a madhouse. The superintendent of the madhouse escorted him to every cell. The king was very interested in the phenomenon of madness, he was studying it. Everybody should be interested because it is everybody's problem. And you need not go to a madhouse – go anywhere and study people's faces. You are studying in a madhouse!

One man was weeping and crying, hitting his head against the bars. His anguish was so deep, his suffering was so penetrating, that the king asked, "Tell me the whole story, how this man became mad."

The superintendent said, "This man loved a woman and couldn't get her, so he went mad."

Then they passed to another cell. There was another man with a picture of a woman, spitting on it. The king asked, "And what is the story of this man? He also seems to be involved with a woman."

The superintendent said, "It is the same woman. This man fell in love with her too, and he got her. That is why he went mad."

If you get what you want you go mad; if you don't get what you want you go mad. The total remains the same. Whatsoever you do, you will repent. A fragment can never be fulfilling. The whole is so big and the fragment is so small that you cannot deduce the whole from the fragment. And if you depend on the fragment and decide your life accordingly, you will always miss. Your whole life will be wasted.

So what should we do? What does Chuang Tzu want us to do? He wants us not to be fragmentary – he wants us to be total. But remember, you can look at the total only when you are total, because only the similar can know the similar. If you are fragmentary, you cannot know the total. How can you know the total if you are fragmented? If you are divided in parts the total cannot be reflected in you. When I speak of meditation I mean a mind which is no longer divided, in which all fragments have disappeared. The mind is one undivided whole.

This one mind looks deeply to the very end. It looks from death to birth, it looks from birth to death. Both polarities are before it. And out of this look, out of this penetrating vision, the action is born. If you ask me what sin is, I will say: action out of the fragmentary mind is sin. If you ask me what virtue is, I will tell you: action out of the total mind is virtue. That is why a sinner always has to repent.

Remember your own life, observe it. Whatsoever you do, whatsoever you choose, this or that, everything goes wrong. Whether you get the woman or lose her, in both cases you go mad. Whatsoever you choose, you choose misery. Hence Krishnamurti goes on insisting on choicelessness.

Try to understand this. You are here listening to me. This is a choice, because you must have left some job undone, some work incomplete. You have to go to the office, to the shop, to the family, to the market and you are here listening to me. This morning you must have decided what to do – whether to go and listen to this man or go to your work, to the office, to the market. Then you decided, you chose to come here.

You will repent – because even while here, you cannot be totally here. Half the mind is there, and you are simply waiting until I finish so you can go. But do you think that if you had chosen otherwise, gone to the shop or to the office, would you have been totally there? No, because that again was a choice. So then you will be there and your mind will be here. And you will repent: "Why am I wasting time, who knows what is happening there, what is being talked about? Who knows what key is to be transferred this morning?"

So whatsoever you choose, whether you come or whether you decide not to come, if it is a choice it means half of the heart, or a little more, has chosen. It is a democratic decision, parliamentary. With the majority of the mind you have decided, but the minority is still there. And no minority is a fixed thing, no majority is a fixed thing. Nobody knows – members go on changing parties.

When you came here you decided. Fifty-one percent of your mind wanted to come, forty-nine wanted to go to the office. But by the time you arrived, the arrangement had changed. With the very decision to go and listen there is a disturbance.

The minority may have become the majority by the time you arrive here. If it has not yet become a majority, by the time you leave it will have become so because by then you will think, "Two hours lost – now, how will I make them up? It would have been better not to come – spiritual things can be postponed, but this world cannot be postponed. Life is long enough, we can meditate later on."

In India people say that meditation is only for old people, those who are on the verge of death. They can meditate; it is not for young people.

Meditation is the last thing on the list, for when you have done everything else. But remember, this point when you have done everything never comes. Or when you cannot do anything because your whole energy has been wasted – then meditation.

But when you cannot do anything, how can you meditate? Meditation needs energy, the purest, the most vital – meditation needs overflowing energy. A child can meditate but how can an old man meditate? A child is easily meditative, an old man – no, he is wasted. There is no movement of energy in him, his river cannot flow, he is frozen. Many parts of his life are already dead.

If you choose to come to the temple, you suffer, you repent. If you go to the office or the market, you suffer, you repent.

It happened once that a monk died. He was a very famous monk, he was known all over the country. Many people worshipped him, he was thought to be enlightened. On the same day a prostitute died. She also lived just in front of the monk's house, the monk's temple. She was also a very famous prostitute, as famous as the monk. They were two polarities living together and they died on the same day.

The angel of death came and took the monk to heaven; other angels of death came and took the prostitute to hell. When the angels reached heaven the doors were closed and the man in charge said, "You are confused. This monk has to go to hell and the prostitute has to come to heaven."

But they said, "What do you mean? This man was a very famous ascetic, continuously meditating and praying. That is why we never inquired, we simply went and brought him. And the prostitute must have reached hell because the other group has taken her, and we never thought of asking why. It was so obvious."

The man who was in charge at the gate said: "You are confused because you have looked only at the surface. This monk was continuously thinking that he was meditating for others. For himself he was always thinking, 'I am missing life. What a beautiful woman, and available. Any moment I can cross the street, and she is available. What nonsense I am doing, just praying, sitting in a buddha posture and attaining nothing.' But because of his fame he didn't dare."

Many people are virtuous because they are cowards. He was virtuous because he was a coward – he could not cross the street. So many people knew him, how could he go to the prostitute? What would people say?

Cowards are always afraid of the opinion of others. So he remained an ascetic, fasting, but his mind was always with the prostitute. When there was singing and dancing, he would listen. He sat before the statue of Buddha, but Buddha was not there. He was not worshipping, he was listening to the sounds coming. He would dream and in his fantasy he would make love to the prostitute.

And what was happening with the prostitute? She was always repenting, repenting and repenting. She knew she had wasted her life, she had wasted a golden opportunity. And for what? Just for money, selling her body and soul. And she would always look at the monk's temple, so jealous of the silent life he was living. "What meditative phenomenon is happening there? When will God give me one chance to go inside the temple?" But she thought, "I am a prostitute, unholy, and I should not enter the temple."

She could not go there, so she would walk around the monk's temple from the outside, she will just look from the street. What beauty, what silence, what blessing inside. And when there was *kirtan* and *bhajan*, singing and dancing, she would weep and cry, and scream about what she was missing.

So the man in charge said, "Bring the prostitute to heaven and take this monk to hell. Their outer life was different, their inner life was different, but like everybody both are repenting." The prostitute repents, the monk repents.

We in India have invented a word which does not exist in any other language in the world. Heaven and hell are found everywhere; all languages have those words. We have different words, *moksha* or nirvana or *kaivalya* – the absolute freedom which is neither hell nor heaven.

If your outer life is hell and you repent, you will reach heaven. If you are a prostitute, but constantly desiring the world of meditation and prayer, you will reach heaven. And if your outer life is heaven and your inner life is hell, like the monk who desired the prostitute, you will go to hell. But if you make no choice, have no regrets, if you are choiceless, then you will reach *moksha*.

Choiceless awareness is *moksha*, absolute freedom. Hell is a bondage, heaven is also a bondage. Heaven may be a beautiful prison, hell may be an ugly prison

– but both are prisons. Neither Christians nor Mohammedans can understand this point, because to them heaven is the ultimate. If you ask them where Jesus is, their answer is wrong. They say: "In heaven with God." This is absolutely wrong. If Jesus is in heaven, then he is not enlightened. Heaven may be golden, but it is still a prison. It may be good, it may be pleasant, but it is still a choice, the choice against hell. The virtue which has been chosen against sin is a decision of the majority, but the minority is waiting for its own chance.

Jesus is in *moksha*, that's what I say. He is not in heaven, he is not in hell. He is totally free of all imprisonments: good/bad, sin/virtue, morality/immorality. He did not choose. He lived a choiceless life. And that is what I go on telling you: live a choiceless life.

But how is a choiceless life possible? It is possible only if you can see the total, the seven; otherwise, you will choose. You will say this should happen in the morning, that in the evening, and you think that just by changing the arrangement you are changing the total. The total cannot be changed. The total remains the same – everybody's total remains the same.

Hence I say there is no beggar, and no emperor. In the morning you are an emperor, in the evening you will be a beggar; in the morning you are a beggar, in the evening you will be an emperor. And the total remains the same. Look at the total, *be* total, and then all choice drops.

That monkey trainer simply looked at the total and said, "Okay, you foolish monkeys, if you are happy with it, let this arrangement be as it is." But if he had also been a monkey, then there would have been a fight. Then he would have insisted, "This is going to be the arrangement. Who do you think is the leader, you or me? Who do you think is the master? Who do you think is to decide, you or me?"

Ego always chooses, decides and forces. The monkeys were rebelling, and if this man had also been a monkey, he would have gone mad. He would have had to put them in their place, where they belonged. He would have insisted, "No more four in the morning. I decide."

It happened once. It was the sixtieth birthday of a man – after a long married life of almost thirty-five, forty years of quarrels and conflict. But he was surprised. When he came home his wife was waiting with two beautiful ties as a present. He never expected it from his wife. It was almost impossible that she would wait with two ties as a present. He felt so happy, he said, "Don't cook the dinner, I will get ready in minutes and we will go to the most beautiful hotel."

He took a bath, got ready, put on one of the ties, and came out. His wife stared and said, "What? Do you mean you don't like the other tie? Isn't the other tie good enough?" A man can only wear one tie, but whichever tie he had chosen, the same would have happened: "So what do you mean? The other tie is no good?"

It is the old habit of quarreling, fighting. It was said about the same woman that every day she would find something to fight about. And she would always find something, because when you search, you will find. Remember this: whatsoever you are in search of you will find. The world is so vast, and existence is so rich, that if you are really keen to find something, you will find it.

So one day she will find some hair on her husband's coat, and then there will be a fight, that he has been with some woman. But once it happened that for seven days she could not find anything. She tried and tried but there was no excuse to fight. So on the seventh day, when her husband came home, she started screaming and beating her chest. He said, "Now what are you doing? What is the matter, what happened?"

So she said, "You rascal, you have finished with other women and now you are going around with bald women!"

The mind is always in search of trouble. And don't laugh, because this is about *your* mind. By laughing you may be simply deceiving yourself. You may think it is about somebody else – it is about you. And whatsoever I say, it is always about you.

Mind chooses and always chooses trouble, because with choice there is trouble. You cannot choose God. If you choose, there will be trouble. You cannot choose sannyas. If you choose, there will be trouble. You cannot choose freedom. If you choose, it will not be freedom.

Then how does it happen? How does godliness happen, sannyas happen, freedom happen, *moksha* happen? It happens when you understand the foolishness of choice. It is not a new choice, it is simply the dropping of all choosing. Just looking at the whole thing you start laughing. There is nothing to choose. The total remains the same. In the end, by the evening, the total will be the same. Then you are not bothered whether in the morning you are an emperor or a beggar. You are happy, because by the evening everything comes to the same, everything is leveled.

Death equalizes. In death nobody is an emperor and nobody is a beggar. Death brings out the total; it is always seven.

The two arrangements were the same. Remember, the amount of chestnuts didn't change. But in one case the monkeys were displeased and in the other case they were satisfied.

The keeper was willing to change his personal arrangement in order to meet objective conditions. He lost nothing by it.

A man of understanding always looks at objective conditions, never at his subjective feelings. When the monkeys said no, if you had been the monkey trainer you would have felt offended. These monkeys were trying to rebel, they were trying to be disobedient. This could not be tolerated; monkeys are animals, and very superior animals. You would have felt hurt inside.

You get angry even at dead things. If you are trying to open the door and it resists, you get mad. If you are trying to write a letter and the pen is not functioning well, smoothly, you get angry. You feel hurt, as if the pen is doing it knowingly, as if there is somebody in the boat. Even in the pen's boat you feel somebody is there and trying to disturb you.

And this is not only the logic of small children, this is your logic also. If a child crashes into a table, he will beat the table, just to put it right. And he will always remain an enemy of that table. But you are the same – with dead things you also get angry, you get mad.

This is subjective, and a wise man is never subjective. A wise man always looks at the objective conditions. He will look at the door, and if it is not open, then he will try to open it. But he cannot get angry – because his boat is empty. There is nobody there trying to shut the door, resisting your efforts.

... In order to meet objective conditions, he changed his personal arrangement. He looked at the monkeys and their minds, he didn't feel offended – he was a monkey trainer, not a monkey. He looked and he must have laughed within, because he knew the total. And he yielded. Only a wise man yields. A foolish man always resists. Foolish people say it is better to die than to bend, it is better to break than to bend.

Lao Tzu and Chuang Tzu always say: When there is a strong wind the foolish egoistic trees resist and die, and the wise grass bends. The storm goes by and again the grass stands straight, laughing and enjoying. The grass is objective, the big tree is subjective. The big tree thinks so much of himself: "I am somebody, who can bend me? Who can force me to yield?" The big tree will fight with a storm. It is foolish to fight with the storm, because the storm has not come for you. It is nothing special, the storm is simply passing and you are there, it is coincidental.

The monkeys are not offending the monkey trainer. Monkeys are just monkeys; that is the way they are. They cannot look at the total, they cannot add up. They can look only at the near, they cannot look at the far – the far is too far. It is impossible for them to conceive of the evening, they only know about the morning.

So monkeys are monkeys, storms are storms. Why get offended? They are not fighting you. They are only following their own routine ways, their own habits.

So the monkey trainer was not offended. He was a wise man, he yielded, he was just like the grass. Remember this whenever you start feeling subjective. Somebody says something, and immediately you feel hurt, as if it has been said to you. You are too much in the boat; it may not have been said to you at all. The other may be expressing his or her subjectivity.

When somebody says, "You have insulted me," what is really meant is something else. If he had been a little more intelligent he would have said it the other way. He would be saying, "I feel insulted. You may not have insulted me, but whatsoever you have said, I feel insulted." This is a subjective feeling.

But nobody considers their subjectivity and everybody goes on projecting their subjectivity onto objective conditions. The other always says, "You have insulted me." And when you hear it you are also subjective. Both boats are filled, much too crowded. There is bound to be a clash, enmity, violence.

If you are wise, when the other says, "You have insulted me," you will look at it objectively and you will think, "Why is the other feeling insulted?" You will try to understand the other's feelings, and if you can put things right you will yield. Monkeys are monkeys. Why get angry, why feel offended?

It is said of Mulla Nasruddin that when he was old he was made an honorary magistrate. The first case to come before him was a man who had been robbed, and he told him his story. Nasruddin heard his story and said, "Yes, you are in the right." But he hadn't yet heard the other's story.

The clerk of the court whispered in his ear, "You are new, Nasruddin. You don't know what you are doing. You have to listen to the other before you give judgment."

So Nasruddin said, "Okay."

So the other man, the robber, told his story. Nasruddin listened and said, "You are right."

The clerk of the court felt confused: "This man is not only inexperienced, he looks absurd." Again he whispered in his ear, "What are you doing? How can they both be right?"

Nasruddin said, "Yes, you are right."

This is the wise man who looks at the objective conditions. He will yield. He is always yielding, he is always saying yes – because if you say no, then your boat is not empty. No always comes from the ego. So if a wise man has to say no, he will still use the terminology of yes. He will not say no outright, he will use the terminology of yes. If a foolish man wants to say yes, even then he feels it difficult to say yes. He will use the terminology of no, and even if he has to yield, he will yield grudgingly. He will yield offended, resisting.

The monkey trainer yielded.

The keeper was willing to change his personal arrangement in order
to meet objective conditions. He lost nothing by it.

No wise man has ever lost anything by saying yes to foolish people. No wise
man can ever lose anything by yielding. He gains everything. There is no ego, so
there cannot be any loss. The loss is always felt by the ego: I am losing. Why do
you feel you are losing? – because you never wanted to lose. Why do you feel you
are a failure? – because you always wanted to be a success. Why do you feel you
are a beggar? – because you always desired to be an emperor.

A wise man simply takes whatsoever is. He accepts the total. He knows –
beggar in the morning, emperor in the evening; emperor in the morning, beggar
in the evening. Which is the better arrangement?

If a wise man is forced to arrange he would prefer to be beggar in the
morning and emperor in the evening. A wise man never chooses, but if you
insist, he will say it is better to be beggar in the morning and emperor in the
evening. Why? – because to be emperor in the morning, then beggar in the
evening, will be very difficult. But this is the choice.

A wise man will choose pain in the beginning and pleasure in the end,
because pain in the beginning will give you the taste, the background, and then
the pleasure will be more pleasing than ever. Pleasure in the beginning will
destroy you, and will give you such a background that the pain will be too much,
unbearable.

East and West have made different arrangements. In the East, for the first
twenty-five years every child had to go through hardship. That was the principle
followed for thousands of years until the West came and started dominating
the East.

That was the principle followed. A child had to go to the master's house in the
jungle, he had to live through every possible hardship. Like a beggar he would
just lie on a mat on the floor – there would be no comforts. He would have to
eat like a beggar; he would have to go to town and beg for the master, he would
have to cut trees for wood, he would have to take the animals to the river to
drink, to the forest to feed.

For twenty-five years he would lead the most simple, austere life whether he
was born a king or a beggar – there was no difference. Even the emperor's son
would have to follow the same routine, there was no distinction. And then life
was so blissful.

If the East was so content, this was the trick, the arrangement, because
whatsoever life gives, it is always more than you know in the beginning. The child
comes to live in a hut, and it looks like a palace. Before, he was just lying there

on the ground, without any shelter, crowded. He has an ordinary bed and it is heavenly. Ordinary food – bread, butter, and salt is paradise enough because even butter was not available at the master's house. So whatsoever life gives, he will be happy.

Now, the Western pattern is quite the opposite. They have things. When you are a student every comfort is given to you. Hostels, beautiful universities, beautiful rooms, classrooms, teachers – every arrangement is made. Medical facilities, food, hygiene, everything is taken care of. And after twenty-five years you are thrown into the struggle of life. You have become a hot-house plant – you don't know what struggle is. Then you become a clerk in an office, a master in a primary school and life is hell. Then your whole life you will be grunting, your whole life will be a long grump, just complaining, complaining, everything is wrong. It is going to be so.

The monkey trainer said, "Three measures in the morning and four in the evening."

But the monkeys insisted: "Four in the morning and three in the evening."

Four in the morning and three in the evening – then the evening is going to be cloudy. You will compare it with the past, with the morning. Emperor in the morning and beggar in the evening – then the evening is going to be miserable. The evening should be a climax, not misery.

The monkeys are not choosing a wise arrangement. In the first place a wise man never chooses, he lives choicelessly because he knows that the total is going to be the same. In the second place, if he has to choose because of objective conditions, he will choose three courses in the morning and four in the evening. But the monkeys said, "No. We will choose. We will have four in the morning." That trainer, the keeper, was willing – *in order to meet objective conditions*. He lost nothing by it. But what happened to the monkeys? They lost something.

So whenever you are near a wise man let him arrange, don't insist on your own arrangements. Because whatsoever you choose, in the first place choice is wrong, in the second place whatever choice you monkeys make, it will be wrong. The monkey mind will only look for immediate, instant happiness, right now. He is not worried about what happens later on. He doesn't know. He has no perspective of the whole. So let the wise man choose.

But the whole arrangement has changed. In the East the wise men decided. In the West there is democracy – the monkeys vote and choose. And now they have converted the whole East to democracy – democracy means that the monkeys vote and choose.

Aristocracy means that the wise men will choose the arrangement and the monkeys will yield and follow. Nothing can work like aristocracy if it is run properly. Democracy is bound to be a chaos. But the monkeys feel very happy because they are choosing the arrangement. The world was happier when the choice was with wise men.

Remember, kings would always go to ask the wise men for a final decision. The wise men were not kings because they would not like it, they couldn't be bothered with it. They were beggars, they were living in their huts in the forest. But whenever there was a problem the king would not run to the constituency to ask the people, "What is to be done?" He would run to the forest to ask those who had renounced all – because they have a perspective of the whole, no attachment, no obsessions. Of their own choice they have nothing. They are choiceless; they can see the whole and decide.

The truly wise man, considering both sides of the question without partiality, sees them both in the light of Tao.

This is called following two courses at once.

To look at the total means to follow two courses at once. Then it is not a question of four in the morning, three in the evening. It is a question of seven in the whole life.

Arrangement is immaterial. Things can be arranged according to objective conditions, but seven in all, two courses together. The wise man looks at the whole of everything. Sex gives you pleasure, but he looks also at the pain that comes out of it. Wealth gives you pleasure, but he looks at the nightmare that comes with it. Success makes you happy, but he knows the abyss that follows the peak, the failure that will become intense, unbearable pain.

He looks at the whole. And when you look at the whole you have no choice. Then you are having two courses at the same time. Morning and evening are together now – four plus three are together now. Now nothing is in fragments, everything has become a whole. And to follow this whole is Tao. To follow this whole is to be religious. To follow this whole is Yoga.

Enough for today.

Chapter 6

The Need to Win

When an archer is shooting for nothing
He has all his skill.
If he shoots for a brass buckle
He is already nervous.
If he shoots for a prize of gold
He goes blind
Or sees two targets –
He is out of his mind!

His skill has not changed. But the prize
Divides him. He cares.
He thinks more of winning
Than of shooting –
And the need to win
Drains him of power.

If the mind is filled with dreams you cannot see rightly. If the heart is filled with desires you cannot feel rightly. Desires, dreams and hopes – the future disturbs you, and whatsoever is, is in the present. When you are divided, desire leads you into the future, and life is here and now. Reality is here and now, and desire leads you into the future. Then you are not here. You see, but still you don't see; you hear, but still you miss; you feel, but the feeling is dim, it cannot be deep, it cannot be penetrating. That is how truth is missed.

People go on asking where to find the divine, where to find the truth. It is not a question of finding the divine or the truth. It is always here, it has never been anywhere else, it cannot be. It is there where you are, but you are not there, your mind is somewhere else. Your eyes are filled with dreams, your heart is filled with desires. You move into the future, and the future is illusion. Or, you move into the past, and the past is already dead.

The past is no more and the future has yet to be. Between these two is the present moment. That moment is very short, as short as possible, it is atomic, you cannot divide it – it is indivisible. That moment passes in the flicker of an eye. If a desire enters, you have missed it; if a dream is there, you are missing it.

The whole of religion consists of not leading you somewhere, but bringing you to the here and now, bringing you back to the whole, back where you have always been. But the head has gone away, very far away. This head has to be brought back. So God is not to be sought somewhere – that is why you are missing him, because you are searching somewhere. He has been here waiting for you.

Once it happened that Mulla Nasruddin came staggering home totally drunk. He knocked at his own door, knocked again and again. It was already half past midnight. The wife came and Nasruddin asked her, "Can you tell me, madam, where Mulla Nasruddin lives?"

The wife said, "This is too much. You are Mulla Nasruddin."

Mulla Nasruddin said, "That's okay, I know that, but that doesn't answer my question. Where does he live?"

This is the situation. Drunk with desires, staggering, you knock at your own door and ask where your home is. You are really asking who you are. This is home, and you have never left it, it is impossible to leave it. It is not something outside you which is going to leave and go away. It is your within, it is your very being.

Asking where God is, is foolish, because you cannot lose God. It is your within, your innermost being, your very core. It is your existence: you breathe him, you live him, and it cannot be otherwise. The only thing that has happened is that you have become so drunk, that you cannot recognize your own face. And unless you come back and get sober you will go on searching and seeking and you will go on missing.

Tao, Zen, Yoga, Sufism, Hassidism, these are all methods to bring you back, to make you sober again, to destroy your drunkenness. Why are you so drunk? What makes you so drunk? Why are your eyes so sleepy? Why aren't you alert? What is the root cause of it all? The root cause is that you desire.

Try to understand the nature of desire. Desire is alcoholic, desire is the greatest drug possible. Marijuana is nothing, LSD is nothing. Desire is the greatest LSD possible – the ultimate in drugs.

What is the nature of desire? When you desire, what happens? When you desire, you are creating an illusion in the mind; when you desire, you have already moved from here. Now you are not here, you are absent, because the mind is creating a dream. This absentness is your drunkenness.

Be present. This very moment the doors of heaven are open. There is no need even to knock because you are not outside heaven, you are inside. Just be alert and look around without eyes filled with desire, and you will have a belly laugh. You will laugh at the whole joke, at what has been happening. It is just like a man dreaming at night.

It happened once: a man was very disturbed – his nights were simply prolonged nightmares. His whole night was a struggle. It was so painful that he was always scared to go to sleep and he was always happy to get out of bed. The whole night was nightmarish – he was having very bad dreams, ferocious. The nature of the dreams was such, that the moment he fell asleep, he would start seeing millions of lions, dragons, tigers, reptiles, crocodiles, millions of them sitting underneath his small bed. So he couldn't sleep because at any moment they would attack.

Knowing they would all be coming back the whole night was just a long disturbance, a torture, a hell. He was treated medically, but nothing would help. Everything failed. He was analyzed by psychologists, psychiatrists, but nobody could succeed. Then one day he walked out of his house laughing.

Nobody had seen him laughing for many years. His face had become hellish, always sad, afraid, scared. So the neighbors asked, "What is the matter? You are laughing? We have not seen you laughing for years. We have completely forgotten that you ever used to laugh. What happened to your nightmares?"

The man said, "I told my brother-in-law, and he cured me."

The neighbors asked, "Is your brother-in-law a great psychoanalyst, psychologist, or something? How could he cure you?"

The man said, "He is a carpenter. He simply cut the legs off my bed. Now there's no more space, so I slept for the first time!"

You create a space – and desire is the way to create that space. The greater the desire, the more space is created. Because if a desire is to be fulfilled in one year, then you have one year's space. You can move in it, but then you will have to encounter many reptiles, many dragons. This space which is created by desire, you call it time. If there is no desire, there is no need for time.

A single moment exists – not even two moments, because the second is needed only by desire, it is not needed by your existence. Existence is completely fulfilled, totally, in one moment.

Remember: if you think that time is something outside you, then you are deceiving yourself. Time is not something outside you.

If man disappears from the earth will there be time? Trees will grow, rivers will flow, clouds will still float in the sky, but I ask, will there be time? There will not be any time. There will be moments, rather, there will be one moment – and when one moment disappears another comes into existence. Another disappears, another comes into existence. But there is no time as such. Only the atomic moment exists.

Trees don't desire anything, they don't desire to flower, flowers will come automatically. It is part of the nature of the tree that flowers will come. But the tree is not dreaming, the tree is not moving, it is not thinking, it is not desiring.

If man is not there, there will be no time, just eternal moments. You create time with desire. The greater the desire, the more time is needed.

For materialistic desires much time is not needed. That is why in the West they say that there is only one life. In the East we have desired *moksha*. That is the greatest desire possible – no other desire can be greater than that. But how can you get *moksha* in one life? One life is not enough. You may get a palace, you may organize a kingdom, you may become very rich and powerful, a Hitler, a Ford. You may become something in this world, but *moksha* is such a great desire that one life is not enough.

So in the East we believe in many lives, in rebirth, because more time is needed, many lives will be needed. Only then can you hope that the desire for *moksha* will be fulfilled. I'm not saying whether there are many lives or not. That is not the point. But in the East people believe in many lives because they desire *moksha*. If there is only one life how can you attain it?

If there is only one life, then only material things can be attained. Then spiritual transformation is not possible. The desire is so big that millions of lifetimes are needed. That is why in the East people live so lazily. There is no hurry because there is no shortage of time. You will be born again and again and again. Why be in a hurry? You have infinite time.

So if the East is lazy and looks so absolutely unaware of time, if things move with such a slow flow, it is because of the concept of many lives. If the West is so time-conscious, it is because there is only one life, and everything has to be attained in it. If you miss, you miss forever – no second opportunity is possible. Because of this shortage of time, the West has become so tense. So many things to do and so little time left – so many desires, and time is always short.

Everyone is always in a hurry, running fast. Nobody is moving slowly, nobody is walking slowly. Everybody is running, and more speed is needed. So the West goes on inventing speedier vehicles and there is never any satisfaction. The West goes on lengthening human life just to give you a little more time to fulfill your desires.

But why is time needed? Can't you be here and now without time? Is this moment not enough, just sitting near me, no past, no future? – this moment in between, which is atomic, which is really as if nonexistential. It is so small that you cannot catch hold of it; if you catch it, it is already past. If you think, it is in the future. You can be *in* it, but you cannot catch hold of it. When you catch hold of it, it is gone; when you think about it, it is not there.

When it is there, only one thing can be done – you can live it, that is all. It is so small that you can only live in it, but it is so vital that it gives life to you.

Remember, it is just like the atom, so small it cannot be seen. Nobody has seen it yet, not even scientists have seen it yet. You can only see the consequences. They have been able to explode it – Hiroshima and Nagasaki were the consequences. We have seen Hiroshima burning, over one hundred thousand people dead – this is the consequence. But nobody has seen what happened in the atomic explosion. Nobody has seen the atom with their own eyes. There are no instruments yet which can see it.

Time is atomic, this moment is also atomic. Nobody can see it, because when you see it, it has already gone. In the time that is taken in seeing, it has past – the river has flowed on, the arrow has moved. Nobody has ever seen time. You go on using the word *time*, but if someone insists on a definition you will be at a loss.

Somebody asked Saint Augustine, "Define God. What do you mean when you use the word *god*?"

Augustine said, "It is just like time. I can talk about it, but if you insist on the definition, I am at a loss."

You can go on asking people, "What is the time?" And they will look at their watches and reply. But if you really ask, "What is time?" If you ask for the definition, then watches won't help.

Can you define time? Nobody has seen it, there is no way to see it. If you look, it is gone; if you think, it is not there. When you don't think, when you don't look, when you simply are, it is there. You live it. And Saint Augustine is right: godliness can be lived, but cannot be seen. Time can be lived, but cannot be seen. Time is not a philosophical problem, it is existential. Godliness is also not philosophical, it is existential. People have lived it, but if you insist on a definition they will remain silent, they cannot answer. And if you can be in this moment, the doors to all the mysteries are open.

So throw off all desires, remove all the dust from your eyes, be at ease within, not longing for something, not even for godliness. Every longing is the same, whether you long for a big car, or a god, or a big house, it makes no difference. Longing is the same. Don't long – just be! Don't even look – just be! Don't think! Let this moment be there, and you in it, and suddenly you have everything – because life is there. Suddenly everything starts showering on you, and then this moment becomes eternal and then there is no time. It is always the now. It never ends, it never begins. But then you are in it, not an outsider. You have entered the whole, you have recognized who you are.

Now try to understand Chuang Tzu's sutra: the need to win. From where does this need arise – the need to win? Everybody is in search of victory, seeking to win, but why does this need to win arise?

You are not in any way aware that you are already victorious, that life has happened to you. You are already a winner and nothing more is possible, all that could happen has happened to you. You are already an emperor, and there is no other kingdom to be won. But you have not recognized it, you have not known the beauty of the life that has already happened to you. You have not known the silence, the peace, the bliss that is already there.

Because you are not aware of this inner kingdom, you always feel that something is needed, some victory, to prove that you are not a beggar.

It happened:

Alexander the Great was coming to India – to win, of course – because if you don't need to win you will not go anywhere. Why bother? Athens was so beautiful, there was no need to bother to go on such a long journey.

On the way he heard that one mystic, Diogenes, lived by the side of a river. He had heard many stories about him. In those days, in Athens particularly, only two names were spoken about – one was Alexander, the other was Diogenes. They were two opposites, two polarities. Alexander was an emperor, and was trying to create a kingdom which stretched from one end of the earth to the other: "The whole world should be in my possession." He was a conqueror, a man in search of victory.

And there was Diogenes, the exact opposite completely. He lived naked, not a single thing did he possess. In the beginning he possessed a begging bowl for drinking water or sometimes to beg for food. Then one day he saw a dog drinking water from the river and immediately he threw away his bowl. He said, "If dogs can do without, why not I? If dogs are so intelligent that they can do without a bowl, I must be stupid to carry this bowl with me, it is a burden."

He took that dog for his master, and invited the dog to be with him because he was so intelligent. He had not been aware that to carry the bowl was an unnecessary burden. Thereafter that dog remained with him. They used to sleep together, to take their food together. The dog was his only companion.

Somebody asked Diogenes, "Why do you keep company with a dog?"

He said, "He is more intelligent than so-called human beings. I was not so intelligent before. Looking at him, watching him, has made me more alert. He lives in the here and now, not bothered about anything, not possessing anything. And he is so happy – having nothing, he has everything. I am not yet so content, some uneasiness remains inside, within me. When I have also become just like him, then I will have reached the goal."

Alexander had heard about Diogenes, his ecstatic bliss, his silent, mirrorlike eyes, just like the blue sky without any clouds. And this man lived naked, even clothes were not needed. Somebody said, "He's just by the river, and we are passing, he's not very far away." Alexander wanted to see him, so he went.

It was morning, a winter morning, and Diogenes was taking his sunbath, lying on the sand naked, enjoying the morning, the sun showering on him, everything so beautiful, silent, the river flowing by ...

Alexander thought, "What should I say?" A man like Alexander cannot think except about things and possessions. So he looked at Diogenes, and said, "I am Alexander the Great. If you need something, tell me. I can be of much help and I would like to help you."

Diogenes laughed, and said, "I don't need anything. Just stand aside a little because you are blocking the sun. That's all you can do for me. And remember, don't block anybody's sun, that's all one can do. Don't stand in my way and nothing else is needed."

Alexander looked at this man. He must have felt like a beggar before him: "He needs nothing, and I need the whole world, and even then I will not be satisfied, even this world is not enough." Alexander said, "I'm happy to see you, I have never seen such a contented man."

Diogenes said, "There is no problem! If you want to be as contented as I, come and lie down by my side, have a sunbath. Forget the future, and drop the past. Nobody is hindering you."

Alexander laughed, a superficial laugh of course, and said, "You are right – but the time is not yet ripe. One day I would also like to relax like you."

Diogenes said, "That one day will never come. What do you need to relax? If I, a beggar, can relax, what else is needed? Why this struggle, this effort, these wars, this conquering, why this need to win?"

Said Alexander, "When I have become victorious, when I have conquered the whole world, I would like to come and learn from you and sit by your side and lie down here on this bank."

Diogenes said, "But if I can lie down on this bank and relax right now, why wait for the future? And why go around the whole world creating misery for yourself and others – just to come to me at the end and relax here? I am already relaxing."

What is the need to win? You have to prove yourself. You feel so inferior within, you feel so vacant and empty, you feel such a nobodiness inside, that the need to prove arises. You have to prove that you are somebody, and unless you have proved it, how can you be at ease?

There are two ways, and try to understand that these are the only ways. One way is to go out and prove that you are somebody. The other way is to go inside and realize that you are nobody. If you go out you will never be able to prove that you are somebody. The need will remain; rather, it may increase. The more you prove, the more you will feel as Alexander felt, like a beggar standing before Diogenes. You will feel it always. Because just by proving to others that you are somebody does not make you become somebody. Deep down the nobodiness remains. It goes on biting in the heart – that you are nobody.

Kingdoms won't help, because kingdoms will not go in and fill the gap. Nothing can go in. The without will remain without; the within will remain within. There is no meeting. You may have all the wealth in the world but how can you bring it in and fill the emptiness? No, even when you have all the wealth you will still feel empty, more even, because now the contrast will be there. That is why Buddha left his palace: seeing all the wealth yet feeling the inner emptiness, feeling that all is useless.

Another way is to go within – not to try to get rid of this nobodiness, but to realize it. This is what Chuang Tzu is saying: Become an empty boat, just go in and realize that you are nobody. The moment you realize you are nobody you explode into a new dimension, because when somebody realizes he is nobody he is also realizing that he is all.

You are not somebody, because you are all. How can the all be somebody? Somebody will always be a part. God cannot be somebody because he is all, he cannot possess anything because he is the whole. Only beggars possess, because possessions have limitations. Possessions cannot become unlimited. Somebodiness has a boundary, somebodiness cannot be without boundaries, it cannot be infinite. Nobodiness is infinite, just like *allness*.

Really, both are the same. If you are moving without you will feel your inner being as nobody. If you are moving within you will feel the same nobodiness as all. That is why Buddha says that *shunya*, the absolute void, is *brahman*. To be nobody is to realize that you are all. To realize that you are somebody is to realize that you are not all. And nothing less will do.

So the other way is to move within, not to fight with this nobodiness, not to try to fill this emptiness, but to realize it and become one with it. Be the empty boat and then all the seas are yours. Then you can move into the uncharted, then there is no hindrance for this boat, nobody can block its path. No maps are needed. This boat will move into the infinite. Now everywhere is the goal, but one has to move within.

The need to win is to prove that you are somebody, and the only way we know how to prove is to prove in the eyes of others, because their eyes become reflections.

Looking in others' eyes Alexander could see that he was somebody; standing near Diogenes, he felt he was nobody. Diogenes would not recognize that it was Alexander. Rather, Alexander must have felt foolish. It is said that he told Diogenes that if God would grant him another birth he would like to be Diogenes rather than Alexander – next time!

The mind always moves in the future. At this very time he could have become Diogenes, there was no barrier, nobody was preventing him. There would be millions of barriers to becoming Alexander the Great because everybody would try to prevent him. When you want to prove that you are somebody you hurt everybody's ego, and they will all try to prove that you are nothing. Unless you kill them, unless you succeed in destroying them, they will go on saying that you are nothing. What are you thinking yourself to be? Who do you think you are? You have to prove it, and it is a very hard way, very violent, destructive.

There was no barrier to being a Diogenes. Alexander felt the beauty, the grace of this man. He said, "If God gives me another opportunity to be born, I would like to be Diogenes – but next time."

Diogenes laughed and said, "If I am asked, only one thing is certain: I would not like ever to be Alexander the Great!"

Alexander must have seen in the eyes of Diogenes that there was no recognition of his victories. Suddenly he must have felt the sinking sensation, the deathlike sensation that he was nobody. He must have escaped, run from Diogenes as soon as possible. Diogenes was a dangerous man.

It is said that Diogenes haunted Alexander his whole life. Wherever he went, Diogenes was with him like a shadow. At night, in his dreams, Diogenes was there laughing. And it is said, it is a beautiful story, that they died on the same day.

Diogenes must have waited for this man to follow. They died on the same day, and while crossing the river which divides this world from that, Alexander met Diogenes again, and the second meeting, the second encounter was more dangerous than before. Alexander was ahead because he had died a few minutes earlier – it had to be so because Diogenes had to follow, he must have waited. Hearing a noise, that somebody was behind on the river, he looked back, and saw Diogenes there laughing. He must have felt numb, because this time things were absolutely different. He was also naked like Diogenes, because you cannot take your clothes to the other world. This time he was again absolutely nobody, not an emperor.

But Diogenes was the same. All that death can take away he had already renounced, so death couldn't take anything from him. He was just the same as on that river bank, and here he was on this river, just the same. So to be nonchalant, to give himself courage and confidence, Alexander also laughed and said, "Great, wonderful! Again the meeting of the emperor and the beggar, the meeting of the greatest emperor and the greatest beggar."

Diogenes replied, "You are absolutely right, only you are a little confused about who is the emperor and who is the beggar. This is a meeting of the greatest emperor and the greatest beggar, but the emperor is behind and the beggar is ahead. And I tell you, Alexander, at the first meeting it was also the same. You were the beggar, but you thought I was. Now look at yourself. What have you gained by winning the whole world?"

What is the need to win? What do you want to prove? In your own eyes you know that you are a nonentity, you are nothing, and this nothingness becomes a pain in the heart. You suffer because you are nothing – so you have to prove yourself in the eyes of others. You have to create some opinion in others' minds that you are somebody, that you are not a nothing. And looking in their eyes you will gather opinions, public opinion, and through public opinion you will create an image. This image is the ego, it is not your real self. It is a reflected glory, it is not your own – it is collected from others' eyes.

This type will always be afraid of others because they can take back whatsoever they have given. A politician is always afraid of the public because they can take back whatsoever they have given. It is just borrowed, his self is a borrowed self. If you are afraid of others, you are a slave, you are not a master.

A Diogenes is not afraid of others. You cannot take anything from him because he has not borrowed anything. He has the self, you only have the ego. This is the difference between the self and the ego – the ego is a borrowed self, it depends on others, on public opinion. Self is your authentic being, it is not borrowed, it is yours. Nobody can take it back.

Look, Chuang Tzu has beautiful lines to say:

When an archer is shooting for fun
he has all his skill.

When an archer is shooting for fun he has all his skill. When you are playing, you are not trying to prove that you are somebody. You are at ease, at home. While playing, just for fun, you are not worried what others think about you.

Have you seen a father in a mock fight with his child? He will be defeated. He will lie down and the child will sit on his chest and laugh, and say, "I am the winner!" – and the father will be happy. It is just fun. In fun you can be defeated and be happy. Fun isn't serious, it is not related to the ego. Ego is always serious.

So remember, if you are serious, you will always be in turmoil, inner turmoil. A saint is always in play, as if shooting for fun. He is not interested in shooting at a particular target, he is just enjoying himself.

One German philosopher, Eugene Herrigel, went to Japan to learn meditation. In Japan they use all types of excuses to teach meditation, including archery. Herrigel was a perfect archer, one hundred percent. He would never miss the target. So he went to a master to learn meditation through archery, because he was already skilled in it.

After three years Herrigel started feeling that it was a waste of time, because the master went on insisting that *he* should not shoot. He told Herrigel, "Let the arrow leave by itself. You should not be there when you aim, let the arrow aim itself."

This was absurd. For a Western man particularly, it was absolutely absurd: "What do you mean, let the arrow shoot by itself? How can the arrow shoot by itself? I have to do something." And he continued. And he would never miss the target.

But the master said, "The target is not the target at all. *You* are the target. I am not looking at whether you are hitting the target or not. That is a mechanical skill. I am looking at you, to see whether you are there or not. Shoot for fun! Enjoy it, don't try to prove that you never miss the target. Don't try to prove the ego. It is already there, you are there, there is no need to prove it. Be at ease and allow the arrow to shoot itself."

Herrigel could not understand. He tried and tried and said again and again, "If my aim is a hundred percent correct, why don't you give me the certificate?"

The Western mind is always interested in the end result and the East is always interested in the beginning, not in the end – in the archer, not in the target. The end is useless. So the master would say, "No!"

Then, completely disappointed, Herrigel asked to leave. He said, "Then I will have to go. Three years is too much and nothing has been gained and you go on saying no, and you go on saying that I am still the same."

The day he was to leave, he had just gone to say goodbye. The master was teaching other disciples. That morning Herrigel was not interested; he was leaving, he had dropped the whole project. So he was just waiting there until the master was not engaged. He would say his goodbye and leave.

Sitting on a bench he looked at the master for the first time. For the first time in three years he looked at the master. Really, he was not doing anything; it was as if the arrow was shooting itself. The master was not serious, he was playing, he was in fun. There was nobody who was interested in a target.

Ego is always target-oriented. Fun has no target to reach, fun is in the beginning when the arrow leaves the bow. If it shoots that is accidental, if it reaches the target that is not relevant; whether it reaches or misses is not the point. But when the arrow leaves the bow, the archer should be in fun, enjoying, not serious. When you are serious you are tense, when you are not serious you are relaxed, and when you are relaxed you are. When you are tense, the ego is; you are clouded.

For the first time Herrigel looked – because now he was not interested. It was none of his business now, he had dropped the whole thing. He was leaving so there was no question of being serious. He had accepted his failure, nothing was to be proved. He looked, and for the first time his eyes were not obsessed with the target.

He looked at the master and it was as if the arrow was shooting itself from the bow. The master was only giving it energy, he was not shooting. He was not doing anything, the whole thing was effortless. Herrigel looked, and for the first time he understood what it meant.

As if enchanted he approached the master, took the bow in his hand and drew back the arrow. The master said, "You have reached. This is what I have been telling you to do for three years." The arrow had not yet left the bow and the master said, "Finished: the target is attained." Now he was having fun, he was not serious, he was not goal-oriented.

This is the difference. Fun is not goal-oriented; it has no goal. Fun itself is the goal, the intrinsic value, nothing else. You enjoy it, that is all. There is no purpose to it; you played, that's all.

When an archer is shooting for fun he has all his skill. When you are shooting for fun, you are not in conflict. There are not two, there is no tension; your mind is not going anywhere. Your mind is not going at all – so you are whole. Then the skill is there.

It is said of one Zen painter, a Zen master ... He was making a drawing, a design, for a new pagoda, a new temple. It was his habit to have his chief disciple by his side. He would draw the design, look at the disciple and ask, "What do you think?"

And the disciple would say, "Not worthy of you." So he would throw it out.

This happened ninety-nine times. Three months passed and the king was continuously asking when the design would be completed, when the work could start. And one day it happened: the master was making the design, and the ink ran dry, so he told the disciple to go out and prepare more ink.

The disciple went out, and when he came back in, he said, "What? You have done it! But why couldn't you do it for three months?"

The master said, "Because of you. You were sitting by my side and I was divided. You were looking at me and I was target-oriented, it was not fun. When you were not there, I relaxed. I felt that nobody is there, I became whole. I have not done this design, it has come by itself. For three months it would not come because I was the doer."

When an archer is shooting for fun he has all his skill ... because his whole being is available. And when the whole being is available, you have a beauty, a grace, a totally different quality of being. When you are divided, serious, tense, you are ugly. You may succeed, but your success will be ugly. You may prove to somebody that you are somebody but you are not proving anything, you are simply creating a false image. But when you are total, relaxed, whole, nobody may know about you, but you are.

And this wholeness is the benediction, the beatitude, the blessing, that happens to a meditative mind, that happens in meditation.

Meditation means wholeness.

So remember, meditation should be fun, it should not be work. You should not do it like a religious man, you should do it like a gambler. Play, for fun. You should be like a sportsman not a businessman. It should be fun, and then all the skill will be available, then it will flower by itself. You will not be needed. No effort is needed. Simply your whole being has to be available, your whole energy has to be available. Then the flower comes by itself.

If he shoots for a brass buckle
he is already nervous.

If he is in a competition just for a brass buckle, if something is to be achieved, some result is there, he is already nervous, afraid. Fear comes in: "Will I succeed or not?" He is divided. One part of the mind says, "Maybe you will succeed"; another part says, "Maybe you will fail." Now his whole skill is not available, now he is half and half. And whenever you are divided your whole being becomes ugly and ill. You are diseased.

If he shoots for a prize of gold
he goes blind
or sees two targets –
he is out of his mind.

Go to the market and see people who are after gold. They are blind. Gold blinds men as nothing else does, gold covers the eyes completely. When you are too much for success, too much for the result, too ambitious, when you are too much after the gold medal, then you are blind and you start seeing two targets. You are so drunk you start seeing double.

I have heard ...

Mulla Nasruddin was teaching his son in a bar: "Always remember when to stop. Alcohol is good, but one needs to know when to stop. And I'm telling you through my experience. Look over at that corner – when those four people sitting at the table start looking like eight, stop."

The boy said, "But father, I see only two people sitting there."

When the mind is drunk, vision becomes double. And gold makes you so unconscious, drunk. Now there are two targets and you are in such a hurry to reach them that you are nervous, trembling inside.

This is the state Chuang Tzu calls:

... he is out of his mind.

Everybody is out of his mind. It is not only mad people who are out of their minds, you are also out of your mind. The difference is only of degree, not of quality, a little more and any moment you can cross the boundary. It is as if you are at ninety-nine degrees. One hundred degrees and you boil, you have crossed the boundary. The difference between those who are in madhouses and those who are outside is only of quantity, not of quality. Everybody is out of his mind, because everyone is after results, goals, purposes. Something has to be achieved. Then comes nervousness, inner trembling, then you cannot be still within. And when you tremble inside, the target becomes two, or even four or eight — and then it is impossible to become an archer.

A perfect archer is always the archer who is having fun.

A perfect man lives life as fun, as play.

Look at Krishna's life. Had Chuang Tzu known about him, it would have been beautiful. Krishna's life is fun. Buddha, Mahavira, Jesus, somehow or other look a little serious, as if something has to be achieved — the *moksha*, the nirvana, the desirelessness. But Krishna is absolutely purposeless — the flute player just living for fun, dancing with girls, enjoying, singing. Nowhere to go, all is here, so why bother about the result. Everything is available right now, why not enjoy it?

Krishna is the perfect man if fun is the sign of a perfect man. In India we never call his life *Krishna charitra*, his character, we never call it that. We call it *Krishna leela*, his play. It is not a character, it is not purposeful; it is absolutely purposeless.

It is just like a small child. You cannot ask, "What are you doing?" You cannot ask, "What is the meaning?" He is enjoying himself just running after butterflies. What will he achieve just jumping in the sun? To what end will this effort lead him? Nowhere! He is not going anywhere. We call him childish and we think ourselves mature, but I tell you that when you are really mature, you will again become childlike. Then your life will again become fun. You will enjoy it, every bit of it, you will not be serious. A deep laughter will spread all over your life. It will be more like a dance and less like a business; it will be more like singing, humming in the bathroom, less like calculating in the office. It will not be mathematics, it will just be enjoyment.

His skill has not changed, but the prize
divides him. He cares.
He thinks more of winning

than of shooting –
and the need to win
drains him of power.

If you look so impotent, so powerless, helpless, it is because of you. Nobody else is draining you of your power. You have infinite sources of power, unending, but you look drained, as if any moment you are going to fall with no energy left.

Where are all these energies going? You are creating a conflict within yourself – your skill is the same.

His skill has not changed, but the prize
divides him. He cares.

I have heard one story. It happened in a village ... A poor man, the son of a beggar, he was young, healthy – so young and so healthy that when the king's elephant passed through the village, he would just catch hold of the elephant's tail and it would not be able to move.

Sometimes it became very embarrassing to the king because he would be sitting on the elephant and the whole market would gather and people would laugh. And all because of the son of a beggar.

The king asked his prime minister, "Something has to be done. This is insulting. I have become afraid to pass through that village, and that boy sometimes visits other villages also. Anywhere he can catch hold of the elephant's tail and it will not move He is so powerful, do something to drain his energy."

The prime minister said, "I will have to go and consult a wise man because I don't know how to drain his energy. There is nothing to drain his energy because he is a beggar. If he had a shop, the energy could be drained. If he was working as a clerk in an office, the energy would be drained. If he was a master in a primary school, his energy could be drained. But he has nothing to do. He lives for fun, and people love him and give him food and milk, so he is never short of food. He is happy, he eats and sleeps. So it is difficult, but I will go."

So he went to a wise old man. The wise old man said, "Do one thing. Go and tell the boy that you will give him one golden rupee every day if he will do a small job – and the job is very small. He has to go to the village temple and put the lamp on. He has just to light the lamp, that is all. And you will give him one golden rupee every day."

The prime minister said, "But how will this help? This may make him even more energetic. He will get one rupee and he will feel more energy. He will not even bother to beg."

The wise man said, "Don't worry, simply do what I say."

This was done, and the next week, when the king passed, the boy tried but he failed, he couldn't stop the elephant. He was dragged along by it.

What happened? Care entered, anxiety entered. He had to remember, for twenty-four hours a day he had to remember that he had to go to the temple every evening and put the light on. That became an anxiety, that divided his whole being. Even in his sleep he started to dream that it was evening: "What are you doing? Go and put the light on and take your rupee."

Then he started to collect those golden rupees – now seven, now eight. Then he started to calculate that by such and such a time he would have one hundred golden rupees – and they would grow to two hundred. Mathematics came in, fun was lost. And he had just a small thing to do to, to put the light on. Just a single minute affair, not even a single minute, just a momentary thing – but it became a worry. It drained him of all his energy.

If you are drained there is no wonder your life is not fun. You have so many temples and so many lamps to put on and off, so many calculations in your life, it cannot be a fun.

His skill has not changed – the skill is the same, but the archer, when he is shooting for fun, has all his skill available. *His skill has not changed. But the prize divides him. He cares.* Anxiety enters, nervousness comes in. He thinks more of winning, now he is not concerned with shooting. Now the question is how to win, not how to shoot. He has moved from the beginning to the end. Now the means is not important, the end is important, and whenever the end is important your energy is divided, because all that can be done is to be done with the means, not with the end. Ends are not in your hands.

Says Krishna to Arjuna in the Gita: "Don't be concerned with the end, with the result. Simply do whatsoever is to be done here and now and leave the result to me, to existence. Don't ask what will happen, nobody knows. You simply leave it to existence, to faith. Whatever happens you simply do whatsoever is to be done. Be concerned with the means and don't think of the end. Don't be result-oriented."

This situation is beautiful and worth considering with Chuang Tzu's sentences, because Arjuna was an archer, the greatest archer India has produced. He was the perfect archer.

But the end entered his mind. He had never worried, it had never happened before. His archery was perfect, his skill was total, absolute, but looking at that vast siege of *Kurukshetra*, two armies confronting each other, he became worried. What was the worry? It was that he had friends on both sides. It was a family affair, a war between cousin-brothers, so everybody was interlinked. Those who were on the other side were also related to those on this side All these families and relatives were divided – it was a rare war, a family war.

Krishna was fighting alongside Arjuna, but his army was fighting on the other side. Krishna had said, "You both love me so you will have to divide half and half. One side can have me, and the other side can have my armies."

Duryodhana, the leader of the other side, was foolish. He thought, "What will I do with Krishna alone – and his army is so big." So he said, "I will choose your army."

So Krishna was with Arjuna and Arjuna was happy, because one Krishna is more than the whole world. What can armies do – unconscious, sleepy people? One awakened man is worth all.

Krishna became the real help when Arjuna was confused and his mind divided. In the Gita it is said that looking at these two armies he became puzzled. And these are the words he spoke to Krishna: "My energy is drained. I feel nervous, I feel impotent, my power has left me" – and he was a man of perfect skill, a perfect archer.

His bow is known as a *gandiva*. He said, "The *gandiva* seems to be too heavy for me. I have become so powerless, my body is numb, and I cannot think and cannot see. Everything has become confused, because these are all relatives and I will have to kill them. What will be the result? Murder, so many people killed, and what will I gain out of it? A worthless kingdom? I am not interested in fighting, it seems to be too costly. I would like to escape and become a sannyasin, to go to the forest and meditate. This is not for me. My energy is drained."

Krishna told him that, "Don't think of the result. That is not in your hands. And don't think that you are the doer, because if you are the doer, then the end is in your hands. The doer is always the divine, and you are just an instrument. Be concerned with the here and now, the means, and leave the end to me. I tell you, Arjuna, that these people are already dead, they are fated to die. You are not going to murder them. You are just the instrument to reveal to them the fact that they have been murdered, they are already murdered. As far as I can see, I see them dead. They have reached the point where death happens – you are just an instrument."

Sanskrit has a beautiful word, there is no equivalent to it in English: it is *nimitta*. *Nimitta* means you are not the doer, you are not the cause, not even one of the causes, you are just the *nimitta*. It means the cause is in the hands of the divine. The divine is the doer, you are just a vehicle of it. You are just like a postman – the postman is the *nimitta*. He comes and delivers a letter to you. If the letter insults you, you don't get angry with him. You don't say, "Why did you bring me this letter?" The postman is not concerned, he is the *nimitta*. He has not written the letter, he has not caused it, he is not concerned about it. He has just fulfilled his duty. You will not be angry with him. You will not say, "Why have you brought this letter to me?"

Krishna said to Arjuna, "You are just like a postman, you have to deliver death to them. You are not the killer; the death is from the divine. They have earned it already, so don't you worry. If you are not going to kill them, then somebody else will. If this postman will not do it then somebody else will deliver the letter. It is not a question of whether or not you are there, or you are on holiday or you are ill, then the letter will not be delivered. A substitute postman will do. But the letter has to be delivered. So don't be bothered, don't get worried unnecessarily; you are just a *nimitta*, neither the cause of it nor the doer of it, just an instrument. Be concerned with the means, don't think about the ends, because once you think about the ends your skill is lost, you are divided.

"That's why you are feeling drained, Arjuna. Your energy has not gone anywhere. It has become a conscience – then you are divided. You are fighting with yourself. One part says go ahead; another part says this is not good. Your wholeness is lost. And whenever the wholeness is lost, one feels impotent."

Such a powerful man as Arjuna says, "I cannot carry this *gandiva*, this bow is too heavy for me. I have become nervous. I feel fear, deep fear, an anxiety arising in me. I cannot fight."

The skill is the same, nothing has changed, but the mind is divided. Whenever you are divided you are powerless; when you are undivided you are powerful. Desires divide you, meditation undivides you. Desires lead you to the future, meditation brings you to the present.

Remember this as a conclusion: don't move to the future. Whenever you feel your mind moving to the future jump back to the present immediately. Don't try to complete it. Immediately, the moment you think, the moment you become alert that the mind has moved into the future, into the desire, jump back to the present. Be at home.

You will lose it again and again. Again and again you will miss it because it has become a long habit; but sooner or later, more and more, you will be at home. Then life is fun, it is a play. And then you are so full of energy that you overflow – a flood of vitality. And that flood is bliss.

Impotent, drained, you cannot be ecstatic. How can you dance? For dancing you will need infinite energy. Drained, how can you sing? Singing is always an overflowing. Dead as you are, how can you pray? Only when you are totally alive, a thankfulness arises from the heart, a gratitude. That gratitude is prayerfulness.

Enough for today.

Chapter 7

Three Friends

There were three friends
Discussing life.
One said:
"Can men live together
And know nothing of it?
Work together
And produce nothing?
Can they fly around in space
And forget to exist
World without end?"

The three friends looked at each other
And burst out laughing.
They had no explanation.
Thus they were better friends than before.

Then one friend died.
Confucius sent a disciple
To help the other two
Chant his obsequies.

The disciple found that one friend
Had composed a song.
While the other played a lute,
They sang:

"Hey, Sung Hu!
Where'd you go?
Hey, Sung Hu!
Where'd you go?
You have gone
Where you really were.
And we are here —
Damn it, we are here!"

Then the disciple of Confucius burst in on them and
Exclaimed: "May I inquire where you found this

In the rubrics for obsequies,
This frivolous caroling in the presence of the departed?"

The two friends looked at each other and laughed:
"Poor fellow," they said, "he doesn't know the new liturgy!"

The first thing about life is that it has no explanation. It is there in its absolute glory, but it has no explanation. It is there as a mystery and if you try to explain it you will miss it. It will not be explained, but you will become blind through your explanations.

Philosophy is the enemy of life. The most inimical thing that can happen to a man is to get fixed and obsessed with philosophical explanations. The moment you think you have the explanation life has left you, you are already dead.

This will look paradoxical. Death can be explained; life cannot be explained – because death is something finished, complete. Life is always an ongoing affair, life is always on the journey, death has arrived. When something has reached and is finished, you can explain it, you can define it. When something is still ongoing, it means that the unknown is still to be traveled.

You can know the past but you cannot know the future. You can put the past into a theory; how can you put the future into a theory? The future is always an opening, an infinite opening, it goes on opening and opening. So when you explain, the explanation always indicates that which is dead.

Philosophy has explanations so it cannot be very alive, and you cannot find people who are more dead than philosophers. Their life has ebbed away, their life has oozed out, they are shrunken heads, like dead stones. They make much noise but there is none of the music of life. They have many explanations, but they have completely forgotten that they have only explanations in their hands.

Explanation is like a closed fist. Life is like an open hand. They are totally different. And when the fist is completely closed there is no sky in it, no air in it, no space to breathe. You cannot grab the sky in your closed fist; the fist will miss it. The sky is there, the hand is open, it is available. Explanation is grabbing, closing, defining – life oozes out.

Even laughter is greater than any philosophy. When somebody laughs about life, he understands it. So all those who have really known have laughed. And their laughter can be heard even after centuries. Mahakashyapa laughed looking at Buddha – Buddha was holding a flower in his hand – and Mahakashyapa laughed. His laughter can be heard even now. Those who have ears to hear, they will hear his laughter, just like a river continuously flowing past, through the centuries.

In Zen monasteries in Japan they still ask, disciples still ask the master, "Tell us, Master, why did Mahakashyapa laugh?" And those who are more alert they ask, "Tell us, Master, why is Mahakashyapa still laughing?" Those who are more alert use the present tense, not the past. And it is said that the master will reply only when he feels that you can hear the laughter of Mahakashyapa. If you cannot hear it, nothing can be said to you about it.

Buddhas have always been laughing. You may not have heard them because your doors are closed. You may have looked at a buddha and you may have felt that he is serious, but this seriousness is projected. It is your own seriousness – you have used the buddha as a screen. Hence, Christians say Jesus never laughed. This seems to be absolutely foolish. Jesus must have laughed and he must have laughed so totally that his whole being must have become laughter – but the disciples couldn't hear it, that is true. They must have remained closed, their own seriousness projected.

They could see Jesus on the cross – because you all live in such suffering that you can only see suffering. Even if they had heard Jesus laughing, they must have omitted it. It was so contradictory to their life, it didn't fit in. A Jesus laughing doesn't fit in with you, he becomes a stranger.

But in the East it has been different, and in Zen, in Tao, the laughter reached its peak. It became the polar opposite of philosophy.

A philosopher is serious because he thinks life is a riddle and a solution can be found. He works on life with his mind, and he gets more and more serious. The more he misses life, the more serious and dead he becomes.

Taoists, Lao Tzu and Chuang Tzu, say that if you can laugh, if you can have a belly laughter that comes from the very core of your being, not just on the surface, not painted – if it comes from the deepest center of your being, spreads all over you, overflows to the universe – that laughter will give you the first glimpse of what life is. It is a mystery. For Chuang Tzu such laughter is prayerful, because now you accept life; you don't hanker for the explanation. How can one find the explanation? We are part of it. How can the part find the explanation for the whole? How can the part look at the whole? How can the part dissect, divide the whole? How can the part go before the whole was there?

Explanation means that you must transcend that which you are trying to explain – you must be there before it existed, you must be there when it has ceased to exist. You must move around it so you can define it, and you must dissect it so you can reach the heart of it. A surgeon can find an explanation for a dead body, but not for life. All medical definitions of life are foolish because the surgeon dissects, and when he comes to know that life is no longer there, it is only a corpse. All explanations are postmortems, life is not there.

Now even scientists have become aware of the phenomenon that when you examine blood, if you take blood out of the body, and then examine it, it cannot be the same. Scientists say this now, because when it was moving in the veins of the body it was alive, it had a different quality; now when it is in the test tube, it is dead. It is not the same blood, because the basic quality – life – is no longer in it. All explanations are of that type.

A flower on the tree is different because life, the shape of life, is flowing in it. When you cut it from the tree, take it to the lab, examine it, it is a different flower. Don't be deceived by the appearance. Now life is no longer flowing in it. You may come to know the chemical composition of the flower, but that is not the explanation.

A poet has a different approach, not through dissection, but through love, not through uprooting the flower from the tree but rather by merging with the flower, remaining in deep love with it, in a participation mystique. He participates, then he comes to know something, and that is not an explanation. Poetry cannot be an explanation, but it has a glimpse of the truth. It is truer than any science.

Watch: when you are in love with someone your heart beats differently. Your lover, your beloved, will listen to your heart – it beats differently. Your lover will take your hand – the warmth is different. The blood moves in a different dance, it pulsates differently.

When the doctor takes your hand in his hand, the pulsation is not the same. He can hear the heart beating but this beat is different. When the heart was beating for a lover it had a song of its own, but only a lover can know the beat, only a lover can know the pulsation, the blood, the warmth of life. The doctor cannot know.

What has changed? The doctor has become the observer and you are the observed – you are not one. The doctor treats you like an object. He looks at you as if he is looking at a thing – that makes the difference. A lover doesn't look at you as an object – he becomes one with you, he merges and melts. He comes to know the deeper core of your being, but he has no explanation. He feels it, but feeling is different. He cannot think about it.

Anything that can be thought will not be alive. Thought deals with death, it always deals with dead objects. That is why in science there is no place for feeling, because feeling gives a different dimension to existence, the dimension of the alive.

This beautiful story has many things to say to you. Move step by step into it, and if you reach a conclusion, then understand that you have missed. If you reach laughter, then you have understood.

There were three friends
discussing life.

Chuang Tzu is very telegraphic. As always, those who know will not utter a single word unnecessarily. They live with the essential.

There were three friends discussing life. The first thing to be understood is that only friends can discuss life. Whenever a discussion becomes antagonistic, whenever a discussion becomes a debate, the dialogue is broken. Life cannot be discussed that way. Only friends can discuss, because then discussion is not a debate, it is a dialogue.

What is the difference between a debate and a dialogue? In debate you are not ready to listen to the other; even if you are listening, your listening is false. You are not listening, you are simply preparing your argument. While the other is speaking you are getting ready to contradict. While the other is talking, you are simply waiting for your opportunity to argue. You have a prejudice already there in you, you have a theory. You are not in search, you are not ignorant, you are not innocent; you are already filled, your boat is not empty. You carry certain theories with you and you are trying to prove them true.

A seeker of truth carries no theories with him. He is always open, vulnerable. He can listen. A Hindu cannot listen, a Mohammedan cannot listen. How can a Hindu listen? He already knows the truth, there is no need to listen. He will try to make you listen to him, but he cannot listen. You try to make him listen but he cannot; his mind is already so filled that nothing can penetrate. A Christian cannot listen, he already knows the truth. He has closed his doors for new breezes to reach him, he has closed his eyes for the new sun to rise; he has reached, he has arrived.

All those who feel that they have arrived can debate, but they cannot move in a dialogue. They can clash, then conflict arises, they oppose each other. In such a discussion you may prove something, but nothing is proved. You may silence the other, but the other is never converted. You cannot convince, because this is a sort of war, a civilized war – you are not fighting with weapons, you are fighting with words.

Chuang Tzu says: Three friends were discussing life – that is why they could reach laughter; otherwise there would have been a conclusion. One theory might have defeated other theories, one philosophy might have silenced other philosophies, then there would have been a conclusion – and conclusion is dead.

Life has no conclusion. Life has no foolish thought to it. It goes on and on endlessly; it is always, eternally, an onward affair. How can you conclude anything about it? The moment you conclude you have stepped out of it. Life goes on and you have stepped out of the way. You may cling to your conclusion but life will not wait for you.

Friends can discuss. Why? Because you can love a person, you cannot love a philosophy. Philosophers cannot be friends. You can be either their disciple or their enemy but you cannot be their friend. Either you are convinced by them or not convinced, either you follow them or don't follow them, but you cannot be friends. A friendship is possible only between two empty boats. Then you are open to the other, inviting to the other, then you are constantly an invitation: "Come to me, enter me, be with me."

You can throw away theories and philosophies but you cannot throw away friendship. When you are in friendship a dialogue becomes possible. In dialogue you listen, and if you have to speak, you speak not to contradict the other, you speak just to seek, to inquire. You speak, not with a conclusion already reached, but with an inquiry, an ongoing inquiry. You are not trying to prove something; you speak from innocence, not from philosophy. Philosophy is never innocent, it is always cunning, it is a device of the mind.

Three friends were discussing life – because between friends a dialogue is possible. So in the East it has been the tradition that unless you find friendship, love, reverence, trust, no inquiry is possible. If you go to a master and your boat is filled with your ideas, there can be no contact, there can be no dialogue. First you have to be empty so that friendship becomes possible, so that you can look without any ideas floating in your eyes, so that you can look without conclusions. And whenever you can look without conclusions, your perspective is vast, it is not confined.

A Hindu can read the Bible, but he never understands it. Really, he never reads it, he cannot listen to it. A Christian can read the Gita, but he remains the outsider. He never penetrates its innermost being, he never reaches the inner realm, he moves round and round. He cannot really read the books, it is impossible because of the conclusions in the mind. He already knows that only Christ is true, he already knows that only through Christ comes salvation; he already knows that Christ is the only son of God. How can he listen to Krishna? Only Christ is truth. Then Krishna is bound to be untrue, at the most a beautiful untruth, but never true. Or if he concedes too much, then he will say it is approximately true.

But what do you mean when you say approximately true? It is untrue. Truth is either there or not. Nothing can be approximately true. Truth is or truth is not. It is always total. You cannot divide it. You cannot say it is true to some degree. No, truth knows no degrees. Either it is or it is not.

So when the mind concludes that Christ is the only truth, then it is impossible to listen to Krishna. Even if he crosses your path, you will not be able to listen to him. Even if you meet Buddha you will not meet him.

The whole world is filled with conclusions. Someone is a Christian, someone is a Hindu, someone is a Jaina, someone is a Buddhist – that is why truth is missing. A religious person cannot be a Christian, a Hindu, or a Buddhist; a religious person can only be a sincere inquirer. He inquires and he remains open without any conclusions. His boat is empty.

Three friends discussing life ... Only friends can discuss because then it becomes a dialogue, then the relationship is of I and thou. When you are debating, the relationship is of I and it. The other is a thing to be converted, convinced, the other is not a thou; the other has no significance, the other is just a number.

In friendship the other is significant, the other has intrinsic value, the other is an end in himself, you are not trying to convert him. How can you convert a person? What foolishness! The very effort to convert a person is foolish. A person is not a thing. A person is so big and so vast that no theory can be more important than a person. No Bible is more important than a person, no Gita is more important than a person. A person means the very glory of life. You can love a person but you can never convert a person. If you are trying to convert, you are trying to manipulate. Then the person has become a means and you are exploiting.

Dialogue is possible when your I says thou, when the other is loved, when there is no ideology behind it. The other is simply loved, and whether he is a Christian or Hindu doesn't matter. This is what friendship means – and friends can discuss life because dialogue is possible.

One said:
"Can men live together
and know nothing of it,
work together
and produce nothing?
Can they fly around in space
and forget to exist,
world without end?"

He is not proposing a theory, he is simply raising a question. And remember, you can raise a question in two ways. Sometimes you raise a question only because you have to supply an answer and the answer is already there – you raise the question just to answer it. Then the question is not real, it is false. The answer is already there. The question is just a trick, rhetorical; it is not real, authentic.

The question is authentic when there is no answer in you, when you question but you don't question from an answer, when you question simply to look; the question leaves you empty, just open, inviting, inquiring.

One said:
"Can men live together
and know nothing of it ... ?"

We live together and we never know anything of what togetherness is. You can live together for years without knowing what togetherness is. Look all over the world – people are living together, nobody is living alone: husbands with wives, wives with husbands, children with parents, parents with children, teachers with students, friends with friends; everybody is living together. Life exists in togetherness, but do you know what togetherness is?

Living with a wife for forty years, you may not have lived with her for a single moment. Even while making love to her you may have been thinking of other things. Then you were not there, the lovemaking was just mechanical.

I have heard ...

Once it happened: Mulla Nasruddin went to a film with his wife. They had been married for at least twenty years. The film was one of those torrid foreign films. When they were leaving the cinema hall, the wife said to Nasruddin, "Nasruddin, you never love me like those actors were doing in the film. Why?"

Nasruddin said, "Are you crazy? Do you know how much they are paid for doing such things?"

People go on living with each other without any love because you love only when it pays. And how can you love if you love only when it pays? Then love has also become a commodity in the market; then it is not a relationship, it is not a togetherness, it is not a celebration. You are not happy being with the other, at the most you just tolerate the other.

Mulla Nasruddin's wife was on her deathbed and the doctor said, "Nasruddin, I must be frank with you, because in such moments it is better to be truthful. Your wife cannot be saved. The disease has gone beyond us, and you must be ready. You should not allow yourself to suffer. Accept it as fate. Your wife is going to die."

Nasruddin said, "Don't be worried about it. If I could suffer with her for so many years, I can suffer for a few hours more."

At the most we tolerate. And whenever you think in terms of toleration, you are suffering, your togetherness is suffering. That is why Jean-Paul Sartre says, "The other is hell," because with the other you simply suffer, the other becomes the bondage, the other becomes the domination. The other starts creating trouble, your freedom is lost, your happiness is lost. Then it becomes tolerance, a routine. If you are tolerating the other how can you know the beauty of togetherness? Really, it has never happened.

Marriage almost always never happens, because marriage means the celebration of togetherness. It is not a license. No registry office can give you marriage; no priest can give it to you as a gift. It is a tremendous revolution in the being, it is a great transformation in your very style of life, and it can happen only when you celebrate togetherness, when the other is no longer felt as the other, when you no longer feel yourself as I. When the two are not really two, but a bridge has happened, they have become one in a certain sense. They remain two bodies, but as far as the innermost being is concerned, they have become one. They may be two poles of one existence but they are not two. A bridge exists. That bridge gives you glimpses of togetherness.

It is one of the rarest things to come across a marriage. People live together because they cannot live alone. Remember this: because they cannot live alone, that is why they live together. To live alone is uncomfortable, to live alone is uneconomical, to live alone is difficult, that is why they live together. The reasons are negative.

A man was going to get married and somebody asked him, "You have always been against marriage, why have you suddenly changed your mind?"

He said, "Winter is coming and they say that this winter is going to be very cold, and central heating is beyond me and a wife is cheaper."

This is the logic. You live with someone because it is comfortable, convenient, economical, cheaper. To live alone is really difficult. A wife is so many things, the housekeeper, the cook, the servant, the nurse, so many things – the cheapest labor in the world, doing so many things without being paid at all. It is exploitation.

Marriage exists as an institution for exploitation, it is not togetherness. That is why no happiness comes out of it as a flowering. It cannot. How can ecstasy be born out of the roots of exploitation?

Then there are your so-called saints who go on saying that you are miserable because you live in a family, because you live in the world. They say, "Leave everything, renounce!" And their logic appears to be right to you also, not because it *is* right, but because you have missed togetherness. Otherwise, all those saints would look absolutely wrong. One who has known togetherness has known the divine; one who is really married has known the divine, because love is the greatest door.

But togetherness is not there and you live together without knowing what togetherness is; you live for seventy, eighty years without knowing what life is. You drift without any roots in life. You just move from one moment to another without tasting what life gives you. And this is not given by birth. It is not hereditary to know life.

Life comes through birth but the wisdom, the experience, the ecstasy, has to be learnt – hence the meaning of meditation. You have to earn it, you have to grow towards it, you have to attain a certain maturity; only then will you be able to know it.

Life can open to you only in a certain moment of maturity. But people live and die childishly. They never really grow, they never attain to maturity.

What is maturity? Just becoming sexually mature? Then you are not mature. Ask the psychologists: they say that the mental age remains nearabout thirteen or fourteen. Your physical body goes on growing but your mind stops at about thirteen. That's why it is no wonder you behave so foolishly, why your life becomes a continuous foolishness. A mind which has not grown up is bound to do something wrong every moment.

And the immature mind always throws responsibility onto the other. You are unhappy because everybody else is creating hell for you: "The other is hell." I say this assertion of Sartre is really immature. If you are mature, the other can also become heaven. The other is whatsoever you are because the other is just a mirror, he reflects you.

When I say maturity, I mean an inner integrity. And this inner integrity comes only when you stop throwing responsibility onto others, when you stop saying that the other is creating your suffering, when you start realizing that you are the creator of your suffering. This is the first step towards maturity: I am responsible. Whatsoever is happening, it is my doing.

You feel sad. Is this your doing? You will feel very much disturbed, but if you can remain with this feeling, sooner or later you will be able to stop doing many things. This is what the theory of karma is all about. You are responsible. Don't say society is responsible, don't say that parents are responsible, don't say the economic conditions are responsible. Don't throw the responsibility onto anybody. *You* are responsible.

Once you accept this burden ... In the beginning it looks like a burden because now you cannot throw responsibility onto anybody else.

It happened ... Mulla Nasruddin was sitting, very sad. Somebody asked him, "Nasruddin, why do you look so sad?"

He said, "My wife has insisted that I stop gambling, smoking, drinking, and playing cards. I have stopped all of them."

The man said, "So your wife must be very happy."

Nasruddin said, "That is the problem. Now she cannot find anything to complain about, so she is very unhappy. She starts talking, but she cannot find anything to talk about. Now she cannot make me responsible for anything and she is so unhappy, I have never seen her so unhappy. I also thought that when

I stop all these things her unhappiness will stop. But she has become more unhappy than ever."

If you go on throwing responsibility onto others and they all do whatsoever you say they do, you will commit suicide. Because there will be nowhere left to throw your responsibilities.

So it is good to have a few faults; it helps others to be happy. A wife will leave a really perfect husband, because how can you dominate a perfect man? So even if you don't want to, go on doing something wrong so the wife can dominate you and feel happy.

A perfect husband – there is bound to be divorce. You will all be against any perfect man, because you cannot condemn him, you cannot say anything wrong about him. Our minds love to throw responsibility onto somebody else, they want to complain. It makes us feel good, because then we are not responsible, we are unburdened. But this unburdening is very costly. You are not really unburdened, you are getting more and more burdened. Only you are not alert.

People live for seventy years. Really, they have lived for many, many lives without knowing what life is. They were not mature, they were not integrated, they were not centered. They lived on the periphery.

When your periphery meets the other's periphery a clash happens, and if you go on being concerned that the other is wrong, you remain on the periphery. Once you realize: "I am responsible for my being; whatsoever has happened, I am the cause, I have done it," suddenly your consciousness shifts from the periphery to the center. Now you become, for the first time, the center of your world.

Now much can be done – because whatsoever you don't like, you can drop; whatsoever you like, you can adopt; whatsoever you feel is true, you can follow, and whatsoever you feel is untrue, there is no need to follow because you are now centered and rooted in yourself.

One friend asked:

One said:
"Can men live together
and know nothing of it,
work together
and produce nothing?
Can they fly around in space
and forget to exist,
world without end?"

The three friends looked at each other ...

Only friends look at each other. When there is someone to whom you feel antagonistic, you never look at him. You avoid the eyes. Even if you have to look, your look is vacant, you don't allow your eyes to absorb him; he is something foreign, rejected.

Eyes are doors. You look towards a person only when you want to absorb, to let him melt in you.

The three friends looked at each other ... One friend inquired, the other two were not in any hurry to answer. They waited, they were patient. If there had been any conclusion in their mind, they would have objected immediately. But they looked at each other. They felt the situation, the inquiry, the heart of the inquirer, the meaning of the question, the depth of the question. Remember, if you can feel the depth of a question, the answer is almost found. But nobody is that patient, nobody is ready to go into the question deeply. You ask, but you never go into the inquiry. You ask for the answer immediately.

The three friends looked at each other
and burst out laughing.

The fact, the question, the penetration of it, the depth, the reality, the fact of it – no answer was needed. Any answer would have been foolish, any answer would have been superficial.

It is said about Buddha that millions of times people would ask questions and he would not answer. If the question was such that any answer would be superficial, he would not answer. If somebody asked, "Is there a God?" he remained silent. But people are foolish. They started thinking that either he was an atheist, and didn't believe in God, or that he was ignorant, he didn't know. Otherwise why should he not say yes or no.

You don't know. When you ask a question like this, whether there is a God, "Does God exist?" you don't know what you are asking. Is this a question to be answered? Then you are stupid. Can such vital questions be answered? Then you don't know the depth of it; this is curiosity, not inquiry.

If the man who was asking Buddha was really an inquirer, an authentic seeker, then he would have remained with Buddha's silence – because the silence was the answer. In that silence he would have felt the question, in that silence the question would have asserted itself. Against the background of the silence it would have become clearer. A clarity would have come to him.

Whenever you ask a deep question, no answer is required. All that is required is to remain with the question. Don't move here and there, remain with the question and wait. The very question will become the answer. If you really go deep into the question, it will lead to the very source from where the answer also flowers. It is in you.

Buddha has not answered any real question – and remember that about me also. I go on answering your questions, but I also cannot answer your real questions – and you have not asked yet. Whenever you ask the real question, I am not going to answer, because no real question can be answered, it is not an intellectual thing. Only from heart to heart the transmission happens, not from head to head.

The three friends looked at each other ... What happened in that look? They were not heads in that look, they became hearts. They looked at each other, they felt, they tasted the question – it was so real that there was no answer to it.

Yes, we live without knowing what life is. Yes, we live together without knowing what togetherness is. Yes, we live, forgetting completely that we exist. We have been flying round and round in the sky without knowing where we are going or why.

The question was so real that if any answer had been given, that answer would be foolish. Only a fool would answer such a question. They looked at each other; they really looked into each other – *and burst out laughing*. Why burst out laughing? The whole situation is so absurd. Really, we live without knowing what life is; we exist without becoming aware of existence, we journey and journey without knowing from where or to what or why.

Life is a mystery. Whenever you confront a mystery laughter will arise. How can you answer a mystery?

What is the most mysterious thing in you? Laughter is the most mysterious thing in you. No animal can laugh, only man. It is the supreme-most glory of man. No animal laughs, no trees laugh – only man laughs. Laughter is the most mysterious element in man.

Aristotle defined man as the rational being. It is not so because reason exists in other animals also. The difference is only of degree, and it is not much. Man can only be defined as the laughing and weeping animal, no other definition will do, because no other animal can weep, no other animal can laugh. This polarity exists only in humanity. This is something mysterious in man, most mysterious.

Anger exists all over, it is nothing. Sex exists all over, it is nothing, it is not so mysterious. If you want to understand sex, you can understand animal sex, and all that is applicable to animal sex will be applicable to man. In that way man is nothing more.

Anger, violence, aggression, possessiveness, jealousy, everything exists and exists more purely and more simply in animals than in you. Everything is confused in you. That is why psychologists have to study rats just to study man. They are simple, clear, less confused, and whatsoever they conclude about rats is true of you. All the psychology laboratories are filled with rats. The rat has become the most important animal for psychologists because it is so human-like. In many ways it is like the human.

The rat is the only animal which follows humanity wherever it goes. It is universal. If you find a man in Siberia, there will be a rat there somewhere. Wherever he goes, the rat follows – I suspect that rats must have reached the moon. No other animal can exist everywhere like the rat. And its behavior is absolutely human. Understand the behavior of the rat and you have understood humanity.

But the rat cannot laugh, the rat cannot weep. Laughter and weeping are two aspects of something which exists only in man. If you need to understand laughter and weeping you have to study humanity; nowhere else can it be studied. That's why I call it the most distinctive quality of the human mind.

Whenever you feel mystery, there are only two ways, either you weep or you laugh. It depends on your personality, your type. It is possible, if they had been of a different personality type, that the three friends would have wept. When such a mystery surrounds you, when you encounter such an unknowable mystery that no explanation is possible, what can you do? How can you respond?

But laughter is better than weeping because weeping comes when the mystery of death surrounds you. Then you weep. And the question was about life so it was relevant to laugh. Whenever you encounter the mystery of death you weep, you feel the relevance of weeping whenever death is there.

The question was about life, not about death. So it seems relevant that they looked into each other, into the life that was in each – the life pulsating, the life dancing all around and with no explanation, with no secret book to reveal the keys: life in its total mystery, in its total unknowability.

What was there to do? They were not philosophers, they were true men, mystics. They laughed, they had no explanation.

Thus they were better friends than before.

This is beautiful. Whenever there is an explanation enmity arises, whenever you believe in something you are divided. Belief creates conflict. The whole world is divided because of belief. You are a Hindu and someone is a Moham-medan, and you are enemies. Why are you enemies? – because of your belief. Belief creates the conflict; foolish explanations, ideologies, create conflict, war.

Look at this: if there is no explanation, who is a Hindu and who is a Moham-medan? And how can you fight? For what? Men have always been fighting over philosophies, shedding blood, murdering each other, just for foolish beliefs. And if you look into beliefs, you can see the foolishness – not of your beliefs, but of others' beliefs. Your belief is something sacred, but every body else's belief looks foolish.

All beliefs are foolish. You cannot see your own because it is so near. Really, explanations are foolish, stupid.

I have heard ...

A flock of birds was flying south for the winter. One bird at the rear asked another, "How come we always follow this idiot leader?"

The other said, "In the first place, all leaders are idiots." Otherwise, who would want to lead? Only the foolish are always ready to lead. A wise man hesitates. Life is so mysterious – it is not a ready-made path. How can you lead? A wise man hesitates and an idiot is always ready to lead.

So the bird said, "In the first place, all leaders are idiots, because nobody is interested in leading except idiots, and in the second place, he has got the map, so every year we have to follow him."

Life has no map and there is no possibility of making a map. It is a pathless path. Without explanations how can you be divided? If there is no explanation, the world will be one. But there are millions of explanations, millions of fragments.

Chuang Tzu says a really very penetrating thing:

They had no explanation,
thus they were better friends than before.

Now there was nothing to be enemies for, nothing to fight about.

They laughed, and the laughter made them one. They laughed, and the laughter led them into togetherness. Explain and you are divided, become philosophical and you are separated from others, become a Hindu, a Mohammedan, a Buddhist, then all others are enemies.

Look at the mystery and laugh, and humanity is one. And then there is no need to say that Christians are brothers of Hindus, Hindus are brothers of Moham-medans. First, divide them by beliefs, make them ill, and then supply them with medicine – you are all brothers. Have you seen brothers? They fight more than enemies! So what is the use of making them brothers?

Man fights for his explanations. All fights are foolish. Man fights for his flags, and look at the flags. What type of foolishness, what type of madness exists in the world? – for flags, for symbols, for beliefs, for ideologies?

Says Chuang Tzu: *They had no explanation* – they laughed. In that mysterious moment they became one, better friends than before.

If you really want to be a friend, have no explanations and no conclusions, don't believe in anything. And then you are not divided, then humanity is one, then there is no barrier.

And love exists not through mind, it exists through feeling.

They laughed. Laughter comes from the heart, laughter comes from the belly, laughter comes from the total being. When three people laugh, they become friends. When three people weep, they become friends. When three people debate, they become enemies.

Then one friend died.
Confucius sent a disciple
to help the other two
chant his obsequies.

Confucius is the most perfect man of manners, par excellence. Nobody can transcend him. So he is always the butt of Chuang Tzu and Lao Tzu. They bring Confucius into their stories just to laugh at his foolishness.

What was his foolishness? He lived by a system, he lived by a formula, by theories and beliefs. He was the perfectly civilized man, the most perfect gentleman the world has ever known. He moves, and he moves according to the rule. He looks, and he looks according to the rule. He laughs, and he laughs according to the rule. He never moves beyond the boundary, he lives in a constant bondage of his own making. So he is the butt of their laughter, and Chuang Tzu and Lao Tzu very much enjoyed bringing him into their stories.

Then one friend died.
Confucius sent a disciple
to help the other two
chant his obsequies.

Neither life nor death is a mystery to him. It is according to a system. Some mannerism has to be followed. So he sent his disciple to see whether the dead man was disposed of according to the rules, the right prayer, the right chanting as given in the books. The dead had to be respected.

This is the difference. A man who lives through manners is always thinking of respect, never of love. And what is respect in comparison to love? Love is something alive; respect is absolutely dead.

The disciple found that one friend
had composed a song
while the other played the lute.

This was unbelievable! This was disrespectful to a person who is dead. The dead body was lying there, and one friend had composed a song. They loved the other man, and when you love a man you want to give him the last farewell through your love, not through books, not through a ready-made song, borrowed, which so many have chanted, so many have used, already rotten, rubbish.

They made up a song of their own, fresh, young. Of course, it was homemade, not produced in a factory, not mass-produced. Just homemade, not very polished of course, because they were not poets, they were friends, and they didn't know how poetry was created. The meter may have been wrong and the grammar incorrect, but love doesn't care about grammar, love doesn't care about meter, love doesn't care about rhythm, because love has such a vital rhythm of its own, it need not care. When there is no love, then everything has to be taken care about, because then you have to substitute.

One was playing the lute – and I know that he was not a lute player. But how do you say goodbye to a friend? It must come from your heart, it must be spontaneous, it cannot be ready-made. That is the point.

They sang:
"Hey, Sung Hu,
where'd you go?

The mystery! They were not saying, "You are going to heaven." They didn't know. Otherwise, when anybody dies you say he has gone to heaven. Then who is going to hell? Nobody seems to go to hell.

In India, they use the word *swargiya* for a dead person. It means one who has gone to heaven. Then who is going to hell?

They didn't know, so what was the point of uttering a falsehood? Who knows where this man had gone, this Sung Hu – to hell or heaven? Who knows whether hell and heaven exist? Nobody knows; it is a mystery, and one should not defile a mystery, one should not make it profane, one should not assert falsehoods. It is such a sacred thing, one should not say anything which is not known directly.

"Hey, Sung Hu,
where'd you go?

It was a question mark.

"Hey, Sung Hu,
where'd you go?
You have gone
where you really were,

and we are here –
damn it, we are here!"

They say, "You have gone to the place from where you came." This is a secret law: the ultimate can only be the beginning. The circle comes round and becomes perfect, complete. It reaches to the same point from where it started. The end cannot be anything else but the beginning, the death cannot be anything else but the birth. The final should be the source, the original. One is born out of nothingness and then one dies and moves into nothingness. The boat was empty when you were born and when you die the boat will be empty again. Just a flash of lightning – for a few moments you are in the body and then you disappear. Nobody knows from where you came, or where you go.

Nobody knows, and they don't claim any knowledge. They say, "This much we feel, Sung Hu: you have gone to the place from where you came, and damn it, we are still here." So they are not sorry for Hu, they are sorry for themselves, "We are hanging in the middle, your circle is perfect."

Whenever somebody dies, have you felt this? Are you sorry for the person who is dead or sorry for yourself? Really, when someone dies, are you sad for him or her, or for yourself? Everybody is sorry for himself because every death brings the news that you are going to die. But a person who can laugh at the mystery of life knows what it is, because only knowledge, real wisdom, can laugh.

Where you really were, you have gone ...

"And we are here –
damn it, we are here!"

And we are still in the middle. Our journey is incomplete; your circle has become perfect. So they are sorry for themselves, and if they weep, they are weeping for themselves. For the friend who has departed they have nothing but a song, nothing but a celebration of the heart. If they are sorry, they are sorry for themselves.

This is something to be understood very deeply. If you understand life, if you can laugh at it, then death is the completion, then it is not the end. Remember, death is not the end of life, it is the completion, it is the climax, the crescendo, the peak from where the wave returns again to the original source.

They are sorry for themselves, that their wave is hanging in the middle. They have not reached the crescendo, the peak, and their friend has reached where he was before. He has reached home. Those who understand life, only they can understand death, because life and death are not two. Death is the peak, the ultimate, the final flowering, the fragrance of life.

Death looks ugly to you because you have never known life, and death creates fear in you because you are afraid of life. Remember, whatsoever your attitude towards life, the same will be your attitude towards death. If you are scared of death you are scared of life; if you love life, you will love death, because death is nothing but the highest peak, the completion. The song reaches its end, the river falls into the ocean. The river came from the ocean in the first place. Now the circle is complete, the river has reached the whole.

> *Then the disciple of Confucius burst in on them and*
> *exclaimed: "May I inquire where you found this*
> *in the rubrics for obsequies,*
> *this frivolous caroling in the presence of the departed?"*

The disciple of Confucius cannot understand them. They look frivolous, disrespectful. What type of song, from where have you got this? It is not authorized, it is not from the Vedas. *Then the disciple of Confucius burst in on them and exclaimed: "May I inquire where you found this?"*

Everything should be according to the books, according to the Bible, to the Vedas. But life cannot be according to the books – life always transcends books, it always goes beyond; life always throws books aside, moves ahead.

"Where have you found this, *this frivolous caroling in the presence of the departed*? You should be respectful. Someone has departed, someone is dead and what are you doing? This is profane!"

> *The two friends looked at each other and laughed:*
> *"Poor fellow, he doesn't know the new liturgy!"*

He doesn't know the new scripture, he doesn't know the new religion. That is what is happening here every day – the new liturgy.

A man was here just a few days ago, a professor of history, and he asked me, "To what tradition do you belong?"

I said, "To no tradition."

He had come here from America to make a film of the meditation techniques, of the camp, of what I say, of what is happening here. The moment he heard that I don't belong to any tradition, he simply disappeared. Then I don't belong to history, it is obvious.

Poor fellow, he does not know the new liturgy!

Enough for today.

Chapter 8

The Useless

Hui Tzu said to Chuang Tzu:
"All your teaching is centered on what has no use."

Chuang replied:
"If you have no appreciation for what has no use
You cannot begin to talk about what can be used.
The earth, for example, is broad and vast
But of all this expanse a man uses only a few inches
Upon which he happens to be standing.

Now suppose you suddenly take away
All that he is not actually using
So that, all around his feet a gulf yawns,
And he stands in the Void
With nowhere solid except right under each foot:
How long will he be able to use what he is using?"

Hui Tzu said: "It would cease to serve any purpose."

Chuang Tzu concluded:
"This shows
The absolute necessity
of what has 'no use.'"

Life is dialectical, that is why it is not logical. Logic means that the opposite is really opposite, and life always implies the opposite in itself. In life the opposite is not really the opposite, it is the complementary. Without it nothing is possible.

For example, life exists because of death. If there is no death there cannot be any life. Death is not the end and death is not the enemy – rather, on the contrary, because of death life becomes possible. So death is not somewhere in the end, it is involved here and now. Each moment has its life and its death; otherwise existence is impossible.

There is light, there is darkness. For logic they are opposites, and logic will say: If it is light, there cannot be any darkness, if it is dark, then there cannot be any light. But life says quite the contrary. Life says: If there is darkness it is because of light; if there is light it is because of darkness. We may not be able to see the other, but it is hidden just around the corner.

There is silence because of sound. If there is no sound at all, can you be silent? How can you be silent? The opposite is needed as a background. Those who follow logic always go wrong because their life becomes lopsided. They think of light, then they start denying darkness; they think of life, then they start fighting death.

That's why there exists no tradition in the world where it is said that God is both light and darkness. There is one tradition which says that God is light, he is not darkness. No darkness exists in God for these people who believe God is light. There is another tradition that says that God is darkness – but for them there is no light. Both are wrong, because both are logical, they deny the opposite. And life is so vast, it carries the opposite in itself. It is not denied, it is embraced.

Once somebody said to Walt Whitman, one of the greatest poets ever born, "Whitman, you go on contradicting yourself. One day you say one thing, another day you say just the opposite."

Walt Whitman laughed and said, "I am vast. I contain all the contradictions."

Only small minds are consistent; the narrower the mind, the more consistent. When the mind is vast, everything is involved – light is there, darkness is there, God is there and the Devil also, in his total glory.

If you understand this mysterious process of life which moves through the opposites, which is dialectical, in which the opposite helps, gives balance, gives tone, makes the background, then only can you understand Chuang Tzu – because the whole Taoist vision is based on the complementariness of the opposites.

They use two words, *yin* and *yang*. They are opposites, male and female. Just think of a world which is totally male or a world which is totally female. It will be dead. The moment it is born it will be dead. There cannot be any life. If it is a female world, only women, and women and women, and no men – they will commit suicide. The opposite is needed because the opposite is attractive. The opposite becomes the magnet, it pulls you; the opposite brings you out of yourself, the opposite breaks your prison, the opposite makes you vast. Whenever the opposite is denied there is going to be trouble. And that is what we have been doing, hence so much trouble in the world.

Man has tried to create a society which is basically male, that's why there is so much trouble – the woman has been denied, she has been thrown out. In past centuries the woman was never to be seen anywhere. She was just hidden in the back chambers of the house; she was not even allowed in the drawing rooms. You couldn't meet her on the streets, you couldn't see her in the shops. She was not part of life. The world went ugly, because how can you deny the opposite? It became lopsided, all balance was lost. The world went mad.

The woman is still not allowed; she is really not yet a part, a vital part of life. Men move in men-oriented groups – the exclusively male club where boys meet, the market, politics, the scientific group. Everywhere it is lopsided. Man dominates, that is why there is so much misery. When one of the polar opposites dominates, there will be misery, because the other feels hurt and there is revenge.

Every woman is taking revenge in the house. Of course, she cannot go out and move in the world and take revenge on humanity, on mankind. She takes revenge on the husband. There is constant conflict.

I have heard ...

Mulla Nasruddin was saying to his son, "It is none of your business, don't ask such things. Who are you to ask me how I met your mother? But I will tell you one thing: she sure cured me of whistling."

Then he said, "And this is the moral of the story: if you don't want to be unhappy like me, never whistle at a girl!"

Why is the wife always in conflict? It is not the person, it is not a personal thing. It is the revenge of the woman, of the female, of the denied opposite. And this man in the house, this husband, is the representative of the whole male world, the male-oriented world. She is fighting.

Family life is so miserable because we have not heard what Chuang Tzu says. There are so many wars because we have not listened – the opposite has to be merged. Negating it, you invite trouble, and on every path, on every level, in every dimension, it is the same thing.

Chuang Tzu says that if you deny the useless, then there will be no use in the world. If you deny the useless, the playful, the fun, there cannot exist any work, any duty. This is very difficult, and the whole emphasis is on the useful.

If you look at a door, you will see the walls. If somebody asks you what a house consists of, you will say, walls. But Chuang Tzu would say, just like his master Lao Tzu, that a house consists not of walls but of doors and windows. Their emphasis is on the other part. They say that walls are useful, but their use depends on the useless space behind.

A room is space, not walls. Of course, space is free and walls have to be purchased. When you purchase a house, what do you purchase? – the walls, the material, the visible. But can you live in the material? Can you live in the walls? You have to live in the room, in the vacant space. You purchase the boat, but you have to live in the emptiness.

So really, what is a house? Emptiness surrounded by walls. And what is a door? There is nothing. *Door* means there is nothing, no wall, emptiness. But you cannot enter the house if there is no door. If there is no window then no sun will enter, no breeze will blow. You will be dead, and your house will become a tomb.

Chuang Tzu says: Remember that the house consists of two things: the walls, the material – from the market, the utilitarian – and the emptiness surrounded by the walls, the non-utilitarian which cannot be purchased, which cannot be sold, which has no economic value.

How can you sell emptiness? But you have to live in the emptiness – if a man lives only in the walls he will go mad. It is impossible to do that – but we try to do the impossible. In life, we have chosen the utilitarian.

For example, if a child is playing you say, "Stop! What are you doing? This is useless. Do something useful. Learn, read, at least do your homework, something useful. Don't go around like a vagabond." If you go on insisting like this to a child, by and by you will kill the useless. Then the child will become just useful, and when a person is simply useful, he is dead. You can use him, he is a mechanical thing now, a means, not an end unto himself.

You are really yourself when you are doing something useless – painting, not to sell, just enjoying; gardening, just to enjoy; lying down on the beach, not doing anything, just to enjoy, useless fun; sitting silently by the side of a friend.

Much could be done in these moments. You could go to the shop, to the market, you could earn something. You could change time into money. You could have a bigger bank balance because these moments will not come back. And foolish people say that time is money – because they know only one use of time – how to convert it into more money and more money and more money. In the end you die with a big bank balance but inside totally poor, because the inner richness arises only when you can enjoy the useless.

What is meditation? People come to me and say, "What is the use of it? What will we gain out of it? What is the benefit of it?"

Meditation ... and you ask about the benefit? You cannot understand it because meditation is just useless. The moment I say useless, you feel uncomfortable because the whole mind has become so utilitarian, so commodity-oriented that you ask for a result. You cannot concede that something can be a pleasure unto itself.

Useless means you enjoy it, but there is no benefit from it; you are deeply merged into it, it gives you bliss. But when you are deeply in it, you cannot accumulate that bliss, you cannot make a treasure out of it.

In the world two types of people have existed: the utilitarians – they become scientists, engineers, doctors. Then there is the other path, the complementary – the poets, the vagabonds, the sannyasins – useless, not doing anything useful.

But they give the balance, they give grace to the world. Think of a world full of scientists and not a single poet – it would be absolutely ugly, not worth living in. Think of a world with everyone in the shops, in the offices, not a single vagabond. It would be hell. The vagabond gives beauty.

Once two vagabonds were caught ... The magistrates and police are the custodians of the utilitarians. They protect, because this useless part is dangerous – it can go on spreading. So nowhere are vagabonds, useless people, allowed. If you are just standing on the street and somebody asks, "What you are doing?" and you say, "Nothing," the policeman will immediately take you to court – because nothing is not allowed. You must do something. "Why are you standing there?" If you say simply, "I am standing and enjoying," you are a dangerous man, a hippy. You may be arrested.

So two vagabonds were caught. The magistrate asked the first one, "Where do you live?"

The man said, "The whole world is my home, the sky is my shelter; I move everywhere, there is no barrier. I am a free man."

Then he asked the other, "And where do you live?"

He said, "Next door to him."

These people give beauty to the world, they are a perfume. A Buddha is a vagabond, a Mahavira is a vagabond. This man, this vagabond, answered that the sky was his only shelter. That is what is meant by the word *digambar*. Mahavira, the last *tirthankara* of the Jainas, is known as a *digambar*. *Digambar* means naked, only the sky for clothing, nothing else. The sky is the shelter, the home.

Whenever the world becomes too utilitarian you create many things, you possess many things, you become obsessed with things – but the inner is lost, because the inner can flower only when there is no outer tension, when you are not going anywhere, just resting. Then the inner flowers.

Religion is absolutely useless. What use is the temple? What use is the mosque? What use is the church? In Soviet Russia they have converted all the temples, mosques, and churches into hospitals and schools, something useful. Why is this temple standing without any use? Communists are utilitarians. That's why they are against religion. They have to be, because religion gives way to the useless, to that which cannot be exploited in any way, to that which cannot be made a means to anything else. You can have it, you can be blissful in it, you can feel the highest ecstasy possible, but you cannot manipulate it. It is a happening. When you are not doing anything, it happens. And the greatest has always happened when you are not doing anything. Only the trivial happens when you are doing something.

Søren Kierkegaard, a Danish philosopher, has written something very penetrating. He said, "When I started praying, I would go to the church and I would talk to God." That's what Christians are doing all over the world – talking very loudly to God, as if God is deaf. They advise him what to do and what not to do, as if God is just a foolish entity. Or, as if God is just a foolish monarch – persuading him, bribing him to fulfill the desires that are inside them.

But Kierkegaard said, "I started talking, then suddenly I realized that this was useless. How can you talk? One has to be silent before God. What is there to be said? And what can I say which will help God to know more? He is omnipotent, he is omniscient, he knows all, so what is the purpose of my telling him?

"So at first I was talking to him for many years. Then suddenly I realized that this was foolish; so I stopped talking, I became silent. Then after many years I realized that even silence wouldn't do. Then the third step was taken, and that was listening. First I was talking, then I was not talking, and then I was listening."

Listening is different from just being silent, because just being silent is a negative thing – listening is a positive thing. Just being silent is passive, listening is an alert passiveness, waiting for something, not saying anything, but waiting with the whole being. It has an intensity. And Kierkegaard said, "When this listening happened, then for the first time prayer happened."

But listening is absolutely useless, and listening to the unknown? – you don't know where it is. Silence is useless, talking seems to be useful. Something can be done through talking, if you are doing many things in the world. And then you think if you are to become religious you will have to do something else, but you will have to *do*!

Chuang Tzu says: Religion begins only when you have understood the futility of all doing, then you have moved to the polar opposite of non-doing, inactivity, of becoming passive, of becoming useless.

Now we shall enter the sutra, *The Useless*.

Hui Tzu said to Chuang Tzu:
"All your teaching is centered on what has no use."

This teaching doesn't seem to be worth much, but Chuang Tzu and his master were always talking about the useless, they even praised men who were useless.

Chuang Tzu talks about a man, a hunchback. All the young people of the town were forcibly entered into the military, into the army, because they were useful. Only one man, a hunchback, who was useless, was left behind. Chuang Tzu said: "Be like the hunchback, so useless that you are not slaughtered in the war."

They go on praising the useless because they say that the useful will always be in difficulty. The world will use you, everybody is ready to use you, to manipulate you, to control you. If you are useless nobody will look at you, people will forget you, they will leave you in silence, they will not bother about you. They will simply become unaware that you are.

It happened to me. I am a useless man. In my childhood days I would be sitting and my mother would be standing just in front of me and she would look all around and say, "I cannot see anybody. I would like to send someone to fetch vegetables from the market." I would be sitting there just in front of her. She would say, "I can't see anyone here!" And I would laugh inside myself – she couldn't send me to the market, I was so useless that she was not aware that I was there.

Once, my aunt had come, and she was not aware of my uselessness. My mother was saying, "Nobody is in to go to the market. All the children have gone out and the servant is ill, so what to do? Someone has to be sent."

So my aunt said, "Why not send Rajneesh? He is sitting there, not doing anything."

So I was sent. I asked the vendor there, "Give me the best vegetables you have got, the best bananas, the best mangoes." Looking at me and the way I was talking he must have thought, "He is a fool," because nobody asks for the best. So he charged me double and gave me all the rotten things he had, and I came home very happy.

My mother threw them out and said, "Look! This is why I say nobody is here."

Chuang Tzu insists very much: Be alert and don't become very useful; otherwise people will exploit you. Then they will start managing you and then you will be in trouble. And if you can produce things, they will force you to produce all your life. If you can do a certain thing, if you are skillful, then you can't be wasted.

He says that uselessness has its own intrinsic utility. If you can be useful for others, then you have to live for others. Useless, nobody looks at you, nobody pays any attention to you, nobody is bothered by your being. You are left alone. In the marketplace you live as if you are living in the Himalayas. In that solitude you grow. Your whole energy moves inwards.

Hui Tzu said to Chuang Tzu:
"All your teaching is centered on what has no use."

Chuang replied:
"If you have no appreciation for what has no use
you cannot begin to talk about what can·be used."

He said that the useless is the other aspect of the useful. You can talk about the useful only because of the useless. It is a vital part. If you drop it completely, then nothing will be useful. Things are useful because there are things which are useless.

But this has happened to the world. We have cut out all playful activities thinking that then the whole energy will be moving towards work. But now work has become a bore. One has to move to the opposite pole – only then one is rejuvenated.

The whole day you are awake, at night you fall asleep – wasting time – and it is not a little time. If you live for ninety years, you will be asleep for thirty years, one-third, eight hours every day. What is the use of it?

Scientists in Russia have been thinking that this is wastage of labor, of energy. This is very uneconomical. So something should be done. Some chemical changes or some hormonal changes are needed, or even if something has to be changed in the very genes, in the very cell, we have to do it. We have to make a man who is aware, alert, awake for twenty-four hours.

Just think ... if they succeed, they will kill! Then they will make you an automaton, just a mechanical device, which goes on working and working, no day, no night, no rest, no work. There is no opposite to move to and forget.

And they have started many things. They have started sleep teaching for small children. Now, when the children are sleeping, thousands of children in Soviet Russia are sleeping with tape recorders plugged to their ears. While they are sleeping, the tape recorder is teaching them. The whole night the tape recorder is repeating something or other. They go on listening to it and it becomes part of their memory – sleep teaching, hypnopedia. And they say that sooner or later all that we do in schools can be done while the child is asleep, and then the day can be used in some other way.

Even sleep has to be exploited. You cannot be allowed to be yourself even in your sleep. You cannot even be allowed the freedom to dream. Then what are you? Then you become a cog in the wheel. Then you are just an efficient part of the wheel, of the mechanism. If you are efficient it is okay; otherwise you can be discarded, thrown in the junkyard, and somebody else who is more efficient will replace you.

What happens after the whole day's work? You fall asleep. What happens? You move from the useful to the useless. And that's why in the morning you feel so fresh, so alive, so unburdened. Your legs have a dancing quality, your mind can sing, your heart can again feel – all the dust of work is thrown off, the mirror is again clear. You have a clarity in the morning. How does it come? It comes through the useless.

That is why meditation can give you the greatest glimpses, because it is the most useless thing in the world. You simply don't do anything, you simply move into silence. It is greater than sleep because in sleep you are unconscious; so whatsoever happens, happens unconsciously. You may be moving in paradise, but you don't know it.

In meditation you move knowingly. Then you become aware of the path: how to move from the useful world of the without to the useless world within. And when you know the path, you can simply move inwards any moment. Sitting in a bus you are not needed to do anything, you are simply sitting; traveling in a car or train or an airplane, you are not doing anything, everything is being done by others; you can close the eyes and move into the useless, the inner. And suddenly everything becomes silent, and suddenly everything is cool, and suddenly you are at the source of all life.

But it has no value in the market. You cannot go and sell it, you cannot say, "I have great meditation. Is anybody ready to buy it?" Nobody will be ready to buy it. It is not a commodity, it is useless.

Chuang Tzu replied:
"If you have no appreciation for what has no use
you cannot begin to talk about what can be used.
The earth, for example, is broad and vast,
but of all this expanse a man uses only a few inches
upon which he happens to be standing at the time.

"Now suppose you suddenly take away
all that he is not actually using,
so that all around his feet a gulf yawns,
and he stands in the void
with nowhere solid except under each foot,
how long will he be able to use what he is using?"

This is a beautiful simile. He has got the point. You are sitting here, you are using only a small space, two by two. You are not using the whole earth, the whole earth is useless; you are using only a small portion, two by two. Says Chuang Tzu: Suppose the whole earth is taken away, only this two by two is left for you; you are standing with each foot using a few inches of earth. Suppose only that is left and the whole earth is taken away — how long will you be able to use this small part that you are using?

A gulf, an infinite abyss, yawns around you — you will get dizzy immediately, you will fall into the abyss. The useless earth supports the useful, and the useless is vast, the useful is very small. And this is true on all levels of being: the useless is vast, the useful is very small. If you try to save the useful and forget the useless, sooner or later you will get dizzy. And this has happened, you are already dizzy and falling into the abyss.

All over the world thinking people have a problem: that life has no meaning, life seems to be meaningless. Ask Sartre, Marcel, Jaspers, Heidegger – they say life is meaningless. Why has life become so meaningless? It was never so before. Buddha never said it; Krishna could dance, sing, enjoy himself; Mohammed could pray and thank God for the blessing of life that he showered upon him. Chuang Tzu is happy, as happy as possible, as happy as a man can be. They never said that life is meaningless. What has happened to the modern mind? Why does life seem so meaningless?

The whole earth has been taken away and you are left only on the part where you are sitting or standing. You are getting dizzy. All around you see the abyss and the danger; and you cannot use the earth on which you are standing now, because you could use it only when the useless was joined with it. The useless must be there. What does it mean? Your life has become only work and no play. The play is the useless, the vast; the work is the useful, the trivial, the small. You have made your life completely filled with work. Whenever you start doing something the first thing that comes to the mind is, what is the use? If there is some use, you do it.

Sartre has a character in one of his stories: in the coming twenty-first century, a very rich man says, "Love is not for me, it is only for poor people. As far as I am concerned my servants can do it."

Of course, why should a Ford go and waste time loving a woman? A cheap servant can do that. Ford's time is more valuable. He should put it to some greater use.

It is possible! Looking at the human mind as it is, it is possible that in the future only servants will make love. When you can depute a servant, why bother yourself? When everything is thought of in terms of economics, when a Ford, a Rockefeller can make so much use of their time, why should they go and waste their time with a woman? They can send a servant, that will be less trouble.

It looks absurd to us hearing this but this has already happened in many dimensions of life. You never play, your servants are doing that. You are never an active participant in any fun, others are doing it for you. You go to see a football match: others are doing it and you are just watching – you are a passive spectator, not involved. You go to a movie to see a film, and others are making love, war, violence – everything – you are just a spectator in the seat. It is so useless you need not bother to do it. Anybody else can do it, you can just watch.

Work you do, others are doing fun for you. Then why not love? – the same logic, somebody else will do it.

Life seems meaningless because the meaning consists of a balance of the useful and the useless. You have denied the useless completely. You have closed the door. Now only the useful is there. The useful has become a burden, you are burdened too much by it.

It is a sign of success that if by the age of forty you get ulcers, it shows that you are successful. If you have passed the age of forty or fifty and still the ulcers have not appeared, you are a failure. What have you been doing all your life? You must have been wasting time.

By fifty you really must have had the first heart attack. Now scientists have calculated that by forty a successful man must have ulcers, by fifty the first heart attack. By sixty he is gone – and he never lived. There was no time to live. He had so many more important things to do, no time to live.

Look all around, look at successful people; politicians, rich men, big industrialists – what is happening to them? Don't look at the things they possess, look at them directly, because if you look at the things you will be deceived. Things don't have ulcers, cars don't have heart attacks, houses are not hospitalized. Don't look at things, otherwise you will be deceived. Look at the person bereft of all his possessions, look directly at him and then you will feel the poverty. Then even a beggar may be a rich man. Then even a poor man may be richer as far as life is concerned.

Success fails, and nothing fails like success, because the man who succeeds is losing his grip on life – on everything. The man who succeeds is really bargaining, throwing away the real for the unreal, throwing away inner diamonds for colored pebbles on the shore; collecting the pebbles, losing the diamonds.

A rich man is a loser, a successful man is a failure. But because you look with the eyes of ambition you look at the possessions. You never look at the politician, you look at the post, the prime ministership. You look at the power. You never look at the person who is sitting there absolutely powerless, missing everything, not even a glimpse of what bliss is. He has purchased power, but in purchasing it he has lost himself. And it is all a bargain.

I have heard ...

After a mass rally, a leader was screaming at his manager. The manager couldn't understand it. The leader said, "I have been cheated!"

The manager said, "I cannot understand, the rally was so successful. So many thousands of people came, and look at your garlands. They have covered you with flowers."

"Count them," the leader said. "Only eleven and I paid for twelve."

In the end, every successful man will feel that he has been cheated. That has to happen, it is bound to happen, it is inevitable, because what are you giving, and what are you receiving? The inner self is being lost for futile possessions. You can deceive others, but how will you be able to deceive yourself? In the end you will look at your life and you will see that you have missed it because of the useful.

The useless must be there. The useful is like a garden, neat, clean; the useless is like a vast forest, natural, it cannot be so neat and clean. Nature has its own beauty, when everything is neat and clean, it is already dead. A garden cannot be very alive, because you go on pruning it, cutting it, managing it. A vast forest has a vitality, a very powerful soul. Go into a forest and you will feel the impact; get lost in a forest and then you will see the power of it. In a garden you cannot feel the power; it is not there, it is man-made. You can look at it – it is cultivated, it is managed, manipulated.

Really, a garden is a false thing – the real thing is the forest. The useless is like a vast forest and the useful is just like a garden you have created around your house. But don't go on cutting the forest. It is okay, your garden is okay, but let it be a part of the vast forest that is not your garden, but God's garden.

And can you think of anything more useless than God? Can you use him in any way? That is the trouble; that's why we cannot find any meaning in God. And those who are very meaning-oriented become atheists. They say there is no God, there cannot be. How can there be a God when God seems so useless? It is better to drop him, then the world is left for us to manage and control. Then we can make the whole world a market, we can change temples into hospitals, into primary schools. But the uselessness of God is the very basis of all the utility that goes on.

If you can play, your work will become pleasure. If you can enjoy simple fun, if you can become like children playing, your work will not be a burden on you. But it is difficult. Your mind keeps thinking in terms of money.

I have heard ...

Once Mulla Nasruddin came home and he found his best friend in bed with his wife. The friend was very embarrassed and became scared. He said, "Listen, I cannot do anything, I am in love with your wife and she is in love with me. And you being a rational man, we should come to some arrangement. It is no use fighting about it."

Nasruddin said, "What arrangement do you suggest?"

The man said, "We should play a game of cards, and let the wife be the stake. If I win, you simply leave; if you win, I will never see your wife again."

Nasruddin said, "Right, it's settled." But then he said, "Place some money, one rupee for each point, because otherwise the whole thing is so useless. Just for a wife the whole thing is so useless. Don't waste my time, place some money in the stake also."

Then the thing becomes useful. Money seems to be the only useful thing. All those who are utilitarians will be money-mad, because money can purchase. Money is the essence of all utility. So if Buddha and people like Buddha renounced, it was not because they were against money, it was because they were against utility, against the useful. So they said: "Keep all your money. I am moving into the forest. This garden is no more for me. I will move in the vast, in the uncharted, where one can be lost. This neat, clean pebbled path, everything known, mapped out, is not for me."

When you move into the vastness of uselessness your soul becomes vast. When you go into the sea with no map you become like the ocean. Then the very challenge of the unknown creates your soul.

When you are secure, when there is no problem, when everything is mathematically planned, settled, your soul shrinks. There is no challenge for it. The useless gives the challenge.

> *"Now suppose you suddenly take away*
> *all that he is not actually using,*
> *so that all around his feet a gulf yawns,*
> *and he stands in the void*
> *with nowhere solid except under each foot,*
> *how long will he be able to use what he is using?"*

Without God the world cannot continue any more. Nietzsche declared just a hundred years ago that God is dead. That very day he was also declaring that we cannot live anymore. He never thought about that, he thought just the contrary. He said: "God is dead and man is now free to live." But I say to you, if God is dead, man is dead already. The news may not have reached him yet, but he is dead – because God is that vast uselessness.

Man's world is the utilitarian world, the useful; without the useless the useful cannot exist. God is the play and man is the work; without God, work will become meaningless, a burden to be carried somehow. God is the fun, man is serious; without the fun the seriousness will be too much, it will be like a disease. Don't destroy the temples, don't destroy the mosques, don't transform them into hospitals. You can make other hospitals, you can create other buildings for schools, but let the useless remain there at the very center of life. That's why we have been placing the temple in the very marketplace, in the very center of the town, just to show that the useless must remain at the very center, otherwise all utility is lost. The opposite must be taken into account, and the opposite is greater.

What is the purpose of life? People go on coming and asking me. There is no purpose, there cannot be any. It is purposeless, fun. You have to enjoy it, you can only enjoy it, you cannot do anything else about it. It is not marketable. And if you miss a moment, you have missed; you cannot go back.

Religion is just a symbol. One man came to me and asked, "In India there are five hundred lakh sannyasins. This is very uneconomical. And what are these people doing? They live on others' labor. They should not be allowed to exist."

In Russia they are not allowed to exist, not a single sannyasin. The whole land has become like a prison. You are not allowed to be useless. In China they are killing Buddhist monks and *bhikkus*, they have killed thousands, and they are destroying all the monasteries. They are turning the whole country into a factory, as if man is just the stomach, as if man can live by bread alone.

But man also has a heart, and man has a being also which is not in any way purpose-oriented. Man wants to enjoy without cause and without reason. Man wants to be blissful, just for nothing.

That man asked, "When are you going to stop these sannyasins in India?" And he was very much against me. He said, "You are increasing the number of them. Stop it. What use are these sannyasins?"

And his question seems relevant. If he had gone somewhere else, if he had asked some other religious head, he would have been given the answer that they have a use. But he was very much disturbed when I said that they have no use.

But life itself is without use. What is the purpose of it? Where are you going? What is the result? No purpose, no result, no goal — life is a constant ecstasy, moment to moment. You can enjoy it but if you start thinking of results you miss enjoying it, your roots are uprooted, you are no longer in it, you have become an outsider. And then you will ask for the meaning, for the purpose.

Have you observed, whenever you are happy you never ask, "What is the purpose of happiness?" When you are in love, have you ever asked, "What is the purpose of all this?" When in the morning you see the sun rising and a flock of birds like an arrow in the sky, have you asked, "What is the purpose of it?" A flower blooming alone in the night, filling the whole night with its fragrance; have you asked, "What is the purpose of it?"

There is no purpose. Purpose is part of the mind, and life exists mindlessly; hence the insistence on the useless. Because if you are too much for the useful, you cannot drop the mind. How can you drop the mind if you are looking for some use, some result? You can drop the mind only when you have come to realize that there is no purpose and mind is not needed. You can put it aside. It is an unnecessary thing. Of course, when you go to the market, take it with you. When you sit in the shop, use it; it is a mechanical device, just like a computer.

Now scientists say that sooner or later we will supply each child with a computer which he can carry in his pocket. He need not carry much mathematics in his mind, he can just push the button and the computer will do it. Your mind is a natural computer. Why be burdened constantly by it? When it is not needed, put it aside. But you think it is needed because you have to do something useful. Who will tell you what is useful and what is useless? The mind is constantly sorting out: This is useful, do this; that is useless, don't do it. Mind is your manager. The mind represents use. Meditation represents the useless.

Move from the useful to the useless, and make this movement so spontaneous and natural that there is no struggle, no conflict. Make it as natural as moving in and out of your house. When the mind is needed, use it as a mechanical device; when it is not in use, when there is no use for it put it aside and forget it. Then be useless and do something useless and your life will be enriched, and your life will become a balance between use and no use. And that balance transcends both. That is transcendental – it is neither use nor non-use.

"How long will he be able to use what he is using?"

Hui Tzu said:
"It would cease to serve any purpose."

Chuang Tzu concluded:
"This shows
the absolute necessity
of what is supposed to have no use."

Even the useful cannot exist without the useless. The useless is the base. I say to you, your mind cannot exist without meditation, and if you try to do the impossible you will go mad. That is what is happening to many people. They go mad. What is madness? Madness is an effort to do without meditation, to live just with the mind, without any meditation. Meditation is the base, even the mind cannot exist without it. And if you try, then the mind goes mad, goes crazy. It is too much. It is unbearable. A madman is a man who is a perfect utilitarian. He has tried the impossible, he has tried to live without meditation, and that's why he goes mad.

Psychologists say that if you are not allowed to sleep for three weeks you will go mad. Why? Sleep is useless. Why will you go mad if you are not allowed to sleep for three weeks? A man can live without food for three months but a man cannot live without sleep for three weeks. And three weeks is the ultimate limit, it is not for you. You will go mad within three days if you are not allowed to sleep. If the useless is cut out you will go mad.

Madness is growing every day because meditation is not thought to be valuable. Do you think that whatsoever can be priced, only that is valuable? Whatsoever can be purchased and sold, only that is valuable? Whatsoever is a market commodity, only that is valuable? Then you are wrong. That which has no price is also valuable. That which cannot be sold and purchased is far more valuable than all that can be purchased and sold.

Love is the basis of sex. If you are deprived of love completely, sex becomes perverted. Meditation is the basis of mind. If you deny meditation, the mind goes mad. Fun, play, is the basis of work. If you deny fun and play, work becomes a burden, a dead weight.

Look at the useless sky. Your house may be useful but it exists in this vast sky of uselessness. If you can feel both, and if you become able to move from one to the other without any trouble, then for the first time the perfect human being is born in you.

The perfect human being does not know what is in and what is out — both are his. The perfect human being does not bother about what is useful and what is useless — both are his wings. The perfect human being uses no-use. The perfect human being flies in the sky with the wings of both mind and meditation, of matter and consciousness, of this world and that, of God, of no God. He is a higher harmony of the opposites.

Chuang Tzu emphasized no-use so much, uselessness so much, because you have emphasized the useful too much. Otherwise that emphasis is not needed. It is just to give you balance. You have gone too much to the left, you have to be pulled to the right.

Remember, because of this over-emphasis you can again move to the other extreme. And that happened to many followers of Chuang Tzu. They became addicted to the useless, they became mad with the useless. They moved too much towards the useless and that was not the point — they missed it.

Chuang Tzu emphasized this only because you have become so extremely addicted to use. That is why he emphasized the useless. But I must remind you — because mind can move to the opposite and remain the same — that the real thing is transcendence. You have to come to a point where you can use the useful and the non-useful, the purposeful and the purposeless. Then you are beyond both, they both serve you.

There are persons who cannot get rid of their mind and there are persons who cannot get rid of their meditation. And remember the disease is the same, you cannot get rid of something. First you were unable to get rid of the mind, somehow you managed. Now you cannot get rid of the meditation. Again you move from one prison to another.

A real, a perfect man, a man of Tao, has no addictions. He can move easily from one extreme to another because he remains in the middle. He uses both wings.

Chuang Tzu should not be misunderstood, that's why I say this. He can be misunderstood. People like Chuang Tzu are dangerous, you can misunderstand them. And there is more possibility for misunderstanding than understanding. The mind says, "Okay, so enough of this shop, enough of this family; now I will become a vagabond." That is misunderstanding. You will carry the same mind, you will become addicted to your vagabond-ness. Then you will not be able to come back to the shop, to the market, to the family. Then you will be afraid of it.

So meditation, like medicine, can become a new disease if you get addicted to it. So the doctor has to see that you get rid of the disease but don't become addicted to the medicine – otherwise he is not a good doctor. First you have to get rid of the disease, and then you have to get rid of the medicine, otherwise the medicine will take the place of the disease and you will always cling to it.

Mulla Nasruddin was teaching his small seven-year-old son how to approach a girl, how to invite her to dance, what to say and what not to say, how to persuade her.

After half an hour, the boy came in and said, "Now teach me how to get rid of her."

That has to be learned too, and that is the difficult part. To invite is very easy but to get rid of is very difficult. And you know well through your own experience: to invite a girl is always easy, to persuade a girl is always easy, but how to get rid of her? Then it becomes a problem. Then you cannot go anywhere, then you forget whistling completely.

Remember, the useless has its own attraction. If you are too troubled by the useful, you may move to the other extreme too much. You may lose your balance.

To me, a sannyasin is a deep balance, standing in the middle, free from all the opposites. He can use the useful and he can use the non-useful, he can use the purposeful and he can use the non-purposeful, and still remain beyond both. He is not used by them. He has become the master.

Enough for today.

Chapter 9

Means and Ends

The purpose of a fish trap is to catch fish,
And when the fish are caught,
The trap is forgotten.

The purpose of words
Is to convey ideas. '
When the ideas are grasped,
The words are forgotten.

Where can I find a man
Who has forgotten words?
He is the one
I would like to talk to.

It is difficult to forget words. They cling to the mind. It is difficult to throw away the net because not only are fish caught in it, the fisher is also caught. This is one of the greatest problems. Working with words is playing with fire, because words become so important that the meaning loses meaning. The symbol becomes so heavy that the content is completely lost; the surface hypnotizes you and you forget the center.

This has happened all over the world. Christ is the content, Christianity is just a word; Buddha is the content, the *Dhammapada* is just a word; Krishna is the content, the Gita is nothing but a trap. But the Gita is remembered and Krishna is forgotten – or if you remember Krishna, you remember him only because of the Gita. If you talk about Christ it is because of the churches, the theology, the Bible, the words. People carry the net for many lives without realizing that it is just a net, a trap, as if one goes on carrying a ladder.

Buddha used to say:

A few men were crossing a river. The river was dangerous, it was in flood – it must have been the rainy season – and the boat saved their lives. Then they thought – they must have been very, very intelligent – they thought, "This boat saved us, how can we leave it now? This is our savior and it will be ungrateful to leave it!" So they carried the boat on their heads into the town.

Somebody asked them, "What are you doing? We have never seen anybody carrying a boat."

They said, "Now we will have to carry this boat for our whole lives, because this boat saved us, and we cannot be ungrateful."

Those intelligent-looking people must have been stupid. Thank the boat but leave it there. Don't carry it. You have been carrying many types of boats in your head – maybe not on your head, but in your head. Look within. Ladders, boats, paths, words – this is the content of your head, of your mind.

The container becomes much too important, the vehicle becomes much too important, the body becomes much too important – and then you are blind. The vehicle was just to give you the message – receive the message and forget the vehicle. The messenger was just to give you the message – receive the message and forget the messenger. Thank him, but don't carry him in your head.

Mohammed insisted again and again, almost every day of his life, "I am just a messenger, a *paigamber*. Don't worship me, I have just carried a message from the divine. Don't look at me, look at the divine who has sent the message to you." But Mohammedans have forgotten the source. Mohammed has become important, the vehicle.

Says Chuang Tzu:

Where can I find a man
who has forgotten words?
He is the one
I would like to talk to.

A man who has forgotten words, he is worth talking to, because he has the innermost reality, the center of being within him. He has the message. His silence is pregnant. Your talking is impotent. What are you doing when you are talking? You are not saying anything in particular. You have got no message, nothing is to be delivered. Your words are empty, they don't contain anything, they don't carry anything. They are just symbols. And when you are talking you are simply throwing out your rubbish. It may be a good catharsis for you, but for the other, it can be dangerous. How can you talk with a person who is filled with words? Impossible. The words don't give space, the words don't give any opening. The words are too much, you cannot penetrate.

To talk with a man who is filled with words is almost impossible. He cannot listen, because for listening one should be silent, for listening one should be receptive. Words don't allow that – words are aggressive, they are never receptive. You can talk but you cannot listen, and if you cannot listen, your talk is the talk of a madman. You are talking and not knowing why, you are talking and not knowing what. You go on talking because it gives you a sort of release.

You feel good after having a good chitchat. You feel good because you are relieved; your talking is part of your tensions. It is not coming from you, it is just a disturbance; it is not a song, it has no beauty of its own. That's why whenever you talk you simply bore the other. But why is he listening? He is not listening, he is just waiting to bore you, waiting for just the right moment when he can take the reins in his hands.

I have heard ...

It happened once that a great leader, a great politician, was speaking, and he spoke and spoke and it was getting near midnight. By and by the audience left until only one person was left in the hall. The leader thanked him and said, "You seem to be the only authentic follower, the only lover. I feel grateful to you. Everybody has left, and you are still here."

The man said, "Don't be deceived, I am the next speaker."

When you listen, you are listening because you are the next speaker. You can tolerate the man – this is a bargain. If you want to bore others you have to allow them to bore you. So, really, when you say that a certain person is a bore, it's that person who will not give you any opportunity to be the next speaker. He goes on and on and you cannot find a gap from where to enter and start boring. That person looks like a bore, but every mind filled with words is a bore.

When will you realize this? Why is one bored? – because there are only words, no fish in them, only traps – useless, meaningless, there is no content. It is like a rattling of something, a noise; no meaning is carried. Whenever there is meaning it is beautiful; whenever there is meaning you grow through it; whenever there is meaning, when you encounter a man who has meaning, it gives you a new upsurge of energy. It is not a wastage, it is a learning, it is an experience. Rare and difficult it is to find a man who is silent.

If you can find a man who is silent and persuade him to talk to you, you will gain much – because when the mind is not filled with words, the heart speaks to the heart. When everything comes out of silence, when a word is born out of silence, it is beautiful, it is alive, it shares something with you. When a word comes only out of the crowd of words, it is mad, it can madden you.

A small boy of five was asked by his teacher, "Has your younger sister learned to talk yet?"

The boy said, "Yes, she has learned to talk – and now we are teaching her to be quiet."

This is the misery. You have to teach words, it is part of life, and then one has to learn how to be silent, how to be wordless. Universities, parents, teachers, they teach you words, and then you have to find a master who can teach you how to keep quiet.

One German scholar came to Ramana Maharshi and said, "I have come from very far away to learn something from you."

Ramana laughed and said, "Then you have come to the wrong place. Go to some university, go to some scholar, some great pundit; there you will be able to learn. If you come to me then be aware that learning is not possible here, we teach only unlearning. I can teach you how to unlearn, how to throw words away, to create space within you. And that space is divine, that space is godliness."

Where are you seeking — in words, in scriptures? Then one day or other you will become an atheist. A pundit, a scholar, cannot remain a theist for long. Remember, howsoever he knows, whatsoever he knows about the Bible and the Gita and the Koran, a scholar is bound to become an atheist some day or other, because that is the logical consequence of gathering words. Sooner or later he will ask: "Where is God?" No Bible can reply, no Gita can supply the answer. Rather, when Bibles and Gitas and Korans are too much on your mind, you miss the divine — because the whole space in you is filled with too much furniture. God cannot move, he may not be able to make any contact with you if the mind is too wordy. Then it is impossible to listen, and if you cannot listen, how can you pray? It is impossible to wait, words are too impatient, they are knocking from within to get out.

I have heard ...

Once it happened ... At three o'clock one morning Mulla Nasruddin phoned the bartender and said, "What time is the bar going to open?"

The bartender said, "This is no time to inquire such a thing. You are a regular customer, Nasruddin, and you know well that not before nine in the morning do we open. Go to sleep and wait until nine."

But after ten minutes he phoned again and he said, "This is urgent. Tell me when the bar is going to open."

Now the bartender felt annoyed. He said, "What are you doing? I told you, not a single minute before nine. And don't go on phoning me again and again."

But after ten minutes he phoned again. The bartender said, "Now you really are something. Have you gone mad? You will have to wait until nine."

Nasruddin said, "You don't understand. I am locked in the bar and I want to get out!"

If your mind is too burdened with words, theories, scriptures, they will go on knocking: "Give way, we want to get out!" And when you want to get out, God cannot enter. When the mind wants to get out, it is not open for anything that is incoming. It is closed, it is one-way traffic — two-way traffic is not possible.

When you are aggressive through words going out, nothing can penetrate you, neither love, nor meditation, nor existence. And all that is beautiful happens as an ingoing process. When you are silent, no words knocking within to get out, when you are waiting ... In that moment of waiting beauty happens, love happens, prayerfulness happens, godliness happens. But if a man is too addicted to words, he will miss it all. In the end he will have a long collection of words and theories, logic, everything – but nothing is worthwhile because the content is missing.

You have the net, the trap, but no fish are there. If you had really caught the fish you would have thrown away the net immediately. Who bothers? If you have really used the ladder, you forget it. Who thinks about it? You have transcended it, it has been used.

So whenever a man really comes to know, knowledge is forgotten. That's what we call wisdom. A wise man is one who has been able to unlearn the knowledge. He simply drops all that is nonessential.

Says Chuang Tzu:

Where can I find a man
who has forgotten words?
He is the one
I would like to talk to.

He is worth talking to. It may not be so easy to persuade him to talk, but just to be near him, just to sit by his side will be a communion, will be a communication, the deepest that is possible. Two hearts will melt into each other.

But why this addiction to words? – because the symbol appears to be the real. And if it is repeated again and again, through repetition you become autohypnotized. Repeat anything, and by and by you will forget that you don't know. The repetition will give you the feeling that you know.

If you go to the temple for the first time, you go in ignorance. It is hypothetical. You don't know whether this temple really contains anything, whether God is there or not. But go every day, again and again, and go on repeating the ritual, the prayers; and whatsoever the priest says, go on doing it day after day, year after year. You will forget the hypothetical state of mind that was there in the beginning. With continuous repetitions the thing goes into the mind and you start feeling that this is the temple, God lives here, this is the abode of God. Now you have moved into the world of appearance.

That's why every religion insists on teaching children as soon as possible, because once you miss childhood it is very difficult to convert people to foolish things, very difficult. Psychologists say that everybody should be caught before the age of seven. He should be converted to be a Hindu, a Mohammedan, a Christian or anything, a communist, theist or atheist, it doesn't make any difference – but catch hold, grab the child before seven. Up to the age of seven the child learns almost fifty percent of all he is going to learn in his whole life. Only fifty percent is left.

And this fifty percent is very meaningful because it becomes the base. He will learn many things, he will create a great structure of knowledge, but all that structure will be based on the knowledge that he received when he was a child. And at this time, before the age of seven, the child has no logic, no argumentativeness. He is trusting, exploring; he is believing. He cannot disbelieve, because he does not know what belief is, what disbelief is.

When the child is born, he has no mind to argue. He does not know what argument is. Whatsoever you say is true, appears true, and if you repeat it the child is hypnotized. That's how all the religions have exploited humanity. The child has to be forced to conform to a pattern, and once the pattern is deeply rooted, nothing can be done. Even if later on the child changes his religion, nothing much will change. Look at a Hindu who has become a Christian – nothing has changed. On the contrary, his Christianity will be just like Hinduism, because of the base.

It happened: there once existed a tribe of cannibals near the Amazon. By and by, they had killed themselves off and all but disappeared, until now only two hundred or so remained. They had killed and eaten each other. One missionary went there to work. The chief of the tribe spoke to him in perfect English. The missionary was surprised and said, "What! You speak perfect English; not only perfect English but with a perfect Oxford accent. And you are still a cannibal?"

The man said, "Yes, I have been to Oxford, and I have learned much. Yes, we are still cannibals, but now I use a knife and fork. I learned that at Oxford."

This much change happens – nothing much can happen. Convert a Hindu to Christianity and his Christianity will be just like Hinduism. Convert a Christian to Hinduism; he will remain a Christian deep down, because you cannot change the base. You cannot make him a child again, you cannot make him innocent. That moment is lost.

If this earth is ever going to be really religious then we will not teach Christianity, Hinduism, Mohammedanism, or Buddhism. That is one of the greatest crimes committed. We will teach prayerfulness, we will teach meditation, but not sects. We will not teach words and beliefs, we will teach a way of life, we will teach happiness, we will teach ecstasy.

We will teach how to look at the trees, how to dance with the trees, how to be more sensitive, how to be more alive and how to enjoy the blessings that existence has given – but not words, not beliefs, not philosophies, not theologies. No, we will not lead them to a church or to a temple or to a mosque, because these places are the sources of corruption. They have corrupted the mind. We will leave the children to nature; that is the temple, the real church.

We will teach children to look at the floating clouds, at the rising sun, at the moon at night. We will teach them how to love, and we will teach them not to create barriers to love, meditation, and prayerfulness. We will teach them to be open and vulnerable, we will not close their minds. And we will of course teach words but simultaneously we will also teach silence, because once words get into the base, silence becomes difficult.

You come to me, your problem is this: at the base there are words and now you are trying to meditate and be silent – and the base is always there. Whenever you are silent the base starts functioning. So you become aware of too much thinking when you meditate – even more than you feel ordinarily. Why? What is happening? When you are silent you go inwards and you become more sensitive to the inner nonsense that goes on and on. When you are not in meditation you are outward-going, extrovert; you are involved with the world and you cannot listen to the inner noise that goes on. Your mind is not there.

The noise is continuously there but you cannot hear it, you are occupied. But whenever you close your eyes and look within, the madhouse opens. You can see and feel and hear, and then you become afraid and scared. What is happening? And you were thinking that through meditation you would become more silent. And this is happening, just the opposite.

In the beginning it is bound to happen because a wrong base has been given to you. The whole society, your parents, your teachers, your universities, your culture, have given you a wrong base. You have already been corrupted, your source is poisoned. That is the problem – how to detoxify you. It takes time, and one of the most difficult things is to get rid of all that you have known, to unlearn.

Says Chuang Tzu:

Where can I find a man
who has forgotten words?
He is the one
I would like to talk to.

Only a sage is worth talking to. Only a sage is worth listening to. Only a sage is worth living with.

What is a sage? An empty boat – no words inside, the empty sky without the clouds; no sound, no noise, nobody mad, no chaos within, a continuous harmony, equilibrium, balance. He lives as if he is not. He is as if he is absent. He moves, but nothing moves within him. He talks, but the inner silence is there. It is never disturbed; he uses words, but those words are only vehicles – through those words he is sending you something which is beyond words. And if you catch and grab the words, you will miss.

When you listen to a sage, don't listen to his words; they are secondary, they are superficial, they are only peripheral. Listen to him, don't listen to his words. When the words reach you, just put them aside, as the traveler will do who has crossed the sea – he leaves the boat there and goes on. Leave the boat there and go on. If you carry the boat, you are mad. Then your whole life will become a burden, you will be burdened by the boat. A boat is not to be carried on the head. Feel grateful, that is okay, but carrying the boat on your head, this is too much.

How many boats are you carrying on your head? Your whole life has become static because of the weight. You cannot fly, you cannot float, because you are carrying such a dead burden, not only from one life, this life, but from many lives. You go on collecting all that is useless, futile. Why does this happen? There must be some deep reason, otherwise everybody would not be doing it.

Why does it happen? In the first place, you think the word is the reality – the word *God* is God, the word *love* is love – the word is the real. The word is *not* the real. You have to make a distinction, a clear-cut distinction, that the word is not the real. The word only symbolizes, indicates, but it is not the real. Once you get into this trap – believing that the word is the real – and somebody says "I love you," then you feel that he loves you because he says he loves you. Then you will be frustrated.

If you cannot see the wordless reality you will be frustrated in all your paths in life, everywhere you will be frustrated because you will take the word as the real.

Many people come to me and say, "This girl loved me, she said it herself." "This man loved me and now the love has disappeared." They are both deceived by words.

Dale Carnegie suggests that even if you have been married for twenty years, don't forget to use the same words you used when you were courting your wife – continue. Every morning say the same as you were doing when you were courting. Don't drop those words. Every day say, "Nobody exists like you. You are the most beautiful person, and I will die without you." Dale Carnegie says that even if you don't feel it, go on saying it, because words are realities. And the wife will be deceived and the husband will be deceived, because we live by words alone.

You don't know anything else, you don't know anything real. How can you be in contact with reality? When someone says, "I love you" – finished! When someone says, "I hate you" – finished! Put aside the words and look at the person.

When someone says, "I love you," don't get entangled with the words, put them aside. Look at the person, at his or her totality. Then nobody can deceive you. Love is such a fire you will be able to see it, you will be able to touch it, you will be able to know whether it is there or not.

Love cannot be hidden. If it is really there, words are not needed. When somebody really loves you, he will not say, "I love you." It is not needed. Love is enough unto itself, it needs no salesmanship. It doesn't need anybody to persuade, to convince; it is enough, it is a fire. Nothing is more fiery than love, it is a flame. When there is a flame in the dark, you need not say anything, it is there. No advertisement is needed, no propaganda is needed.

Try to separate words from reality. In your day-to-day life when someone says, "I hate you," don't believe in the words. This may be just a momentary thing, it may be just a phase. Don't go for the word, otherwise you will make an enemy for life. As you have made friends because of words so you have made enemies because of words. Don't go for the words, look into the person, look into the eyes, feel the whole – it may be just a momentary reaction. Ninety-nine times out of a hundred it will be just a momentary thing. He feels hurt by something, he reacts and says, "I hate you." Wait, don't decide, don't say, "This is an enemy." If you say that, you are not only deceived by others' words, you are also deceived by your own. If you say, "This is an enemy," now this word will cling. And even if he changes tomorrow, you will not be so ready or so willing to change, you will carry it within you. And then through your insistence you will create an enemy. Your enemies are false, your friends are false, because words are not reality.

Words can do only one thing: if you go on repeating them they give you the appearance of reality. Says Adolf Hitler in his autobiography, *Mein Kampf*: "I know only one difference between the truth and the lie – a lie repeated many times becomes true." And he knows by experience, he says that he did it – he continuously repeated lies, and he went on repeating them.

In the beginning they looked foolish. He started saying that it was because of the Jews that Germany had been defeated in the first world war. It was absolutely absurd, but he repeated it so many times that people became aware of the words, and became addicted to them.

It is said that once he was speaking at a meeting and he asked, "Who is responsible for the defeat of Germany?"

One man stood up and said, "The bicycle riders."

Hitler was surprised. He said, "What? Why?"

The man said, "Then why the Jews?" He was a Jew. "Why Jews?"

Even when Hitler was dying and again Germany had been defeated and completely destroyed, he didn't believe that it was because of Stalin, Churchill and Roosevelt. He didn't believe that he had been defeated because his enemies were superior, more powerful than him. His last verdict was still the same: that it was a Jewish conspiracy, that they were working behind the scenes, and because of them he had been defeated. And the whole of Germany believed him – one of the most intelligent peoples on the earth.

But intelligent people can be stupid because intelligent people always believe in words. That is the problem. The Germans, highly intelligent, scholarly people, have produced the greatest professors, philosophers; the whole country is intelligent. How could such a stupid man as Adolf Hitler persuade them?

But this is nothing illogical, this is the logic. A land of professors, intelligentsia, so-called intellectuals, is always word-addicted. If you go on repeating a word again and again and again, hammering and hammering, people listening again and again, they start feeling that this is true. Truth is created out of lies if you go on repeating them. Repetition is the method to convert a lie into a truth. But can you convert a lie into a truth? Just in appearance you can. Try it. Go on repeating something and you will start believing it. It may be that you are not as miserable as you look. Because you have been repeating, "I am in misery, I am in misery, I am in misery," and you have repeated it so often, now you look miserable.

Just look into your misery. Are you really miserable, really in such hell as you show by your face? Have a second thought. Immediately you will not feel so miserable because nobody can be as miserable as you look. It is impossible. God doesn't allow that. It is repetition, it is autohypnosis.

One French psychologist, Emile Coué, used to treat people. His method was simply repetition, suggestion, autohypnosis. You could go to him and say, "I have a headache, a constant headache, and no medicine helps. I have tried all the 'pathies,' even naturopathy; nothing helps."

He would say that there was no need for treatment because there was no headache. You have simply believed in it. And in going to this doctor and that, all have helped you to believe that yes, a headache is there – because if they don't believe in your headache they cannot live. So they cannot say that you don't have any headache. When you go to a doctor, even if you have nothing wrong he will find something. A doctor exists on it.

Talking with Coué would help you immediately, almost fifty percent of the headache would disappear just by talking to him – without any medicine. And he would feel the relaxation coming over your head and then he would know that talking would do the trick. Then he would give you a formula that you had to repeat continuously day and night, whenever you remembered – that there was no headache. Every morning when you got up you had to repeat: "I am getting better and better every day." Within two or three weeks the headache would disappear.

A real headache cannot disappear that way. In the first place the headache was created by words; in the first place, you hypnotized yourself that you had a headache, and then you dehypnotized yourself. A real illness cannot disappear. But your illnesses – ninety percent of them – are unreal. Through words you have created them. Coué helped thousands, Mesmer helped thousands, just by creating the feeling that you are not ill. That doesn't show that autohypnosis cures illness; it only shows that you are such great autohypnotists already that you *create* illnesses. You believe in them.

And doctors cannot say that your diseases are mental. You don't feel good if someone says that your disease is mental, you feel very bad, and you immediately change your doctor. Whenever a doctor says that you have a very great disease, very serious, you feel very good – because a man like you, so great, a somebody, he *must* have a big disease. Small diseases are for small people, ordinary diseases for ordinary people. When you have cancer, TB, or something dangerous, you feel superior, you are somebody. At least as far as illness is concerned you are not ordinary.

A man graduated from the college, became a doctor, and came home. His father was very tired of working and working – he was also a medical doctor – so he went on a holiday. He said, "I am going to the hills for at least three weeks rest, so now you start working."

After three weeks the father came back. The boy said "I have a surprise for you. The lady you have been treating for years and couldn't cure, I have cured her in three days."

The father beat him on the head and said, "You fool, that lady was paying for your education and I was hoping that through her all my children would get through college. Her stomachache was not real. And I was worried while in the hills. I forgot to tell you not to touch that woman. She is rich and she needs a stomachache, and I have been helping her. For years she has been the source of our livelihood."

Ninety percent of all diseases are psychological. They can be cured by mantra, they can be cured by suggestion, they can be cured by Satya Sai Baba, because in the first place you have already done the real miracle in creating them. Now anybody can cure them.

Continuously repeating a word creates the reality, but this reality is hallucinatory. It is illusion, and you cannot come to reality unless all words have disappeared from the mind. Even a single word may create illusion. Words are great forces. If even a single word is in the mind, your mind is not empty. Whatsoever you are seeing, feeling, is through the word, and that word will change the reality.

You have to be completely wordless, thoughtless. You have to be just consciousness.

When you are just consciousness then the boat is empty, reality is revealed to you. Because you are not repeating anything, nor are you imagining anything, you are not autohypnotizing yourself. Only then the real appears, is revealed.

Chuang Tzu is right. He says:

Where can I find the man
who has forgotten words?
He is the one
I would like to talk to.

The purpose of a fish trap is to catch fish …

You have forgotten the purpose completely. You have gathered so many fish traps, you are so constantly worried about them – that somebody might steal them, that they might get broken, or go rotten – so constantly worried about the traps, and completely forgotten the fish!

The purpose of a fish trap is to catch fish,
and when the fish are caught,
the trap is forgotten.

If you cannot forget the trap it means that the fish is not yet caught. Remember, if you are continuously obsessed with the trap, it shows that the fish are not yet caught. You have forgotten completely about them and become so entangled with the fish traps that you have fallen in love with them.

Once I knew a neighbor, he was a professor, a man of words. He purchased a car. Every morning he would work on it, cleaning it. It always remained in showroom condition, and he never took it on the road. For years I watched him in front of me. Every morning he would take much trouble, cleaning it, polishing it, doing everything. But the car remained there.

Once we were traveling in the same railway compartment, so I asked, "Is something wrong with the car? You never bring it out. It is always in your porch."

He said, "No, I have fallen in love with it. I love it so much that I am always afraid that if I take it out something may go wrong – some accident, some scratch, anything can go wrong. And it is unbearable even to think of it."

A car, a word, a trap, they are means not ends. You can fall in love with them and then you never use them.

I used to stay in a house. The lady of the house had three hundred sarees but she always used two — she was preserving the rest for some special occasion. When will that special occasion come? As far as I know, and I have known her for fifteen years, that special occasion has not come yet. It is not going to come, because she is becoming older every day; sooner or later she will die and those three hundred sarees will live on.

What happened? Fallen in love with sarees? You can fall in love with things. It is difficult to fall in love with persons, it is very easy to fall in love with things because things are dead, you can manipulate them. Sarees will never say, "Wear us! We would like to go out and have a look around." The car will never say, "Drive me, I am getting bored."

With people it is difficult. They will demand, they will ask, they would like to go out, they have their own desires to be fulfilled. When you fall in love with a person there is always conflict, so those who are clever never fall in love with persons, they always fall in love with things: a house, a car, clothes. They are always easy, manageable, and you always remain the master and the other never creates trouble. Or, if you fall in love with a person, you immediately try to convert him into a thing, a dead thing. A wife is a dead thing, a husband is a dead thing, and they torture each other. Why do they torture each other? What is the point of it? Through torture they make the other dead so the other becomes a thing, manipulatable. Then they are not worried.

Two matrons were looking at a bookshop display window. One said to the other, "Look, there is a book entitled *How to Torture Your Husband*."

But the other was not excited. She didn't even look at the book — she said, "I don't need it, I have a system of my own."

Everybody has his own system of torturing the other, because only through torture and destruction can a person be changed into a thing.

It happened once that Mulla Nasruddin walked into the coffee house looking very angry, very aggressive and dangerous, and he said, "I hear that someone has called my wife an ugly old hag. Who is this guy?"

One man stood up, a very tall, strong, giantlike man. He said, "I called your wife that, what about it?"

Looking at the person, Nasruddin immediately calmed down. The man was dangerous. He came near and said, "Thank you, this is my feeling too, but I couldn't gather the courage to say so. You have done it, you are a brave man."

What is happening in a relationship? Why does it always turn ugly? Why is it so impossible to love? Why does everything become poisoned? Because the mind is always happy to manipulate things, because things never rebel; they are always obedient, they never disobey. A person is alive, you cannot predict what he is going to do. And you cannot manipulate – the other's freedom becomes the problem.

Love is such a problem because you cannot allow the other the freedom to be. And remember this: if you really love, real love is possible only when you allow the other total freedom to be himself or herself. But then you cannot possess, then you cannot predict, then you cannot be secure, then everything has to move from moment to moment. And mind wants to plan, to be secure and safe.

Mind wants life to run on a track because mind is the most dead thing inside you. It is as if you are a river and part of the river is floating frozen ice. Your mind is just like the ice – the frozen part of you – and the mind wants to make you completely frozen, so there is no fear. Because whenever the new is there, there is fear – with the old there is no fear. Mind is always happy with the old.

That is why mind is always orthodox, never revolutionary. There has never been a mind which can be called revolutionary. Mind cannot be revolutionary. Buddha is revolutionary, Chuang Tzu is revolutionary – because they have no minds. Lenin is not revolutionary, Stalin absolutely not. They cannot be. With minds, how can you be revolutionary? Mind is always orthodox, mind is always conformist, because mind is the dead part in you. This has to be understood.

There are many dead parts in you, and the body has to throw them out. Your hairs are dead, that's why you can cut them easily and there is no pain. Your nails are dead, that is why you can cut them easily and there is no pain, no hurt. The body goes on throwing out. Consciousness also has to throw off many things, otherwise they will accumulate. Mind is the dead part like the hair. And this is symbolic: Buddha told his disciples to shave their heads just as a symbol. As you shave your hair completely, so shave the inner consciousness also, shave it completely of the mind.

Both are dead, don't carry them. It is beautiful. Don't allow the dead part to accumulate. What is mind? – your past, your experiences, your learning, all that has been. Mind is never present – how can it be? Here and now, mind cannot be.

If you simply look at me, where is the mind? If you simply sit here and listen to me, where is the mind? If you start arguing, the mind comes in; if you start judging, the mind comes in. But how do you judge? You bring the past to the present, the past becomes the judge of the present. How do you argue? You bring up the past as an argument, and when you bring up the past, the mind comes in.

Mind is the dead part of you, it is the excreta. And just as there are constipated people who suffer very much, so there is mind constipation, accumulated excreta. You never throw it out. Your mind thinks: only take in, never throw out.

Meditation is an unburdening, throwing the mind out. The excreta has not to be carried, otherwise you will become more and more dull. That's why a child has a fresh mind — because it has no accumulation. So sometimes children can say things that your philosophers cannot say. Sometimes they look and penetrate into realities that your man of knowledge misses. Children are very, very penetrating. They have a clarity, their look is fresh, their eyes are not filled. A sage is again a child. He has emptied his boat, he has emptied himself of all the cargo. The excreta has been thrown out, he is not constipated. His consciousness is a flow, it has no frozen parts.

The purpose of a fish trap is to catch fish,
and when the fish are caught,
the trap is forgotten.

The purpose of words
is to convey ideas.
When the ideas are grasped,
the words are forgotten.

If you really understand me, you will not be able to remember what I said. You will catch the fish but you will drop the trap. You will be what I said but you will not remember what I said. You will be transformed through it but you will not become a more learned man through it. You will be more empty through it, less filled; you will go away from me refreshed, not burdened.

Don't try to gather what I say because whatsoever you gather will be wrong. Gathering is wrong: don't accumulate, don't fill your treasure chest from my words. Words are excreta, they are of no worth. Throw them out, then the meaning will be there, and meaning has not to be remembered. It never becomes part of the memory, it becomes part of your wholeness. You have to remember a thing only when it is part of the memory, just of the intellect. You never need to remember a real thing that has happened to you. If it happens to you, it is there — what is the need to remember? Don't repeat, because repetition will give you a false notion.

Listen, but not to the words — just by the side of the words the wordless is being given to you. Don't be too focused on the words, just look a little sideways, because the real thing is being given there. Don't listen to what I say, listen to me! I am also here, not only the words. And once you listen to me, then all words will be forgotten.

It happened ... Buddha died, and the *bhikkus*, the disciples, were very disturbed because none of his sayings had been collected while he was alive.

They had completely forgotten. They did not think that he would die so soon, so suddenly. Disciples never think of that — that the master may disappear suddenly.

Suddenly one day Buddha said, "I am going." There was no time, and he had been speaking for forty years. When he was dead, how could his words be collected? A treasure would be lost, but what was there to do?

And it is beautiful that Mahakashyapa could not repeat anything. He said, "I heard him, but I don't remember what he said. I was so much in it, it never became part of my memory, I don't know." And he had become enlightened.

Sariputta, Moggalyan, all these who had become enlightened, shrugged their shoulders: "It is difficult, he has said so much, but we don't remember." And these were the disciples who had reached.

Then Ananda was approached. He had not become enlightened while Buddha was alive; he became enlightened after Buddha died. He had remembered everything. He was with Buddha continuously for forty years, and he dictated everything word by word — a man who was not enlightened! It looks paradoxical. Those who had reached should have remembered, not this man who had not yet reached the other shore. But when the other shore is reached, this shore is forgotten, and when one has oneself become a buddha, who cares to remember what Buddha said?

The purpose of a fish trap is to catch fish,
and when the fish are caught,
the trap is forgotten.

The words of the Buddha were traps, Mahakashyapa caught the fish. Who bothers about the trap now? Who bothers where the boat has gone? He has crossed the stream. Mahakashyapa said, "I don't know what this fellow said. And you cannot rely on me, because with me it is difficult to separate what he said and what I say."

Of course it will be so. When Mahakashyapa has become a buddha himself, how can they be separate? The two are not two. But Ananda said, "I will relate his words," and he related very authentically. Humanity is in great debt to this fellow Ananda, who was still ignorant. He had not caught the fish so he remembered the trap. He was still thinking to catch the fish so he had to carry the trap.

The purpose of words
is to convey ideas.
When the ideas are grasped,
the words are forgotten.

Remember this as a basic law of life – that the useless, the meaningless, the peripheral, looks so significant because you are not aware of the center. This world looks so significant because you are not aware of God. When the God is known, the world is forgotten. And it is never otherwise.

People have tried to forget the world so that they can know God – it has never happened and it will never happen. You can go on trying and trying to forget the world, but you cannot. Your every effort to forget will become a continuous remembering. Only when God is known is the world forgotten. You can go on struggling to drop thinking, but you cannot drop thinking unless consciousness is achieved. Thinking is a substitute – how can you drop the trap when the fish is not yet caught? The mind will say, "Don't be foolish. Where is the fish?"

How can you drop the words when you have not realized the meaning? Don't try to fight with the words, try to reach the meaning. Don't try to fight with thoughts. That's why I insist again and again that if thoughts disturb you, don't create any struggle with them, don't wrestle with them. If they come, let them come. If they go, let them go. Don't do anything, just be indifferent, just be a watcher, an onlooker, not concerned. That's all that you can do right now – be unconcerned.

Don't say, "Don't come." Don't invite, don't reject, don't condemn and don't appreciate. Simply remain indifferent. Look at them, they come as clouds, and then they go, as clouds disappear. Let them come and go, don't get in their way, don't pay attention to them. Because if you are against them, you start paying attention to them, and then immediately you are disturbed: "My meditation is lost." Nothing is lost. Meditation is your intrinsic nature. Nothing is lost. Is the sky lost when clouds come? Nothing is lost.

Be indifferent, don't be bothered by thoughts, this way or that. And sooner or later you will feel and you will realize that their coming and going has become slower. Sooner or later you will come to see that now they come, but not so much; sometimes the traffic stops, the road is vacant. One thought has passed, another has not come yet; there is an interval. In that interval you will know your inner sky in its absolute glory. But if a thought enters, let it enter; don't get disturbed.

If you can do this much, and only this much can be done; nothing else is possible. Be inattentive, indifferent, not caring. Just remain a witness, watching, not interfering, and the mind will go, because nothing can be retained inside if you are indifferent.

Indifference is cutting the roots, the very roots. Don't feel antagonistic because that is again feeding. If you have to remember friends, you have to remember enemies also, even more so. Friends you can forget, how can you forget enemies? You have to constantly remember them because you are afraid.

People are disturbed by thoughts, ordinary people. Religious people are disturbed more because they are constantly fighting. But through fighting you pay attention – and attention is food. Everything grows if you pay attention, grows fast, becomes more vital. You just be indifferent.

Buddha used the word *upeksha*; it means absolute indifference, neither this nor that – just in the middle – neither friendly nor inimical, neither for nor against, just in the middle, looking as if you are not concerned, as if these thoughts don't belong to you, as if they are part of the great world. Let them be there. Then one day suddenly, when the indifference is total, the consciousness shifts from the periphery to the center.

But it cannot be predicted and cannot be planned; one has to go on working and waiting. Whenever it happens, you can laugh. Those thoughts were there because you wanted them to be there, those thoughts were there because you were feeding them constantly, and those thoughts were there because the fish was not yet caught. How could you throw away the trap? You had to carry it.

I remember:

Once it happened in Mulla Nasruddin's country that the king was in search of a wise man. His old wise man had died and had said as he was dying, "When you replace me, find the most humble man in the kingdom, because ego is anti-wisdom. Humbleness is wisdom, so find the most humble man."

Secret agents were sent all over the kingdom to spy and seek out the most humble man. They reached Nasruddin's village. He had heard that the old man had died, so he thought about what he should suggest as an indication of a wise man. He had read, he knew the ancient lore that the humblest is the most wise. So he logically inferred, concluded, that the old man must have said to find the humblest man. So he became the humblest man.

The king's men came in search. Mulla Nasruddin was very rich, but when they saw him, the richest man in the town, he was carrying a fishing net, coming from the river, as if from the humblest job in the town. So they thought, "This man seems to be very humble," and they asked Nasruddin, "Why do you carry this fishing net? You are so rich, you need not go on fishing."

Nasruddin said, "I became so rich through fishing. I started my life as a fisherman. I have become rich, but just to pay respect to the original profession that gave me so much, I always carry this fish net on my shoulder." A really humble man …

Otherwise if a poor man becomes rich he starts cleaning his whole past, so that nobody knows that he was ever a poor man. He will drop all contacts which show that once he was a poor man. He doesn't want to see his relatives, he doesn't want to be reminded of the past. He simply drops the past completely.

He creates a new past as if he is a born aristocrat. But this man was humble. So they informed the king that Mulla Nasruddin was the humblest man they had ever seen and he was appointed as the wise man.

The day he was appointed, he threw away the net. The men who had recommended him asked, "Nasruddin, where is your net now?"

He said, "When the fish is caught, the net is thrown away."

But you cannot throw it away before – it is impossible, you have to carry it. But carry it indifferently. Don't get attached, don't fall in love with it, because one day it has to be thrown away. If you fall in love with it then you may never catch the fish, just afraid that if you catch the fish you will have to throw away the net.

Don't fall in love with the mind. It has to be used and it is there because you don't know the no-mind yet, you don't know the innermost core of your being. The periphery is there and you have to carry it but carry it indifferently. Don't become a victim of it.

One story:

It happened ... A man used to go to the race course every year on his birthday. The whole year he accumulated the money just for one stake on his birthday. And he was losing and losing for many years, but hope always revived him, again and again. Every time he decided not to go again, but one year is so far away. For a few days he would remember and then again hope returned: "Who knows? This year I may become rich, and why not one effort more?"

By the time his birthday came he was again ready to go to the race course. And it was his fiftieth birthday, so he thought, "I should try wholeheartedly."

So he sold all his possessions, gathered a small fortune, all that he had earned in his whole life, all that he had, and he said, "Now I have to decide this way or that. Either I am to become a beggar or an emperor; no more in the middle, enough!"

He went there, to the window, he looked at the names of the horses: "There is a horse, Adolph Hitler. It will do well. Such a great man, such a victorious man, he threatened the whole world. This horse must be ferocious and strong." So he staked all, and he lost – as all those who stake on Hitler will lose. Now he had nowhere to go, even his house was lost. So what to do? There was nothing to do but commit suicide.

So he went to a cliff, just to jump and finish it. When he was just about to jump he suddenly heard a voice, he couldn't recognize it, whether it came from the outside or from the inside. He heard, "Stop! Next time I will give you the name of the winning horse – one more try. Don't kill yourself."

Hope revived, he came back. He worked hard that year, because it was going to be the victory for which he had been waiting his whole life. The dream had to be fulfilled. He worked hard day and night, he earned much. Then with a trembling heart he reached the window and waited. The voice said, "Okay, choose this horse, Churchill." Without any argument, without thinking about it, without his mind coming in, he staked all and won. Churchill came first.

He went back to the window, and waited. The voice said, "Now back Stalin." He staked all. Stalin came in first. Now he had a big treasure.

The third time he waited, and the voice said, "No more."

But he said, "Keep quiet, I am winning, my stars are high and nobody can defeat me now." So he chose Nixon and Nixon came last.

The whole treasure was lost, he was again a beggar. Standing there, he muttered to himself, "Now what to do?"

Said the inner voice, "Now you can go to the cliff and jump!"

In moments when you are going to die, the mind stops because there is nothing for it to work on. The mind is part of life, it is not part of death. When there is no life ahead, mind stops; there is no work, it is unemployed immediately. And when mind stops, the inner voice comes in. It is always there, but there is so much noise that a still small voice cannot be heard.

The voice had not come from beyond, there is nobody beyond, everything is within. God is not in the skies, it is in you. He was going to die – the last decision taken by the mind. But then the mind retired, there was no more work, and suddenly he heard the voice. This voice came from his innermost core, and the voice that comes from the innermost core is always right.

Then what happened? Twice the voice worked, but then the mind entered again and the mind said, "Don't listen to such nonsense, the stars are high and we are winning."

Remember this: whenever you win, you win because of the inner voice. But the mind always comes in and takes charge. Whenever you feel happiness it is always from the inner. Then mind immediately jumps in and takes control and says, "It is because of me." When you are in love, it is like death, you feel blissful. Immediately mind comes in and says, "Okay, this is me, this is because of me."

Whenever you meditate, there are glimpses. Then the mind comes in and says, "Be happy! Look, I have done it." And immediately the contact is lost.

Remember this: with mind you will always be a loser. Even if you are victorious, your victories will be just defeats. With mind there is no victory, with no-mind there is no defeat.

You have to shift your whole consciousness from mind to no-mind. Once no-mind is there, everything is victorious. Once the no-mind is there, nothing goes wrong, nothing *can* go wrong. With no-mind everything is absolutely as it should be. One is content, not a single fragment of discontent remains, one is absolutely at home. You are an outsider because of the mind.

This shift is possible only if you become indifferent; otherwise this shift will never be possible. Even if you have glimpses, those glimpses will be lost. You have had glimpses before – it is not only in prayer and meditation that glimpses happen. Glimpses happen in ordinary life too. Making love to a woman, the mind stops. That is why sex is so appealing; it is a natural ecstasy. For a single moment suddenly mind is not there, you feel blissful and content – but only for a single moment. Immediately the mind comes in and starts – how to get more, how to stay longer? Planning, control, manipulation comes in, and you have missed.

Sometimes, without any reason or rhyme, you are walking down the street under the trees and suddenly a sunray comes and falls on you, a breeze touches your face. Suddenly it is as if the whole world has changed, for a single moment you are ecstatic. What was happening? You were walking, unworried, not going somewhere, just having a walk, a morning or evening walk. In that relaxed moment, suddenly, without your knowing, consciousness shifted from mind to no-mind. Immediately there is beautitude. But the mind comes in and says, "I must get more and more moments like this." Then you can stand there for years, for lives, but it will never happen again – because of the mind.

In ordinary life, in day-to-day life, not only in temples, in shops and offices also, the moments come – the consciousness shifts from the periphery to the center. But the mind controls again immediately. Mind is the great controller. You may be the master but he is the manager, and the manager has absorbed so much control and power that the manager thinks he is the master. And the master is completely forgotten.

Be indifferent to mind. Whenever moments come which are wordless, silent, if the mind comes in, don't help and don't cooperate with it. Just look. Let it say whatsoever it says, don't pay much attention. It will withdraw.

In meditation, it is happening to you every day. Many come to me and say, "It happened on the first day but since then it has not been happening."

Why did it happen on the first day? You are more prepared now, on the first day you were not so prepared. Why did it happen on the first day? It happened on the first day because the manager was unaware of what was going to happen. It couldn't plan. The next day the manager knows well what is to be done: breathing fast, then crying and screaming, then Hoo, Hoo! Now the manager knows, and the manager does it. Then it will not happen, the manager has taken charge.

Remember this: whenever a blissful moment happens, don't ask for it again. Don't ask for it to be repeated, because all repetition is of mind. Don't ask for it again. If you ask, then the mind will say, "I know the trick. I will do it for you."

When it happens, feel happy and grateful and forget. The fish is caught, forget the trap. The meaning is caught, forget the word.

And the last thing: whenever meditation is complete, you will forget meditation. And only then, when you forget meditation, has it come to fulfillment, the climax has been reached. Now you are meditative for twenty-four hours a day. It is nothing to be done; it is there, it is you, it is your being.

If you can do this, then meditation becomes a continuous flow, not an effort on your part – because all effort is of the mind.

If meditation becomes your natural life, your spontaneous life, your Tao, then I tell you, some day Chuang Tzu will catch hold of you. Because he asks:

Where can I find a man
who has forgotten words?
He is the one
I would like to talk to.

He is searching. I have seen him here many times wandering around you, just waiting, waiting. If you forget the words he will talk to you. And not only Chuang Tzu – Krishna, Christ, Lao Tzu, Buddha, they are all in search of you; all the enlightened people are in search of the ignorant. But they cannot talk because they know a language which is of silence, and you know a language which is of madness. That cannot lead anywhere. They are in search. All the buddhas that have ever existed are in search. Whenever you are silent you will feel that they have always been all around you.

It is said that whenever the disciple is ready the master appears. Whenever you are ready the truth will be delivered to you. There is not even a single moment's gap. Whenever you are ready, it happens immediately. There is no time gap.

Remember Chuang Tzu. Any moment he may start talking to you, but before he starts talking, your talking must go.

Enough for today.

Chapter 10

Wholeness

"How does the true man of Tao
Walk through walls without obstruction,
Stand in fire without being burnt?"

Not because of cunning or daring;
Not because he has learned,
But because he has unlearned.

His nature sinks to its root in the One.
His vitality, his power
Hide in secret Tao.

When he is all one,
There is no flaw in him
By which a wedge can enter.
So a drunken man, falling out of a wagon,
Is bruised but not destroyed.
His bones are like the bones of other men,
But his fall is different.
His spirit is entire.
He is not aware of getting into a wagon
Or falling out of one.

Life and death are nothing to him.
He knows no alarm, he meets obstacles
Without thought, without care,
Takes them without knowing they are there.

If there is such security in wine,
How much more in Tao.
The wise man is hidden in Tao.
Nothing can touch him.

This is one of the most basic and secret teachings. Ordinarily we live through cunningness, cleverness and strategy; we don't live like small children, innocent. We plan, we protect, we make all the safeguards possible – but what is the result? Ultimately, what happens? All the safeguards are broken, all cunningness proves foolishness – ultimately death takes us away.

Tao says that your cunningness will not help you, because what is your cunningness but a fight against the whole? With whom are you cunning – with nature, with Tao, with existence? Whom do you think you are deceiving – the source from where you are born and the source to which you will finally go? The wave is trying to deceive the ocean, the leaf trying to deceive the tree, a cloud trying to deceive the sky? Whom do you think you are trying to deceive? With whom are you playing?

Once it is understood, a man becomes innocent, drops his cunningness, all his strategies, and simply accepts. There is no other way than to accept nature as it is and flow with it. Then there is no resistance, then he is just like a child who is going with his father, in deep trust.

It happened once ... Mulla Nasruddin's son came home and said that to a boy he believed to be his friend he had given his toy to play with. Now he was not returning it. "What should I do?" he asked.

Mulla Nasruddin looked at him and said, "Go up this ladder." The boy trusted his father so he did so. When he was ten feet high, Nasruddin said, "Now jump into my arms."

The boy hesitated a little, and said, "If I fall, I will get hurt."

Nasruddin said, "I am here, you need not worry. Take a jump." The boy jumped, and Nasruddin stood aside. The boy fell down, and started crying and weeping.

Then Nasruddin said, "Now you know. Never believe anybody, not even anything your father says, not even your father, don't believe anybody. Otherwise you will be deceived all your life."

This is what every father, every parent, every school, every teacher, is teaching you. This is your learning. Don't believe in anybody, don't trust, otherwise you will be deceived. You become cunning. In the name of cleverness you become cunning, untrusting. And once a man is untrusting he has lost contact with the source.

Then your whole life is wasted; you fight an impossible fight in which defeat is bound to happen. Trust is the only bridge and it is better to realize it sooner, because at the moment of death everybody realizes that it has been a defeat. But then nothing can be done.

Real intelligence is not cunningness, it is totally different. Real intelligence is to look into things. And whenever you look into things deeply, you will come to know that you are just a wave, that this whole is the ocean and there is no need to worry. The whole has produced you, it will take care of you. You have come out of the whole, it is no enemy to you. You need not worry, you need not plan. And when you are not worried, not planning, for the first time life starts. For the first time you feel free of worries and life happens to you.

This intelligence is religion. This intelligence gives you more trust, and finally, total trust. This intelligence leads you to the ultimate nature, acceptance – what Buddha called *tathata*. Buddha said: Whatsoever happens, happens. Nothing else can happen, nothing else is possible. Don't ask for it to be otherwise; be in a let-go, and allow the whole to function. And when you allow the whole to function and you are not a barrier, a resistance, then you cannot be defeated.

In Japan, through Buddha, Lao Tzu and Chuang Tzu, they have developed a particular art they call *zendo*. *Zendo* means the Zen of the sword, the art of the warrior – and nobody knows it like they do. The way they have developed it is supreme. It takes years, even a whole lifetime, to learn *zendo* because the learning consists of acceptance. You cannot accept in ordinary life – how can you accept when a warrior is standing before you to kill you? How can you accept when the sword is raised against you and every moment, any moment, death is near?

The art of *zendo* says that if you can accept the sword, the enemy, the one who is going to kill you, and there is no distrust; if even the enemy is the friend, and you are not afraid, you are not trembling, then you become a pillar of energy, unbreakable. The sword will break on you, but you cannot be broken. There will not even be any possibility that you could be destroyed.

It happened ... Once there was a great *zendo* master, he was eighty, and traditionally, the disciple who could defeat him would succeed him. So all the disciples hoped that someday he would accept their challenge, and now he was getting old.

There was one disciple who was the cleverest, a strategist, very powerful, but not a master of zendo, just skilled in the art. He was a good warrior, knowing everything about swordsmanship, but he was not yet a pillar of energy. He was still afraid while fighting. The *tathata* had not yet happened to him.

He went to the master again and again saying, "Now the time has come, and you are getting old. You may become too old to challenge, even dead. So I challenge you. Accept my challenge, Master, and give me a chance to show what I have learned from you." The master laughed and avoided him.

The disciple started thinking that the master had become so weak and old that he was afraid, just trying to evade the challenge. So one night he insisted and insisted and said, "I will not leave until you accept my challenge for tomorrow morning. You have to accept, I challenge you." He became angry, "You are getting old and soon there will be no chance for me to show what I have learned from you. This has been the tradition always."

The master said, "If you insist, your very insistence shows that you are not ready or prepared. There's too much excitement, your ego is challenging. You have not yet become capable; but if you insist, okay. Do one thing. Go to the nearby monastery; there is a monk there, he was my disciple ten years ago. He became so efficient in *zendo* that he threw away his sword and became a sannyasin. He was my rightful successor. He never challenged me, and he was the only one who could have challenged and even defeated me. So first go and challenge that monk. If you can defeat him, then come to me. If you cannot defeat him, then just drop the idea."

The disciple immediately started out for the monastery. By the morning he was there. He challenged the monk. He couldn't believe that this monk could be a *zendo* master – lean and thin, continuously meditating, eating only once a day. The monk listened and laughed, and he said, "You have come to give me a challenge? Even your master cannot challenge me, even he's afraid."

Listening to this, the disciple got completely mad! He said, "This is insulting, I will not listen! Stand up immediately! Here is a sword I have brought for you knowing well that you are a monk and you may not have one. Come out in the garden."

The monk looked absolutely undisturbed. He said, "You are just a child, you are not a warrior. You will be killed immediately. Why are you asking for death unnecessarily?"

This made him still more angry, and then they both went out. The monk said, "I will not need the sword, because a real master never needs it. I am not going to attack you, I am only going to give you a chance to attack me so your sword is broken. You are no match for me. You are a child, and people will laugh at me if I take up the sword against you."

It was too much! The young man jumped up – but then he saw that the monk was standing. Up until now the monk had been sitting; now he stood up, closed his eyes, and started swaying from side to side, left to right – and suddenly the young man saw that the monk had disappeared. There was only a pillar of energy – the face was no longer there, just a solid pillar of energy, swaying. He became afraid and started retreating, and the pillar of energy started moving towards him, swaying. He threw away his sword and screamed, "Save me!"

The monk sat down again and started laughing. His face came back, the energy disappeared, and he said, "I told you before: even your master is no match for me. Go and tell him."

Perspiring, trembling, nervous, the disciple went back to his master and said, "How grateful I am for your compassion towards me. I am no match for you. Even that monk destroyed me completely. But one thing I couldn't tolerate, why I got involved in it. He said, 'Even your master is no match for me.'"

The master started laughing and said, "So that rascal played the trick on you too? You got angry? Then he could see through you, because anger is a hole in the being. And that has become his basic trick. Whenever I send somebody to him, he starts talking against me, and my disciples of course become angry. When they are angry, he finds out that they have loopholes, and when you have holes you cannot fight."

Whenever you are angry, your being has leakages. Whenever you desire, your being has holes in it. Whenever you are jealous, filled with hatred, sexuality, you are not a pillar of energy. Hence buddhas have been teaching us to be desireless, because whenever you are desireless energy does not move outwards, energy moves within. It becomes an inner circle, it becomes an electric field, a bioelectric field. When that field is there, without any leakage, you are a pillar; you cannot be defeated. But you are not thinking of victory, remember, because if you are thinking of victory you cannot be a pillar of energy. Then that desire becomes a leakage.

You are weak – not because others are strong – you are weak because you are filled with so many desires. You are defeated, not because others are more cunning and clever – you are defeated because you have so many leakages.

Tathata – acceptance, total acceptance, means no desire. Desire arises out of non-acceptance. You cannot accept a certain situation, so desire arises. You live in a hut and you cannot accept it; this is too much for the ego, you want a palace. You are a poor man, but not because you live in a hut, no. Emperors have lived in huts. Buddha lived under a tree, and he was not a poor man. You could not find a richer man anywhere.

No, your hut doesn't make you poor. The moment you desire the palace you are a poor man. And you are not poor because others are living in palaces, you are poor because the desire to live in the palace creates a comparison with the hut. You become envious. You are poor.

Whenever there is discontent, there is poverty; whenever there is no discontent, you are rich. And you have such riches that no thief can steal them; you have such riches, no government can take them by taxation; you have riches which cannot be taken away from you in any way. You have a fort of a being, unbreakable, impenetrable.

Once a desire moves and your energy starts falling you become weak through desire, you become weak through longing. Whenever you are not longing and are content, whenever nothing is moving, when your whole being is still, then you are an impenetrable fort, says Chuang Tzu. Fire cannot burn you, death is impossible – that's the meaning. Fire cannot burn you; death is impossible, you cannot die. You have the secret key to eternal life.

And sometimes this happens in ordinary circumstances too. A house is on fire – everybody dies but a small child survives. There is an accident – the old people die and the small children survive. People say that this is a miracle, God's grace. No, it is nothing of the sort, it is because the child accepted that situation too. Those who were cunning started running and trying to save themselves; they got themselves into trouble. The child rested. He was not even aware that something was happening, that he was going to die. The child is saved through his innocence.

It happens every day. Go and watch near a bar, a wine shop at night, drunkards are falling down in the street, lying in the drain, absolutely happy. In the morning they will get up. They may be bruised a little but no harm has happened to their bodies. Their bones are intact. They have got no fractures.

You try to fall like a drunkard on the street – immediately you will have fractures. And he falls like this every day, every night, many times, but nothing happens to him. What is the matter, what is the secret? When he is drunk there is no desire. He is absolutely at ease, here and now. When he is drunk he is not afraid, there is no fear, and when there is no fear, there is no cunningness.

Cunningness comes out of fear. So the more fearful a person, the more cunningness you will find in him. A brave man is not cunning, he can depend on his bravery, but a man who is afraid, who is a coward, can depend only on cunningness. The more inferior a person, the more cunning – the more superior a person, the more innocent. Cunningness is a substitute. When one is drunk, absolutely drunk, future disappears and past disappears.

I have heard ...

Once it happened ... Mulla Nasruddin was walking with his wife, absolutely drunk. She had found him lying in the street and was bringing him home. Of course, she was arguing, and winning all the arguments, because she was alone. Mulla Nasruddin was not there; he was simply coming along with her.

Then suddenly she saw a mad bull approaching. There was no time to alert Nasruddin, so she jumped into a bush. The bull came up and spun Nasruddin almost fifty feet in the air. He fell into a ditch, and as he crawled out of it he looked at his wife and said, "If you do this to me again, I shall really lose my temper. This is too much!"

Ordinary wine gives so much power when one is drunk, what about Tao, the absolute drunkenness? What about Krishna or Buddha, the greatest drunkards – so drunk with the divine that not even a trace of the ego is left? You cannot hurt them because they are not there, you cannot insult them because there is no one who will resist the insult and create a wound. Your insult will pass through them, as if passing through an empty house. Their boats are empty. A breeze comes in and passes with no barrier. When the breeze has gone the house is not even aware that the breeze has been there.

The appeal of wine is really because you are so egoistic. You are too burdened by it and sometimes you want to forget it. The world will have to follow alcohol or Tao – these are the alternatives. Only a religious man, a really religious man, can be beyond alcohol, marijuana, LSD – any type of drug. Only a religious man can be beyond them; otherwise how can you be beyond them? The ego is too much, the burden is so much, it is constantly on your head. You *have* to forget yourselves.

But if wine can do so much, you cannot conceive of what the divine wine can do. What is the wine doing? For certain moments, through chemical changes in the brain, in the body, you forget yourself. But this is momentary. Deep down you are there, and after a few hours the chemical effect is gone, your body has thrown the wine out and the ego asserts itself again.

But there is a wine, I tell you – God is that wine, Tao, or whatsoever name you like to call it. Once you taste it, the ego is gone forever. Nobody ever comes back from that drunkenness.

That's why Sufis always talk of wine, Sufis always talk of women. Their woman is not the woman you know – God is the woman. And their wine is not the wine that you know – God is the wine. Omar Khayyam has been misunderstood, tremendously misunderstood; because of Fitzgerald he has been misunderstood all over the world. Omar Khayyam's *Rubaiyat* appears to be written as if in praise of wine and women, not at all. Omar Khayyam is a Sufi, a mystic. He talks of the wine which comes through Tao; he talks of this wine in which you are lost forever and forever. This intoxicant, this divine intoxicant, is not temporary, it is non-temporal, it is not momentary – it is eternal.

Sufis talk of God as the woman. Then the embrace is eternal, it is ultimate; then there is no separation. If you can understand this then you are intelligent, but not through your strategies, cunningness, arithmetic, your logic.

If you can, look deep into existence. From where have you come? Where are you going? With whom are you fighting, and why? These same moments that you are losing in fighting can become ecstatic.

Now look at the sutra: *Wholeness.*

You think of yourself as the individual. You are wrong. Only the whole exists. This is false, this appearance, that I think I am. This is the most false thing in the world. And because of this *I am*, fight arises. If I am, then this whole seems inimical; then everything seems to be against me.

It is not that anything is against you – it cannot be! These trees have helped you, this sky has helped, this water has helped, this earth has created you. Then nature is your mother. How can the mother be against you? You have come out of her. But you think of *I* as an individual, and then the fight arises. It is one-sided. You start the fight, and nature goes on laughing, existence goes on enjoying. Even in a small child, the moment he starts feeling *I*, the fight arises.

In a supermarket, a small child was insisting on a toy. The mother said positively, "No, I am not going to purchase it. You have got enough."

The child got angry and said, "Mum, I have never seen a meaner girl than you, you are the meanest."

The mother looked at the child, at his face, the anger, and she said, "Just wait, you will certainly meet a really mean girl. Just wait!"

In one house, the mother was insisting that the child do his homework. He was not listening and went on playing with his toys, so she said, "Are you listening to me or not?"

The child looked up and said, "Who do you think I am – Daddy?"

Only a small child, and the fighting starts – the ego has arisen. He knows Daddy can be silenced, but not him. The moment the child feels he is separate the natural unity is broken, and then his whole life becomes a struggle and a fight.

Western psychology insists that the ego should be strengthened. That is the difference between the Eastern attitude and the Western. Western psychology insists that the ego should be strengthened; the child must have a strong ego, he must fight, struggle; only then will he be mature.

The child is in the mother's womb, one with the mother, not even aware that he is – he is, but without any consciousness. In a deeper sense all consciousness is illness. Not that he is unconscious – he *is* aware. His being is there, but without any *self*-consciousness. The *am* is there, but the *I* has not been born yet. The child feels, lives, is fully alive, but never feels that he is separate. The mother and the child are one.

Then the child is born. The first separation happens, and the first cry. Now he is moving, the wave is moving away from the ocean. Western psychologists say: we will train the child to be independent, to be individual. Jung's psychology is known as the way of individuation. He must become an individual, absolutely separate. He must fight. That's why, in the West, there is so much rebellion in the new generation. This rebellion was not created by the new, younger generation; this rebellion was created by Freud, Jung, Adler and company. They have provided the basis.

Fight will give you a stronger ego. It will shape you. So fight the mother, fight the father, fight the teacher, fight the society. Life is a struggle. And Darwin started the whole trend when he said only the fittest survive; the survival of the fittest. The stronger you are in your ego, the more likely you will survive.

The West lives through politics, the East has a totally different attitude — and Tao is the core, the very essence of the Eastern consciousness. It says: No individuality, no ego, no fight; become one with the mother; there is no enemy, the question is not of conquering.

Even a man, a very knowledgeable man, a very penetrating, logical man like Bertrand Russell, thinks in terms of conquest — conquering nature, the conquest of nature. Science seems to be a struggle, a fight with nature: how to break the lock, how to open the secrets, how to grab the secrets from nature.

Eastern consciousness is totally different. Eastern consciousness says: Ego is the problem, don't make it stronger, don't create any fight. And not the fittest but the humblest survive.

That's why I insist again and again that Jesus is from the East; that's why he could not be understood in the West. The West has misunderstood him. The East could have understood him because the East knows Lao Tzu, Chuang Tzu, Buddha, and Jesus belongs to them. He says: "Those who are last will be the first in my kingdom of God." The humblest, the meekest, will possess the kingdom of God. Poor in spirit is the goal. Who is poor in spirit? The empty boat, he who is not at all — no claim on anything, no possession of anything, no self. He lives as an absence.

Nature gives her secrets. There is no need to grab, there is no need to kill, there is no need to break the lock. Love nature, and nature gives you her secrets. Love is the key. Conquering is absurd.

So what has happened in the West? This conquering has destroyed the whole of nature. Now there is a cry for ecology, how to balance. We have destroyed nature completely, because we have broken all the locks and we have destroyed the whole balance. And now through that imbalance humanity will die sooner or later.

Chuang Tzu can be understood now, because he says: Don't fight with nature. Be in such deep love, become so one that through love, from heart to heart, the secret is given. And the secret is that you are not the individual, you are the whole. Why be satisfied with just being a part? Why not be the whole? Why not possess the whole universe? Why possess small things?

Ramateertha used to say, "When I close my eyes I see stars moving within me, the sun rising within me, the moon rising within me. I see oceans and skies. I am the vast, I am the whole universe."

When he went to the West for the first time and started saying these things, people thought he had gone crazy. Somebody asked him, "Who created the world?"

He said, "I, it is within me."

This *I* is not the ego, not the individual; this *I* is the universe, existence.

He looks crazy. This claim looks too much. But look in his eyes: there is no ego. He is not asserting anything, he is simply stating a fact.

You are the world. Why be a part, a tiny part, and why unnecessarily create trouble when you can be the whole?

This sutra is concerned with wholeness. Don't be the individual, be the whole. Don't be the ego. When you can become the divine, why be satisfied with such a small, tiny, ugly thing?

How does the true man of Tao
walk through walls without obstruction
and stand in fire without being burned?

Somebody asked Chuang Tzu, "We have heard that a man of Tao can walk through walls without obstruction. Why?" If you don't have any obstruction within you, no obstruction can obstruct you. This is the rule. If you have no resistance within you, in your heart, the whole world is open for you. There is no resistance. The world is just a reflection, it is a big mirror; if you have resistance, then the whole world has resistance.

It happened once ... A king built a palace, a palace made of millions of mirrors – all the walls were covered with mirrors. A dog entered the palace and he saw millions of dogs all around. So, being a very intelligent dog, he started barking to protect himself from the millions of dogs all around him. His life was in danger. He must have become tense, he started barking. And when he started barking, those millions of dogs started barking too.

In the morning the dog was found dead. There he was, alone, there were only mirrors. Nobody was fighting with him, nobody was there to fight, but he looked at himself in the mirror and became afraid. And when he started fighting, the mirror reflection also started fighting. He was alone, with millions and millions of dogs around. Can you imagine the hell he lived through that night?

You are living in that hell right now; millions and millions of dogs are barking around you. In every mirror, in every relationship, you see the enemy. A man of Tao can walk through walls because he has no wall in his heart. A man of Tao finds the enemy nowhere because he is not the enemy inside. A man of Tao finds all mirrors vacant, all boats empty, because his own boat is empty. He is mirrored, he has no face of his own, so how can you mirror, how can you reflect a man of Tao? All mirrors remain silent. A man of Tao passes – no footprints are left behind, no trace. All mirrors remain silent. Nothing reflects him, because he is not there, he is absent.

When the ego disappears you are absent, and then you are whole. When the ego is there you are present, and you are just a tiny part, a very tiny part, and very ugly at that. The part will always be ugly. That's why we have to try to make it beautiful in so many ways. But a man with ego cannot be beautiful. Beauty happens only to those who are without egos. Then the beauty has something of the unknown in it, something immeasurable.

Remember this: ugliness can be measured. It has limits. Beauty, the so-called beauty, can be measured. It has limits. But the real beauty cannot be measured – it has no limits. It is mysterious – it goes on and on and on. You cannot be finished with a buddha. You can enter him, and you will never come out. Endless! His beauty is never finished.

But the ego goes on trying to be beautiful. Somehow you remember the beauty of the whole; somehow you remember the silence of the womb; somehow deep down you know the bliss of being one, in unison, the unity with existence. Because of that, many desires arise. You know the beauty of being a god and you have to live like a beggar. So what do you do? You create faces, you paint yourself. But deep down the ugliness remains, because all paints are just paints.

It happened once ... A woman was walking on the seashore. She found a bottle, opened the bottle and a genie came out. And, just like all good genies the genie said, "You have broken my prison, you have set me free. So now you can ask anything, and I will fulfill your fondest desire or wish."

Genies are not found every day, on every shore, in every bottle. It rarely happens, and only in stories. But the woman didn't think even for a single moment. She said, "I want to become a beautiful person – hair like Elizabeth Taylor, eyes like Brigitte Bardot, body like Sophia Loren."

The genie looked again, and said, "Honey, put me back in the bottle!"

And this is what you are asking for – everybody is asking for this – that's why genies have disappeared from the world. They are so afraid of you, you are asking the impossible. It cannot happen because the part can never be beautiful.

Just think: my hand can be cut off – can that hand be beautiful? It will grow more and more ugly, it will deteriorate, it will start smelling. How can my hand be beautiful, separate from me? The separation brings death; unison brings life. In the whole you are alive; alone and separate, you are already dead or dying.

Take my eyes out, then what are they? Even stones, colored stones, will be more beautiful than they because they are still with the whole. Pluck a flower; then it is not beautiful, the glory is gone. It was beautiful just a moment ago when it was joined with the roots, with the earth. Uprooted, you float like egos. You are ill, and you will remain ill, and nothing can be of any help. All your efforts, however clever, are going to fail.

Only in the whole are you beautiful. Only in the whole are you lovely. Only in the whole is grace possible.

It is not because of cunningness that the man of Tao walks through walls without obstruction, and stands in fire without being burned.

Not because of cunning or daring,
and not because he has learned –
but because he has unlearned.

Learning goes into the ego; learning strengthens the ego. That's why pundits, brahmins, scholars, have the subtlest egos. Learning gives them scope, learning gives them space. They become tumors, egos. Their whole being is then exploited by the ego.

The more learned a man, the more difficult he is to live with, the more difficult to relate to him, the more difficult for him to reach the temple. It is almost impossible for him to know God because he himself now lives like a tumor, and the tumor has its own life – now it is the ego tumor. And it exploits. The more you know, the less is the possibility for prayerfulness to happen.

So Chuang Tzu says it is not because of cunning, he is not calculating, he is not cunning or daring, because daring, cunning, calculating, are all part of the ego. A man of Tao is neither a coward nor a brave man. He does not know what bravery is, what cowardice is. He lives. He is not self-conscious, not because he has learned but because he has unlearned. The whole of religion is a process of unlearning. Learning is the process of the ego, unlearning is the process of the non-ego. Learned, your boat is full, filled with yourself.

It happened ... Mulla Nasruddin used to have a ferryboat, and when times were not good he would carry passengers from one bank to the other.

One day a great scholar, a grammarian, a pundit, was crossing to the other shore in his ferryboat. The pundit, the scholar, asked Nasruddin, "Do you know the Koran? Have you learned the scriptures?"

Nasruddin said, "No, no time."

The scholar said, "Half your life has been wasted."

Then suddenly there arose a storm and the small boat was caught on the waves, any moment they could be drowned. Asked Nasruddin, "Schoolmaster, do you know how to swim?"

The man was very afraid, perspiring. He said, "No."

Said Nasruddin, "Then your whole life has been wasted. I am going!"

Now, this boat cannot go to the other shore. But people think learning can become a boat, or learning can become a substitute for swimming. No! Can scriptures become boats? No, they are too heavy. You can drown with them but you cannot cross the river. Unlearning will make you weightless; unlearning will make you innocent again.

When you don't know, in that not knowing what happens? The most beautiful phenomenon, the greatest ecstasy happens when you don't know — there is a silence when you don't know. Somebody asks a question and you don't know. Life is a riddle, and you don't know. Everywhere is mystery and you are standing there not knowing, wondering. When you don't know there is wonder, and wonder is the most religious quality. The deepest religious quality is wonder. Only a child can wonder. A man who knows cannot wonder, and without wonder no one has ever reached the divine. It is the wondering heart to which everything is a mystery — a butterfly is a mystery, a seed sprouting is a mystery.

And remember, nothing has been solved; all your science has done nothing. The seed sprouting is still a mystery and it is going to remain a mystery. Even if science can create the seed, the sprouting will remain a mystery. A child is born; it is a mystery that is born. Even if the child can be produced in a test-tube, it makes no difference. The mystery remains the same.

You are here. It is such a mystery. You have not earned it, you cannot say to the universe, "I am here because I have earned it." It is a sheer gift, you are here for no reason at all. If you were not here, what difference would it make? If you were not here, to what court could you appeal?

This sheer existence, this breathing that goes in and out, this moment that you are here, listening to me, to the breeze, to the birds, this moment that you are alive, is such a mystery. If you can face it without any knowledge you will enter into it. If you face it with knowledge and you say, "I know, I know the answer," the doors are closed — not because of the mystery, the doors are closed because of your knowledge, your theories, your philosophy, your theology, your Christianity, your Hinduism — they close the door.

A man who thinks he knows does not know. The Upanishads go on saying that a man who thinks that he does not know, knows. Says Socrates: When a man really knows, he knows only one thing, that he does not know. Chuang Tzu says it is because he has unlearned. Whatsoever the world taught him, whatsoever society taught him, whatsoever the parents and the utilitarians taught him, he has dropped. He has again become a child, a small child. His eyes are again filled with wonder. He looks all around and everywhere is mystery.

Ego kills the mystery. Whether it is the ego of a scientist or whether it is the ego of a scholar or of a philosopher, makes no difference. The ego says, "I know," and the ego says, "If I don't know now, then sooner or later I will come to know." The ego says that there is nothing unknowable.

There are two aspects for the ego: the known and the unknown. The known is that part which the ego has already traveled, and the unknown is that part which the ego will travel. It is possible to travel, there is nothing unknowable.

The ego leaves no mystery in the world. And when there is no mystery around you, there cannot be any mystery within. When mystery disappears, all songs disappear; when mystery disappears, poetry is dead; when mystery disappears, God is not in the temple, then there is only a dead statue. When mystery disappears there is no possibility for love, because only two mysteries fall in love with each other. If you know, then there is no possibility for love – knowledge is against love. And love is always for unlearning. But because he has unlearned:

His nature sinks to its root in the one.
His vitality, his power,
hide in secret Tao.

His nature sinks to its root ... The ego exists in the head, remember, and you carry your head very high. The root is just at the other pole of your being.

Chuang Tzu and Lao Tzu used to say: Concentrate on the toe. Close your eyes and move into the toe and remain there. That will give you a balance. The head has given you much imbalance. The toe ... ? It looks like they are joking. They mean it, they are not joking. They are right. Move from the head, it is not the root, but we are in the head too much.

His nature sinks to its root, to the very source. The wave goes deeper into the ocean, into the one. And remember, the source is one. The waves may be many millions, but the ocean is one. You are separate there, I am separate here, but just look a little deeper, to the roots, and we are one; we are like branches of the same tree. Look at the branches and they are separate, but deep down they are one.

The deeper you go, you will find less and less multiplicity, more and more unity. At the deepest it is one. That's why Hindus talk of the non-dual, the one, *advait.*

His vitality, his power,
hide in secret Tao.

And whatsoever vitality comes to the man of Tao is not manipulated, is not created by him, it is given by the roots. He is vital because he is rooted; he is vital because he has rejoined the ocean, the one. He is back at the source, he has come to the mother.

When he is all one,
there is no flaw in him
by which a wedge can enter.

And whenever one is rooted in the deepest core of one's being, which is one, then there is no flaw. You cannot penetrate such a man. Swords cannot go into him, fire cannot burn him. How can you destroy the ultimate? You can destroy the momentary, how can you destroy the ultimate? You can destroy the wave, how can you destroy the ocean? You can destroy the individual, but you cannot destroy the soul. The form can be killed, but the formless ... ? How will you kill the formless? Where will you find the sword that can kill the formless?

Krishna said in the Gita, "*Nainam chhedanti sashtrani* – no sword can kill it, no fire can burn it." Not that if you go and kill Chuang Tzu you will not be able to kill him. You will be able to kill the form, but the form is not Chuang Tzu – and he will laugh.

It happened ... Alexander was coming back from India when suddenly he remembered Aristotle, his teacher, one of the greatest logicians.

Aristotle is the original source of all Western stupidity, he is the father. He created the logical mind. He created analysis, he created the method of dissection, he created the ego and the individual, and he was the teacher of Alexander.

He had told Alexander to bring a Hindu mystic, a sannyasin, when he came back, because polar opposites are always interesting. He must have been deeply interested – what is this Hindu mystic? What type of man lives beyond logic, who says there is only one not two, who joins all the contradictions and paradoxes, whose whole attitude is of synthesis, not of analysis? He never believes in the part, he always believes in the whole, what type of man can he be?

So he told Alexander, "When you come back, bring with you a Hindu mystic, a sannyasin. I would like to see one. A man who lives beyond mind and says that there is something beyond mind, is a rare phenomenon." Aristotle never believed that there could be anything beyond mind; for him mind was all.

When Alexander was returning, he suddenly remembered. So he asked his soldiers to go and find a great Hindu mystic, a great sannyasin, a saint, a sage. They inquired in the town. They said, "Yes, just by the side of the river stands a naked man. For years he has been standing there, and we think he is a mystic. We cannot be certain because he never speaks much, and we cannot be certain because we don't understand him much. Whatsoever he says seems to be very illogical. Maybe it is true, maybe it is not true."

Alexander said, "This is the right man. My master, who has created logic, would like to see this illogical man. Go and tell him that Alexander invites him."

The soldiers went and they told this naked man that Alexander the Great invites him; he would be a royal guest, every comfort and convenience would be given to him, so he shouldn't worry.

The man started laughing and said, "The man who calls himself the Great is a fool. Go and tell him I don't keep company with fools. That's why I have been standing here alone for many years. If I want to keep company with fools, do you think that India has less than his country? The town is full of them."

They were very disturbed, those soldiers, but they had to report. Alexander asked what the man had said – Dandami was the name of this man. Alexander has used the name Dandamas in his reports. Alexander felt annoyed, but this was the last village at the border, they would be moving out of India. So he said, "It is best that I go and see what type of man this is."

He may have remembered Diogenes – maybe he was the same type, standing naked near a river. The same thing happened with Diogenes. He also laughed and thought Alexander a fool.

So he came with a naked sword and said, "Follow me, or I will cut your head off immediately. I don't believe in discussion, I believe in orders."

The man laughed and said, "Cut it off – don't wait! The head that you will be cutting off, I have cut it off long ago. This is nothing new, I am already headless. Cut it off, and I tell you, that when the head falls down onto the earth you will see it fall and I will also see it fall, because I am not the head."

The man of Tao can be burned, but still the man of Tao cannot be burned. The form is always on fire. It is burning already. But the formless is never touched by any fire. From where does this power come, from where does this vitality come? They hide in secret Tao. Tao means the great nature, Tao means the great ocean, Tao means the great source.

So a drunken man who falls out of a wagon
is bruised, but not destroyed.
His bones are like the bones of other men,
but his fall is different.

The ego is not there, his spirit is entire.

He is not aware of getting into a wagon,
or falling out of one.

Life and death are nothing to him.
He knows no alarm, he meets obstacles
without thought, without care,
and takes them without knowing they are there.

If there is such security in wine,
how much more in Tao?
The wise man is hidden in Tao,
nothing can touch him.

Watch a drunkard, because the man of Tao is in many ways similar to him. He walks, but there is no walker; that's why he looks unbalanced, wobbling. He walks, but there is no direction, he is not going anywhere. He walks, but the boat is empty, only momentarily, but it is empty.

Watch a drunkard. Follow him and see what is happening to him. If somebody hits him he is not annoyed. If he falls down he accepts the falling, he doesn't resist, he falls down as if dead. If people laugh and joke about him he is not worried. He may even joke with them, he may start laughing with them, he may start laughing at himself. What has happened? Momentarily, through chemicals, his ego is not there.

The ego is a construction; you can also drop it through chemicals. It is a construction; it is not a reality, it is not substantial in you. It is through society that you have learned it. Alcohol simply drops you out of society. That's why society is always against alcohol, the government is always against alcohol, the university is always against alcohol, all the moralists are always against alcohol – because alcohol is dangerous, it gives you a glimpse of the outside of society. That is why there is so much propaganda against drugs in America and in Western countries.

The governments, the politicians, the church, the pope, they have all become scared because the new generation is too much into drugs. They are very dangerous for society, because once you have glimpses beyond society you can never become a really adjusted part of it. You will always remain an outsider. Once you have a glimpse of the non-ego then society cannot dominate you very easily. And if one goes too much into drugs then it is possible that the ego may be shattered completely. Then you will just become mad.

Once or twice a drug will give you a glimpse, just as if a window opens and closes. If you persist and you become addicted to it, the ego may suddenly drop. And this is the problem: the ego will drop, but the non-ego will not arise. You will go mad, schizophrenic, split.

Religion works from the other corner, from the other end; it tries to bring up the non-ego first. And the more the non-ego comes up, the more the whole asserts, the more the ego will drop automatically, by and by. Before the ego drops, the whole has taken possession. You will not go mad, you will not become abnormal, you will simply be natural. You will fall outside society into nature.

Through drugs you can also fall out of society, but into madness. That's why the religions are also against drugs. Society has given you a working arrangement for the ego. Through it you manage somehow, you steer your life somehow. But if the whole takes possession then there is no problem – you become a man of Tao. Then there is no need for this ego, you can throw it to the dogs.

But you can do otherwise also. You can simply destroy this ego through chemicals. This can be done. Then there will be problems, you will simply become abnormal. You will feel certain power, but that power will be false, because the whole has not taken possession of you.

Many people, many cases have been reported. One girl in New York, under LSD, just jumped out of a window on the thirtieth floor because she thought she could fly. And when you are under a drug, if the thought comes that you can fly, there is no doubt. You believe in it totally, because the doubter, the ego, is not there. Who is there to doubt? You believe it. But the whole has not asserted itself.

Chuang Tzu might have flown. Chuang Tzu might have gone out of the window like a bird on the wing, but under LSD you cannot. The ego is not there so you cannot doubt, but the whole has not taken possession so you are not powerful. The power is not there, only the illusion of power. That creates trouble.

You can do certain things under alcohol. Once it happened in a circus: a cage was broken. The circus was traveling in a special train from one town to another; a cage was broken and a lion escaped. So the manager collected all his strong men and said, "Before you go into the night, into the jungle to find the lion, I will give you some wine. It will give you courage."

All twenty of them took big shots. The night was cold and dangerous and courage was needed – but Mulla Nasruddin refused. He said, "I will only take soda."

The manager said, "But you will need courage!"

Nasruddin said, "In such moments I don't need courage. These moments are dangerous – night time and the lion, and courage can be dangerous. I would rather be a coward and alert."

When you don't have power and a drug can give you courage, it is dangerous. You can move madly on a certain path – this is the danger of drugs.

But society is not afraid because of this; society is afraid that if you have a glimpse beyond society then you will never be adjusted to it. And society is such a madhouse – to be adjusted to it you must not be allowed any glimpse outside.

Religions are also against drugs for a different reason. They say: Be a drunkard, a drunkard of the divine wine, because then you are rooted, centered. Then you are powerful.

If there is such security in wine,
how much more in Tao?
The wise man is hidden in Tao,
nothing can touch him.

Absolutely nothing can touch him. Why? If you follow me rightly, only the ego can be touched. It is very touchy. If somebody just looks at you in a certain way, it is touched. He has not done anything. If somebody smiles a little, it is touched; if somebody just turns his head and does not look at you, it is touched. It is very touchy. It is like a wound, always green, fresh. You touch it and the pain arises. A single word, a single gesture – the other may not even be aware of what he has done to you, but he has touched it.

And you always think the other is responsible, that he has wounded you. No, you carry a wound. With the ego your whole being is a wound. And you carry it around. Nobody is interested in hurting you, nobody is positively waiting to hurt you; everybody is engaged in safeguarding his own wound. Who has got the energy? But still it happens, because you are so ready to be wounded, so ready, just on the brink, just waiting for anything.

You cannot touch a man of Tao. Why? – because there is no one to be touched. There is no wound. He's healthy, healed, whole. This word *whole* is beautiful. The word *heal* also comes from *whole*, and the word holy also. He is whole, healed, *holy*.

Be aware of your wound. Don't help it to grow, let it be healed; and it will be healed only when you move to the roots. The less in the head, the more the wound will heal – no head, no wound. Live a headless life. Move as a total being, and accept things. Just for twenty-four hours, try it – total acceptance, whatsoever happens. Somebody insults you, accept it, don't react, and see what happens. Suddenly you will feel an energy flowing in you that you have not felt before. Somebody insults you: you feel weak, you feel disturbed, you start thinking of how to get your revenge. That man has hooked you, and now you will move round and round. For days, nights, months, even years you will not be able to sleep or dream. People can waste their whole life over a small thing, just because someone insulted them.

Just look back into your past and you will remember a few things. You were a small child and the teacher in the class called you an idiot, and you still remember it and you feel resentment. Your father said something. They have forgotten, and even if you remind them, they will not be able to remember it. Your mother looked at you in a certain way and since then the wound has been there. And it is still fresh; if anybody touches it, you will explode. Don't help this wound to grow. Don't make this wound your soul. Go to the roots, be with the whole. Try it for twenty-four hours, just twenty-four hours, try not to react, not to reject, whatsoever happens.

If someone pushes you and you fall to the ground – fall! Then get up and go home. Don't do anything about it. If somebody hits you, bow down your head, accept it with gratitude. Go home, don't do anything, just for twenty-four hours, and you will know a new upsurge of energy that you have never known before, a new vitality arising from the roots. And once you know it, once you have tasted it, your life will be different. Then you will laugh at all the foolish things you have been doing, at all the resentments, reactions, revenge, with which you have been destroying yourself.

Nobody else can destroy you except you; nobody else can save you except you. You are the Judas and you are the Jesus.

Enough for today.

Chapter 11

Chuang Tzu's Funeral

When Chuang Tzu was about to die, his disciples began planning a
splendid funeral.

But he said:
"I shall have heaven and earth for my coffin;
The sun and moon will be the jade symbols
Hanging by my side;
Planets and constellations
Will shine as jewels all around me,
And all beings will be present
As mourners at the wake.
What more is needed?
Everything is amply taken care of!"

But they said:
"We fear that the crows and kites
Will eat our Master."

"Well," said Chuang Tzu, "above ground I shall be eaten
by crows and kites, below it by ants and worms.
In either case I shall be eaten. Why are you so partial to birds?"

Mind makes everything a problem; otherwise life is simple, death is simple, there is no problem at all. But mind gives the deception that every moment is a problem and has to be solved. Once you take the first step of believing that everything is a problem, then nothing can be solved because the first step is absolutely wrong.

Mind cannot give you any solution, it is the mechanism which gives you problems. Even if you think you have solved a problem, thousands of new problems will arise out of the solution. This is what philosophy has been doing continuously. Philosophy is the business of the mind. The moment mind looks at anything it looks with a question mark, it looks with the eyes of doubt.

Very simple is life, and very simple is death – but only if you can see without the mind. Once you bring the mind in, then everything is complex, then everything is a riddle, then everything is confusion. And mind tries to solve the confusion when really it is the source of all confusions, so more confusion is created. It is as if a small stream is flowing in the hills. Some carts have passed, and the stream is muddy, and you jump into the stream to clean it. You will only make it more muddy. It is better to wait on the bank. It is better to let the stream itself become tranquil again, to calm down until the dead leaves are gone, the mud has settled, and the stream is again crystal clear. Your help is not needed. You will only confuse it more.

So if you feel that there is a problem, please don't poke your nose in it. Sit by the side. Don't allow the mind to get involved, tell the mind to wait. And it is very difficult for the mind to wait – it is impatience incarnate.

If you tell the mind to wait, meditation happens. If you can persuade the mind to wait, you will be prayerful – because waiting means no thinking, it means just sitting on the bank not doing anything with the stream. What can you do? Whatsoever you do will make it more muddy; your very entering into the stream will create more problems. So wait.

All meditation is waiting. All prayerfulness is infinite patience. The whole of religion consists of not allowing the mind to create more problems for you. Every simple thing which even animals enjoy, which even trees enjoy, man cannot enjoy – because immediately it becomes a problem and how can you enjoy a problem?

You fall in love, and the mind immediately says: "What is love? Is this love or sex? Is this true or false? Where are you going? Can love be eternal or is it just momentary?" First decide everything, then take the step. But with the mind there is never any decision, it remains indecisive; indecision is its inherent nature. It says, "Don't take the jump." And when mind tells you these things, it seems very clever, it seems very intelligent, because you may go wrong. So don't take the jump, don't move, remain static.

But life is movement and life is trust. Love happens – one has to move into it. Where it leads is not the point. The goal is not the point. The very movement of your consciousness in love is a revelation. The other is not the point; the beloved or the lover is not the point. The point is that you can love, that it could happen to you; that your being opens in trust, without any doubt, without any questioning. This very opening is a fulfillment.

But the mind will say, "Wait, let me think and decide; one should not take any step in haste." Then you can wait and wait. That's how you have been missing life.

Every moment life knocks at your door, but you are thinking. You say to life, "Wait, I will open the door, but let me first decide." It never happens. Your whole life will come and go, and you will be simply dragging, neither alive nor dead, and both are good because death has a life of its own.

So remember, the first thing: don't allow the mind to interfere. Then you can be like trees, even greener. Then you can be like birds on the wing, and no bird can reach to heights which you can touch. Then you can be like fish which go to the very bottom of the sea – you can go to the very bottom of the ocean. Nothing is comparable to you. Human consciousness is the most evolved phenomenon, but you are missing. Even less evolved states are enjoying more. A bird is a bird, a very much less evolved being than you; a tree is almost not evolved at all, but enjoying more, flowering more. More fulfillment is happening all around it. Why are you missing?

Your mind has become a burden. You have not been using it; rather, on the contrary, you are being used by it. Don't allow the mind to interfere with your life, then there will be a flow. Then you are unobstructed, then you are transparent, then each moment is bliss because you are not worried about it.

A man was advised by his psychoanalyst to go to the hills. He was always complaining and complaining about this and that, asking about this and that. He was never at ease with anything, never at home. He was advised to go for a rest.

The next day a telegram arrived for the psychoanalyst. In it the man said, "I am feeling very happy here. Why?"

You cannot even accept happiness without asking why. It is impossible for the mind to accept anything – the *why* is immediately there, and the *why* destroys everything. Hence so much insistence in all religions on faith. This is the meaning of faith – not allowing the mind to ask why.

Faith is not belief, it is not about believing in a certain theory – faith is believing in life itself. Faith is not about believing in the Bible or the Koran or the Gita. Faith is not belief – faith is a trust, a non-doubting trust. And only those who are faithful, those who are capable of trust, will be able to know what life is and what death is.

For us life is a problem, so death is bound to be a problem. We are constantly trying to solve it, and wasting time and energy in solving it. It is already solved. It has never been a problem. It is you who are creating the problem. Look at the stars, there is no problem; look at the trees, there is no problem. Look all around ... If man were not there everything would be already solved. Where is the problem? The trees never ask who created the world – they simply enjoy it. What foolishness to ask who created the world. And what difference does it make who created the world: *a, b, c* or *d*, what difference does it make? And whether it was created or it is uncreated, what difference does it make? How will it affect you if *a* created the world, or *b* created the world, or nobody created the world? You will remain the same, life will remain the same. So why ask an unnecessary, irrelevant question and get entangled in it?

The rivers go on flowing never asking where they are going. They reach the sea. If they start asking, they might not; their energy might be lost on the way. They might become so afraid – where they are going, where is the goal, what is the purpose? They may become so obsessed with the problem that they might go mad. But they go on flowing, unworried where they are going, and they always reach the sea.

When trees and rivers can do this miracle, why can't you do it? This is the whole of Chuang Tzu's philosophy, his whole way of life: When everything is happening, why are you worried? Allow it to happen. If rivers can reach, man will reach. If trees reach, man will reach. When this whole existence is moving, you are part of it. Don't become a whirlpool of thinking, otherwise you go round and round, round and round, and the flow is lost. Then there is no oceanic experience in the end.

Life is a riddle to you because you look through the mind; if you look through the no-mind, life is a mystery. Life is already dead if you look through the mind; and life never dies if you look through the no-mind. Mind cannot feel the alive. Mind can only touch the dead, the material. Life is so subtle and mind is so crude – an instrument not as subtle as life. And when you touch with that instrument it cannot catch the throbs of life. It misses. The throbbing is very subtle – you are the throbbing.

Chuang Tzu is on his deathbed, and when a man like Chuang Tzu is on his deathbed the disciples should be absolutely silent. This moment is not to be missed, because death is the peak. When Chuang Tzu dies, he dies at the peak. It happens rarely that consciousness reaches its absolute fulfillment. The disciples should be silent; they should watch what is happening; they should look deep into Chuang Tzu. They should not interfere with their minds, they should not start asking foolish questions. But the mind always starts asking. They are worried about the funeral and Chuang Tzu is still alive. But the mind is not alive, it is never alive; the mind is always thinking in terms of death. For the disciples the master is already dead. They are thinking about the funeral – what to do, what not to do. They are creating a problem which doesn't exist at all because Chuang Tzu is still alive.

I have heard ...

Three old men were sitting in a park, discussing the inevitable, death. One old man of seventy-three said, "When I die I would like to be buried with Abraham Lincoln, the greatest man, loved by all."

Another said, "I would like to be buried with Albert Einstein, the greatest scientist, humanitarian, philosopher, lover of peace."

Then they both looked at the third, who was ninety-three. He said, "I would like to be buried with Sophia Loren."

They both felt annoyed, angry and they said, "But she is still alive."

That old man said, "So am I!"

This old man must have been something rare. Ninety-three, and he said, "So am I!" Why should life be worried about death? Why should life think about death? When you are alive, where is the problem? But the mind creates the problem. Then you get puzzled.

Socrates was dying, and the same thing happened as happened with Chuang Tzu. The disciples were worried about the funeral. They asked him, "What should we do?"

Socrates is reported to have said, "My enemies are giving poison to kill me and you are planning how to bury me — so who is my friend and who is my enemy? You are both concerned with my death, nobody seems to be concerned with my life."

Mind is somehow death-obsessed. The disciples of Chuang Tzu were thinking what to do — and the master was dying, a great phenomenon was happening right then.

A buddha, Chuang Tzu, was reaching the ultimate peak there. It happens rarely, once or twice in millions of years. The flame was burning. His life had come to a point of absolute purity where it is divine, not human, where it is total, not partial, where the beginning and the end meet, where all the secrets are open and all the doors are open, where everything is unlocked. The whole mystery was there ... And the disciples were thinking of the funeral — blind, absolutely blind, not seeing what was happening. Their eyes were closed.

But why does it happen? These disciples, do you think that they knew Chuang Tzu? How could they? If they were missing Chuang Tzu in his supreme glory, how can we believe that they didn't miss him when he was working with them, working on them, moving with them, digging a hole in the garden, planting a seed, talking to them, just being present with them?

How can we think that they knew who this Chuang Tzu was? When his total glory was missed, it is impossible not to think that they had missed him always. They must have missed. When he was talking, then they must have been thinking: "What is he talking about? What does he mean?"

When an enlightened person speaks, meaning is not to be discovered by you; it is there, you have simply to listen to it. It is not to be discovered, it is not hidden, it is nothing to be interpreted. He is not talking in theories, he is giving you simple facts. If your eyes are open, you will see them; if your ears can hear, you will hear them. Nothing more is needed.

That's why Jesus goes on saying again and again, "If you can hear, hear me." If you can see, see. Nothing more is expected — just open eyes, open ears.

Buddha, Chuang Tzu or Jesus are not philosophers like Hegel, or Kant. If you read Hegel the meaning has to be discovered. It is very arduous, as if Hegel is making every effort to make it more and more difficult, weaving words around words, making everything riddle-like. So when you first encounter Hegel he will look superb, a very high peak, but the more you penetrate and the more you understand, the less of a man he becomes. The day you understand him, he is just useless.

The whole trick is that you cannot understand him, that's why you feel he is so great. Because you cannot understand, your mind is baffled, because you cannot understand, your mind cannot comprehend, the thing seems to be very mysterious, incomprehensible. It is not, it is only verbal. He is trying to hide, he is not saying anything. Rather, he is saying many words without any substance.

So persons like Hegel are immediately appreciated, but as time passes appreciation of them disappears. Persons like Buddha are not immediately appreciated, but as time passes you appreciate them more. They are always before their time. Centuries pass, and then their greatness starts emerging, then their greatness starts appearing, then you can feel it. Because their truth is so simple, there is no garbage, there is no rubbish around it. It is so factual you can miss it if you think about it.

When you are listening to a Chuang Tzu, just listen. Nothing else but a passive receptivity, a welcome, is needed on your part. Everything is clear, but you can make it a mess, and then you can get confused by your own creation. These disciples must have missed Chuang Tzu – they are missing him again. They are worried about what is going to be done.

And this point has to be understood: a man of wisdom is always concerned with the being, and a man of ignorance is always concerned with questions of doing, what is to be done. Being is not a question to him.

Chuang Tzu is concerned with being; the disciples are concerned with doing. If death is coming then what is to be done? What should we do? The master is going to die, so what about the funeral? We must plan it.

We are mad about planning. We plan life, we plan death, and through planning the spontaneity is destroyed, the beauty is destroyed, the whole ecstasy is destroyed.

I have heard ...

An atheist was dying. As he was an atheist, he didn't believe in heaven or hell but still he thought it best to get properly dressed before dying. He didn't know where he was going because he didn't believe in anything, but still he was going somewhere, so before going one must get properly dressed.

He was a man of manners, etiquette, so he was dressed in the right dress for the evening, the tie, everything – and then he died. The rabbi was called to bless him. The rabbi said, "This man never believed, but look how he has planned! He did not believe, he had nowhere to go, but how beautifully dressed and ready!"

Even if you feel that you are not going anywhere, you plan it, because the mind always wants to play with the future. It is very happy planning for the future, it is very unhappy living in the present. But planning for the future seems beautiful. Whenever you have time you start planning for the future, whether of this world or of that, but the future. And the mind enjoys planning. Planning is just fantasy, dreaming, daydreaming.

Persons like Chuang Tzu are concerned with being, not becoming. They are not concerned with doing, they are not concerned with the future. No planning is needed. Existence takes care of itself.

Jesus said to his disciples: "Look at these flowers, these lilies, so beautiful in their glory that even Solomon was not so beautiful." And they don't plan, and they don't think for the future, and they are not worried about the next moment.

Why are the lilies so beautiful? Of what does their beauty consist? Where is it hidden? The lilies exist here and now. Why is the human face so sad and ugly? Because it is never here and now, it is always in the future. It is a ghostlike thing. How can you be real if you are not here and now? You can only be a ghost, either visiting the past or moving into the future.

Chuang Tzu was dying. At the moment of Chuang Tzu's death the disciples should have been silent. That would have been the most respectful thing to do, the most loving thing to do. The master was dying. They never listened to his life, at least they could have listened to his death. They could not be silent while he was talking to them throughout his life; now he was going to give his last sermon through his death.

One should be watchful when a wise man dies because he dies in a different way. An ignorant man cannot die that way. You have your life and you have your death. If you have been foolish in your life, how can you be wise in your death? Death is the outcome, the total outcome, the conclusion. In death your whole life is involved, in essence your whole life is there, so a foolish man dies in a foolish way.

Life is unique, death is also unique. Nobody else can live your life and nobody else can die your death, only you. It is unique, it never happens again. Styles differ, not only in life but also in death. When Chuang Tzu dies, one has to be absolutely silent so that one does not miss it — because you *can* miss.

Life is a long affair, seventy, eighty, a hundred years. Death is in one moment. It is an atomic phenomenon, concentrated. It is more vital than life because life is spread out. Life can never be as intense as death can be, and life can never be as beautiful as death can be, because it is spread out. It is always lukewarm.

At the moment of death the whole of life has come to a boiling point. Everything evaporates from this world to the other, from the body to the bodiless. It is the greatest transformation that happens. One should be silent, one should be respectful, one should not be wavering, because it will happen in a single moment and you may miss it.

And the foolish disciples were talking about the funeral and thinking of making a grand thing out of it. And the grandest thing was happening, the greatest thing was happening, but they were thinking of the show. The mind always thinks of the exhibition – it is exhibitionistic.

Mulla Nasruddin died. Somebody informed his wife who was taking her afternoon tea – half the cup was finished. The man said, "Your husband is dead, he fell under a bus." But Mulla Nasruddin's wife continued sipping her tea.

The man said, "What! You have not even stopped drinking. Do you hear me? Your husband is dead, and you have not even said a single thing!"

The wife said, "Let me first finish my tea, and then – boy, will I give a scream! Just wait a little."

The mind is exhibitionistic. She will give a scream, just give her a little chance to arrange, to plan.

I have heard about an actor whose wife died. He was crying his heart out, screaming, tears rolling down.

One man said, "I never thought that you loved your wife so much."

The actor looked at the man and said, "This is nothing. You should have seen me when my first wife died."

Even when you show your anguish you are looking at others: what do they think about it? Why think of a grand funeral? Why grand? You make an exhibition out of death also. Is this really respectful? Or is death also something on the market, a commodity?

Our master has died, so there is a competition, and we must prove that he received the greatest funeral – no other master ever received one like it and no other will ever receive one like it again.

Even in death you are thinking of the ego. But disciples are like that, they follow. But they never really follow, because if they had followed Chuang Tzu then there would be no question about a grand funeral. They would have been humble in that moment. But the ego is assertive.

Whenever you say that your master is very great, just look within. You are saying, "I am very great, that's why I follow this great man, I am a great follower." Every follower claims that his master is the greatest – but not because of the master. How can you be a great follower if the master is not great? And if somebody says that this is not so, you get annoyed, irritated, you start arguing and fighting. It is a question of the survival of the ego.

Everywhere the ego asserts. It is cunning and very subtle. Even in death it will not leave you; even in death it will be there. The master is dying, and the disciples are thinking of the funeral. They have not followed the master at all – a master like Chuang Tzu whose whole teaching consists of being spontaneous.

When Chuang Tzu was about to die, his disciples began planning a
grand funeral.

He is not yet dead and they have started planning – because the question is not Chuang Tzu, the question is the egos of the disciples. They must do something grand, and everybody must come to know that never, never before has such a thing happened.

But you cannot deceive Chuang Tzu. Even when he is dying he will not leave you alone; even when he is dying he cannot be deceived; even when he is leaving, he will give you his heart, his wisdom; even at the last moment he will share whatsoever he has known and realized. Even his last moment is going to be a sharing.

But Chuang Tzu said:
"I shall have heaven and earth for my coffin;
the sun and moon will be jade symbols
hanging by my side;
planets and constellations
will shine as jewels all around me,
and all beings will be present
as mourners at the wake."

What more is needed? Everything is simple, amply taken care of. What more is needed? What more can you do? What more can you do for a Chuang Tzu, for a buddha? Whatsoever you do will be nothing, whatsoever you plan is going to be trivial. It cannot be grand because the whole universe is ready to receive him. What more can you do?

Chuang Tzu said: "The sun and the moon and all the beings on earth and in heaven are ready to receive me. And all beings, the whole existence, will be the mourners. So you need not worry, you need not engage mourners." You can engage mourners – now they are also available on the market. There are people – you pay them and they mourn. What type of humanity is coming into being? If a wife dies, a mother dies, and nobody is there to mourn, you have to engage professional mourners. They are available in Mumbai, Kolkata; in big cities they are available, and they do such a good job you cannot compete with them. Of course they are more efficient, they get daily practice, but what ugliness when you have to pay for it.

The whole thing has become false. Life is false, death is false, happiness is false. Even mourning is false. And this has to be; it has a logical meaning to it. If you have never been really happy with a person, how can you be really mournful when he dies? It is impossible. If you have not been happy with your wife, if you have never known any blissful moment with her, when she dies how can authentic tears come to your eyes? Deep down you will be happy, deep down you feel a freedom: "Now I am independent, now I can move according to my desires." The wife was like an imprisonment.

I have heard ...

A man was dying and his wife was consoling him, saying, "Don't worry, sooner or later I will join you."

The man said, "But don't be unfaithful to me." He must have been afraid. Why this fear at the last moment? This fear must have always been there.

The wife promised, "I will never be unfaithful to you."

So the man said, "If you commit even a single act of unfaithfulness towards me I will turn in my grave. It will be very painful for me."

Then after ten years the wife died. At the gate, Saint Peter asked her, "Who would you like to see first?"

She said, "My husband, of course."

Saint Peter asked, "What is his name?"

So she said, "Abraham."

But Saint Peter said, "It is difficult because there are millions of Abrahams, so give me some clue." The wife thought. She said, "At the last moment he said that if I commit any act of unfaithfulness towards him he would turn in his grave."

Saint Peter said, "No more is needed. You mean twirling Abraham, who is constantly twirling in his grave. For ten years he has not had a single moment of rest. And everybody knows about him. There is no problem, we will call him immediately."

No faith, no trust, no love, no happiness, has ever happened out of your relationships. When death comes, how can you mourn? Your mourning will be false. If your life is false, your death is going to be false. And don't think that you are the only false one – all around, those who are related to you are false. And we live in such a false world, it is simply amazing how we can continue.

One politician was out of work. He was an ex-minister. He was in search of work because politicians are always in difficulty when they are not in office. They cannot do anything other than politics, they don't know anything else but politics. And they don't have any qualifications either. Even for a puny job certain qualifications are needed — but for a minister none are needed. For a chief minister or a prime minister qualifications are not needed at all.

So this minister was in trouble. He met the manager of a circus, because he thought, "Politics is a great circus, and I must have learned a little, enough to be of some use in the circus." So he said, "Can you find me a job? I am out of work, and in much trouble."

The manager said, "You have come at the right moment. One of the bears has died, so we will give you a bear's costume. You don't have to do anything, just sit the whole day in the cage in the bear's costume. Just sit and nobody is going to know the difference. You are not required to do anything, just sit from morning to evening so people know that the bear is there."

The job looked good, so the politician accepted. He entered the cage, put on his costume, and sat down. He was just sitting there, when fifteen minutes later another bear was shoved in. He panicked and ran to the bars, started shaking them and cried out, "Help, let me out of here!"

Then suddenly he heard a voice. The other bear was speaking. He said, "Do you think you are the only politician out of work? I am an ex-minister too. Don't be so afraid."

The whole of life has become false, root and all, and how you exist in it is a sheer miracle — talking with a false face, talking to a false face, false happiness, false misery. And then you hope to find the truth! With false faces the truth can never be found. One has to realize his own true face and drop all the false masks.

Said Chuang Tzu:

"I shall have heaven and earth for my coffin..."   ·

So why are you worried? And how can you manage a greater coffin than that? Let heaven and earth be my coffin — and they will be.

"... The sun and moon will be jade symbols
hanging by my side..."

So you need not burn candles around me; they will be momentary, and sooner or later they will not be there. Let sun and moon be the symbols of life around me. And they are.

"... Planets and constellations
will shine as jewels all around me,
and all beings will be present ...

This is something to be understood: *all beings will be present*. It is also said of Buddha and Mahavira, but nobody believes it because it is impossible to believe. Even Jainas read it, but they don't believe it. Buddhists read it, but suspicion enters their minds.

It is said that when Mahavira died all the beings were present there. Not only human beings – animals, the souls of the trees, angels, deities, all the beings from all the dimensions of existence were present there. And this should be so because a Mahavira is not only revealed to you; the glory is such, the height is such that all the dimensions of existence become acquainted with him. It is said that when Mahavira would speak angels, deities, animals, ghosts, all types of beings were there to listen to him, not only human beings. It looks like a story, a parable, but I tell you that this is a truth – because the higher you reach, the higher your being grows, and other dimensions of existence become available to you.

When one reaches the highest point – Jainas call it the point of *arihanta*, Buddhists call it the point of *arhat*, Chuang Tzu, the man of Tao calls it the point of the perfect Tao – then the whole existence listens.

Says Chuang Tzu:

"... and all beings will be present
as mourners at the wake."

What more is needed, and what more can you do? What more can you add to it? You need not do anything, and you need not worry.

"Everything is amply taken care of."

This is the feeling of one who becomes silent: *"Everything is amply taken care of."* Life and death, everything, you need not do anything – everything is already happening without you. You come into it unnecessarily and you create confusion, you create chaos. Without you everything is perfect – as it is, it is perfect. This is the attitude of a religious man: everything is perfect as it is. Nothing more can be done to it.

In the West, Leibnitz is reported to have said that this is the most perfect world. He has been criticized, because in the West you cannot assert such things. How is this world the most perfect world? This seems to be the most imperfect, the most ugly, ill; there is inequality, suffering, poverty, illness, death, hatred, everything – and this Leibnitz says that this is the most perfect world.

Leibnitz has been criticized severely, but Chuang Tzu would have understood what he means. I understand what he means. When Leibnitz said, "This is the most perfect world possible," he was not making any comment on the political or economic situation. He was not making any comment on equality, inequality, socialism, communism, wars. He was not making any comment on it. The comment is not objective, the comment is not concerned with the without; the comment is concerned with the inner feeling – it comes from the very being.

That everything is perfect means there is no need to worry.

"Everything is amply taken care of."

And you cannot make it better, you just cannot make it better. If you try you may make it worse, but you cannot make it better. It is very difficult for the scientific mind to understand that you cannot make it better, because the scientific mind depends on this idea – that things can get better. But what have you done?

For two thousand years since Aristotle, we have been trying in the West to make the world a better place. Has it become better in any way? Is man even a little happier? Is man even a little more blissful? Not at all. Things have become worse. The more we have been treating the patient, the more he is falling to his death. Nothing has been helpful. Man is not happier at all.

We may be having more things to be happy with, but the heart which can be happy is lost. You may have palaces, but the man who can be an emperor is here no longer, so palaces become graves. Your cities are more beautiful, richer, wealthier, but they are just like graveyards, no living person lives there. We have made a mistake in trying to make the world better. It is not better, it may be worse.

Look back: man was totally different, poorer but richer. It looks paradoxical; he was poorer, there was not enough food, not enough clothing, not enough shelter, but life was richer. He could dance, he could sing.

Your song is lost, your throat is choked by things; no song can come out of the heart. You cannot dance. At the most you can make some movements, but those movements are not dance, because dancing is not just a movement. When a movement becomes ecstatic then it is dance. When the movement is so total that there is no ego, then it is a dance.

And you must know that dancing came into the world as a technique of meditation. The beginning of dancing was not for dance, it was to achieve an ecstasy where the dancer was lost, only the dance remained – no ego, nobody manipulating, the body flowing spontaneously.

You can dance, but only in dead movements. You can manipulate the body; it may be good exercise, but it is not ecstasy. You still embrace each other, you still kiss, you still make all the movements of lovemaking, but love is not there, only the movements are there. You make them and you feel frustrated. You make them and you know nothing is happening. You do everything, and still a constant feeling of frustration follows you like a shadow.

When Leibnitz says that this is the most perfect world, what he is saying is what Chuang Tzu is saying:

"Everything is amply taken care of."

You need not worry about life, you need not worry about death – the same source which takes care of life will take care of death. You need not think about a grand funeral. The same source which has given me birth will absorb me, and the same source is enough, we need not add anything to it.

The disciples listened but couldn't understand, otherwise there would have been no need to say anything any more. But the disciples still said:

"We fear that the crows and kites
will eat our master."

If we don't make any preparation, if we don't plan, then crows and kites will eat our master.

Chuang Tzu replied:
"Well, above ground I shall be eaten
by crows and kites,
and below ground by ants and worms.
In either case I shall be eaten –
so why are you favoring the birds?"

So why make any choice? I have to be eaten anyhow, so why make a choice? Chuang Tzu says: Live choicelessly and die choicelessly. Why make a choice?

You try to manipulate life and then you try to manipulate death also. So people make wills and legal documents, so that when they are gone they will manipulate. Dead, but they will still manipulate. Manipulation seems to be so enchanting that even after death people go on manipulating. A father dies, and makes conditions in his will that the son will receive his inheritance only if he fulfills a condition, else the money will go to a charity fund. But these conditions have to be fulfilled – the dead man is dominating still.

There is a university in London. The man who built it made a will. He was the president of the college trust. The will read: "When I die, my body is not to be destroyed. It has to be maintained, and I will continue to sit in the chairman's seat. And he still sits there. Whenever the trust meets, his dead body is sitting in the chairman's place. He is still sitting at the head of the table, still dominating.

Your life is a manipulation of others, you would like your death to be a manipulation also. Chuang Tzu says there is no choice. If you leave my body on the
ground, well, it will be eaten; if you bury it deep down it will be eaten. So why
favor the birds or the worms? Let it be as it is going to happen. Let the source
decide.

Decision gives you ego: I will decide. So let the source decide, let the ultimate
decide how it wants to dispose of this body. It was never asked of me how the
source had to construct this body, why should I decide how it has to be disposed
of? And why fear that it should be eaten? It is good.

We are afraid of being eaten – why? This is something to be understood. Why
are we so afraid of being eaten? All our lives we are eating, and we are destroying
life through eating. Whatsoever you eat, you kill. You have to kill, because life
can eat only life. There is no other way. So nobody can really be a vegetarian –
nobody. Everybody is a non-vegetarian, because whatever you eat is life. You eat
fruit, it is life; you eat vegetables, the vegetable has life; you eat wheat, rice, they
are seeds for more life to sprout. Whatsoever you depend on has life.

Everything is a food for somebody else, so why protect yourself, why try to
protect yourself from being eaten? Simple foolishness! You have been eating
your whole life, now give it a chance to eat you, allow life to eat you.

That is why I say that the Parsees have the most scientific method of disposing
of a dead body. Hindus burn it. This is bad, because you are burning food. If every
tree burns its fruit, and every animal dies and other animals burn it, what will
happen? They will all be Hindu but there will be nobody here. Why burn? You
have been eating, now allow it, give life a chance to eat you. And be happy about
it because food means you are being absorbed. There is nothing wrong. It means
the existence has taken back, the river has fallen back into the ocean.

And this is the best way to be absorbed – to be eaten, so that whatsoever
is useful in you is alive somewhere in somebody. Some tree, some bird, some
animal, will be alive through your life. Be happy, your life has been distributed.
Why take it as something wrong?

Mohammedans and Christians bury their dead in the ground in caskets,
in coffins, to protect them. This is bad, this is just foolishness, because
we cannot protect life, so how can we protect death? We cannot protect
anything, nothing can be protected. Life is vulnerable, and you even try to
make death invulnerable. You want to protect, to save.

The Parsees have the best method – they simply leave the body on the walls,
then vultures and other birds come and eat it. Everybody is against the Parsees,
even Parsees, because the whole thing looks so ugly. It is not ugly. When you are
eating, is it ugly? Then why is a vulture ugly when he is eating? When you eat,

then it is a dinner, and when a vulture is eating you then it is also a dinner. You have been eating others, let others eat you; be absorbed.

So Chuang Tzu says: "There is no choice, why favor this or that? Let life do whatsoever it chooses to do, I am not going to decide." Really, Chuang Tzu lived a choiceless life so he was ready to die a choiceless death. And when you are choiceless, only then you are. When you have a choice, the mind is. The mind is the chooser; the being is always choiceless. The mind wants to do something; the being simply allows things to happen. Being is a let-go.

How can you be miserable if you don't choose? How can you be miserable if you don't ask for a particular result? How can you be miserable if you are not moving toward a particular goal? Nothing can make you miserable. Your mind asks for goals, for choices, for decisions – then misery comes in.

If you live choicelessly and allow life to happen, then you simply become a field. Life happens in you, but you are not the manager. You don't manage it, you don't control it. When you are not the controller all tensions dissolve; only then there is relaxation, then you are totally relaxed. That relaxation is the ultimate point, the alpha and the omega, the beginning and the end.

Whether it is life or it is death, you should not take any standpoint. That is the meaning. You should not take any standpoint. You should not say this is right and that is wrong. You should not divide. Let life be an undivided whole.

Chuang Tzu said: If you divide, by even one inch's division, heaven and hell are set apart, and then they cannot be bridged.

It happened once ... I knew a young man. He used to come to me and he was always worried about one thing. He wanted to get married, but whatsoever girl he will bring to the home, his mother would not approve. It had become almost impossible. So I told him, "Try to find a girl who is almost like your mother: face, figure, the way she walks, her clothes. Just find a mirror image, a reflection of your mother."

He searched and searched and finally found a girl. He came to me and said, "You were right, my mother instantly liked her. She is just like my mother; not only does she dress like my mother, she walks, talks, she even cooks like my mother."

So I asked him, "Then what happened?"

He said, "Nothing, because my father hates her."

The polarity – if one part of your mind loves one thing, you can immediately find another part of the mind hating it. If you choose one thing, just look behind – the other part which hates is hiding there. Whenever you choose, it is not only the world that is divided, you are also divided through your choice. You are not whole. And when you are not whole, you cannot allow life to happen. And all benediction comes in life as grace, as a gift; it is not achieved through effort.

So don't choose religion against the world, don't choose goodness against badness, don't choose grace against sin, don't try to be a good man against the bad man, don't make any distinction between the Devil and God, this is what Chuang Tzu says. He says: Don't choose between life and death. Don't choose between this type of death and that type of death. Choose not, remain whole, and whenever you are whole, there is a meeting with the whole, because only like meets like.

It has been said continuously by mystics for centuries: As above, so below. I would like to add one thing more to it: As within, so without. If you are whole within, the whole without happens to you immediately. If you are divided within, the whole without is divided.

It is you who is eternal, who becomes the whole universe, you become projected, it is you – and whenever you choose you will be divided. Choice means division, choice means conflict, for this, against that.

Don't choose. Remain a choiceless witness and then nothing is lacking. Then this existence is the most perfect existence possible. Nothing can be more beautiful, nothing can be more blissful. It is there, all around you, waiting for you. Whenever you become aware it will be revealed to you. But if your mind goes on working inside, dividing, choosing, creating conflicts, it will never happen to you.

You have been missing it for lives. Don't miss it any more.

Enough for today.

About Osho

Osho defies categorization. His thousands of talks cover everything from the individual quest for meaning to the most urgent social and political issues facing society today. Osho's books are not written but are transcribed from audio and video recordings of his extemporaneous talks to international audiences. As he puts it, "So remember: whatever I am saying is not just for you... I am talking also for the future generations."

Osho has been described by *The Sunday Times* in London as one of the "1000 Makers of the 20th Century" and by American author Tom Robbins as "the most dangerous man since Jesus Christ." *Sunday Mid-Day* (India) has selected Osho as one of ten people – along with Gandhi, Nehru and Buddha – who have changed the destiny of India.

About his own work Osho has said that he is helping to create the conditions for the birth of a new kind of human being. He often characterizes this new human being as "Zorba the Buddha" – capable both of enjoying the earthy pleasures of a Zorba the Greek and the silent serenity of a Gautama the Buddha.

Running like a thread through all aspects of Osho's talks and meditations is a vision that encompasses both the timeless wisdom of all ages past and the highest potential of today's (and tomorrow's) science and technology.

Osho is known for his revolutionary contribution to the science of inner transformation, with an approach to meditation that acknowledges the accelerated pace of contemporary life. His unique OSHO Active Meditations are designed to first release the accumulated stresses of body and mind, so that it is then easier to take an experience of stillness and thought-free relaxation into daily life.

Two autobiographical works by the author are available:
Autobiography of a Spiritually Incorrect Mystic,
St Martins Press, New York (book and eBook)
Glimpses of a Golden Childhood,
OSHO Media International, Pune, India

OSHO International Meditation Resort

Location
Located 100 miles southeast of Mumbai in the thriving modern city of Pune, India, the OSHO International Meditation Resort is a holiday destination with a difference. The Meditation Resort is spread over 28 acres of spectacular gardens in a beautiful tree-lined residential area.

Uniqueness
Each year the Meditation Resort welcomes thousands of people from more than 100 countries. The unique campus provides an opportunity for a direct personal experience of a new way of living – with more awareness, relaxation, celebration and creativity. A great variety of around-the-clock and around-the-year program options are available. Doing nothing and just relaxing is one of them!

All programs are based on the OSHO vision of "Zorba the Buddha" – a qualitatively new kind of human being who is able *both* to participate creatively in everyday life and to relax into silence and meditation.

OSHO Meditations
A full daily schedule of meditations for every type of person includes methods that are active and passive, traditional and revolutionary, and in particular the OSHO Active Meditations™. The meditations take place in what must be the world's largest meditation hall, the OSHO Auditorium.

OSHO Multiversity
Individual sessions, courses and workshops cover everything from creative arts to holistic health, personal transformation, relationship and life transition, work-as-meditation, esoteric sciences, and the "Zen" approach to sports and recreation. The secret of the OSHO Multiversity's success lies in the fact that all its programs are combined with meditation, supporting the understanding that as human beings we are far more than the sum of our parts.

OSHO Basho Spa
The luxurious Basho Spa provides for leisurely open-air swimming surrounded by trees and tropical green. The uniquely styled, spacious Jacuzzi, the saunas, gym, tennis courts...all these are enhanced by their stunningly beautiful setting.

Cuisine

A variety of different eating areas serve delicious Western, Asian and Indian vegetarian food – most of it organically grown especially for the Meditation Resort. Breads and cakes are baked in the resort's own bakery.

Night life

There are many evening events to choose from – dancing being at the top of the list! Other activities include full-moon meditations beneath the stars, variety shows, music performances and meditations for daily life.

Or you can just enjoy meeting people at the Plaza Café, or walking in the nighttime serenity of the gardens of this fairytale environment.

Facilities

You can buy all your basic necessities and toiletries in the Galleria. The Multi-media Gallery sells a large range of OSHO media products. There is also a bank, a travel agency and a Cyber Café on-campus. For those who enjoy shopping, Pune provides all the options, ranging from traditional and ethnic Indian products to all of the global brand-name stores.

Accommodation

You can choose to stay in the elegant rooms of the OSHO Guesthouse, or for longer stays opt for one of the OSHO Living-In program packages. Additionally there is a plentiful variety of nearby hotels and serviced apartments.

www.osho.com/meditationresort
www.osho.com/guesthouse
www.osho.com/livingin

For More Information

www.**OSHO**.com

a comprehensive multi-language website including a magazine, OSHO Books, OSHO Talks in audio and video formats, the OSHO Library text archive in English and Hindi and extensive information about OSHO Meditations. You will also find the program schedule of the OSHO Multiversity and information about the OSHO International Meditation Resort.

http://OSHO.com/AllAboutOSHO
http://OSHO.com/Resort
http://OSHO.com/Shop
http://www.youtube.com/OSHO
http://www.Twitter.com/OSHO
http://www.facebook.com/pages/OSHO.International

To contact OSHO International Foundation:
www.osho.com/oshointernational,
oshointernational@oshointernational.com